The Toughest JOB in Baseball

What Managers Do,
How They Do It, and
Why It Gives Them Ulcers

Peter Pascarelli

Simon & Schuster

New York   London   Toronto
Sydney   Tokyo   Singapore

SIMON & SCHUSTER
Simon & Schuster Building
Rockefeller Center
1230 Avenue of the Americas
New York, New York 10020

Designed by Hyun Joo Kim
Manufactured in the United States of America

10 9 8 7 6 5 4 3 2 1

Library of Congress Cataloging-in-Publication Data

Pascarelli, Peter.
   The toughest job in baseball: what managers do, how they
do it, and why it gives them ulcers / Peter Pascarelli.
      p.   cm.
   1. Baseball—Management. 2. Baseball—Managers. I. Title.
GV875.7.P37   1993
796.357'06—dc20   93-16572
                                                           CIP

ISBN: 0-671-79331-4

Acknowledgments

◆ This book was first contemplated during the Reagan administration. It finally took the untimely demise of *The National* to create the relative unemployment that left me the necessary time to turn speculation into reality.

Until going through this whole process, I always thought that authors thanked their editors in order to get paid more quickly. But now I know why authors, at least those lucky ones who have Jeff Neuman as an editor, thank their editors. He kept this idea alive and maintained faith in this author long after saner people would have given up hope. I can never thank him enough for staying with me to the bitter end when the personal pressures were almost too much to bear.

At many points in this book, conversations from private meetings are related. Obviously, I was not in the room for all of them. What is related is as accurate a portrayal as possible, drawn from the memories of either actual participants or those close to the participants to whom details were related.

Thanks must go to Jim Leyland, the best manager in baseball and, more important, one of the best people in baseball. Thanks also to Ted Simmons, Rich Donnelly, Ray Miller, and the other coaches, players, and staff of the Pittsburgh Pirates. And thanks to Tony LaRussa, Wally Haas, Sandy Alderson, and members of the Oakland Athletics; Gene Lamont; Lou Piniella; Tom Lasorda; Jeff Torborg; Johnny Oates; Buck Showalter; Bobby Cox; Roger Craig; and Sparky Anderson.

Paul Meyer's help was invaluable throughout this project. Jerry Crasnick also provided needed assistance.

I learned what major-league baseball was all about from Earl Weaver and the Baltimore Orioles' organization.

Jim Frey, whose counsel dates back to my rookie years covering Baltimore, remains a valued friend to this day.

Peter Gammons has been more than a trusted colleague for years. He is also a loyal friend who has been there in trying times.

Thanks to Bruce Connal, Jed Drake, Jay Rothman, Marc Payton, Jon Miller, Joe Morgan, and the rest of ESPN's "Sunday Night Baseball" production team. They leave every other baseball telecast in their dust, and their patience with this ink-stained wretch's electronic ignorance has been appreciated.

Thanks to Jeff Rimer and Jeff Beauchamp, who have allowed me to keep in touch with Baltimore and make a fool of myself occasionally on the radio.

My father taught me to love baseball. My mother taught me to love books. And my greatest sadness is that they couldn't be here to read their son's first baseball book.

I've never adequately been able to tell David, Patrick, Robyn, Greg, and the youngest, Elizabeth, how proud I am of them. They are always in my thoughts.

Paige will hopefully soon know why her daddy had to lock himself in the office so many late nights. May she also grow up to love baseball and books.

And finally to my Elizabeth, this, like everything else, is for you. I began loving you when you mentioned Carl Yastrzemski in the first note you ever wrote to me. And I've never stopped since.

Contents

Introduction

◆ It was a typical summer night for Jim Leyland. He managed a 3-hour 10-minute major-league game in which he made the usual two or three dozen decisions every major-league manager is required to make every night. He then spent 30 minutes being interviewed by print and electronic media. Then Leyland met with his coaches and GM, because his Pittsburgh Pirates were contemplating a change in the team's roster.

It was well after midnight by the time Leyland had showered, dressed, and headed for his car and the 30-minute ride home. He was home all of eight hours. Then he said good-bye to his wife and infant son and headed back to the ballpark for an afternoon game and its new menu of managerial decisions, after which the Pirates left on a ten-day road trip.

There was nothing unusual about all this; major-league managers all over the country were doing the same thing. It was a schedule common to the lives of the 26 men who managed major-league teams in 1992.

Their existence is a nonstop meat grinder that begins in February amid rather benign spring training settings and then hurtles relentlessly for 180 days from April through September. Since most of the team's 162 games are played at night, a manager lives the timetable of a second-shift factory worker. He leaves for the ballpark shortly after noon and usually doesn't get to his home or hotel until after midnight.

For the lucky ones who reach the play-offs, the merry-go-round then continues through October. Although the pressure may ease over the winter, there are still the baseball winter meetings and assorted public relations functions and meetings over personnel decisions to attend and contract negotiations that can affect players' moods to monitor, all leading to the next February when the cycle spins again.

The job's complexity just begins with the time demands. Managing entails a myriad of responsibilities, constituencies, and stresses that only begin with 162 nine-inning baseball games.

A manager must oversee a coaching staff that usually includes six men. He also must deal with his players, 25 athletes of widely differing personalities, salaries, and backgrounds. The manager must answer to his GM and his club's ownership. He must deal with umpires and marketing people and the media, many of whom travel with the club throughout the season. The manager must often huddle with his club's medical personnel or scouts or minor-league officials. He performs his duties in a climate of economic chaos that can change half his roster from one season to the next. He must also present a product entertaining enough to satisfy fans who have never had more entertainment options and whose cynicism has made them extremely demanding customers.

For better or worse, the manager usually becomes the lightning rod for the entire franchise. No matter that the payroll is out of his hands. No matter that marketing and salaries and the acquisition of personnel and the cleanliness of the ballpark are all beyond his control. When a team loses, there is a very good chance that it will be the manager who will pay the price for the organization's failure.

Jim Leyland is one of the few who have become largely immune to such scrutiny. He entered the 1992 season having won back-to-back division titles and in the process having earned a reputation as one of baseball's best managers. As a reward, he was given a five-year contract extension that would begin in 1993. So he is secure—at least until the Pirates encounter some losing seasons.

However, the truth of the matter is that Leyland and the 25 other men who opened the 1992 baseball season as major-league managers are in the most ephemeral of occupations. Even the Leylands and Tony LaRussas and Sparky Andersons and Tommy Lasordas are second-guessed, their decisions challenged by players, the media, and their own front offices; their job status questioned; their lives potentially turned upside down by the pressures and demands of their chosen profession.

The 1992 season, which is chronicled here, was actually stable by modern standards. "Only" three managers were fired during the season. But three more teams changed managers in the weeks immediately following the season. Even more indicative of the profession's insecurity was the fact that when spring training opened in February 1992, 11 of the 26 managers were in their first springs with their respective clubs.

Although the spectre of being fired is always lurking, the manager's multiple responsibilities and the demands on him serve to sublimate the natural fear of the future. But for those many managers working on short-term contracts, every losing streak magnifies the paranoia. Every whispered conversation between front-office executives is viewed as a possible conspiracy. The body language of the general manager or owner is scrutinized for some indication of where the manager stands. A newspaper columnist's criticism becomes a threat.

Baseball has become a business in which player salaries are an absurd obscenity. Rosters change virtually overnight because loyalty is given more to an agent or a dollar sign than to a team. Thus, fans have waning loyalty to their home teams because new faces arrive all the time. Ownership is no longer in the hands of sportsmen who at least had a long-standing identification with the game; most clubs are now owned by millionaire businesses or business people who view their teams as just one more piece of a financial portfolio.

In this atmosphere, the manager is even more clearly the most disposable of parts. So when the owner tells his general manager to go get some players and millions are spent on a bunch of guys who end up being round pegs in square holes, the modern owner asks his general manager for answers. In the most common scenario, the general manager, who often has a final say on the team's coaches, which enables him to insert a spy or two onto the staff, will advise the owner that the team was really better than it performed. The general manager won't fire himself or the scouts who advised him to sign all those round pegs, and those round pegs make so much money that it is usually difficult to hand them over to another team.

The manager is a much easier target. He is usually making a fraction of what the players make, and there are a dozen other guys anxious for the chance to have his job and willing to take less money for the opportunity. So the manager is the one who gets the axe.

What it's like to manage a major-league team is one of the game's most fascinating elements. Even though the manager plies his trade under the scrutiny of rabid fans and intrusive media, and even though many managers are celebrities in their own right, their job demands have much in common with middle-level managers everywhere in the business world. Nonetheless, what a manager really goes through is rarely studied.

The great irony of it all is that with all the stress and strain and injustice and insecurity, those who manage feel fortunate to have the chance. There are only 28 (with the 1993 addition of new franchises in Colorado and Florida) major-league managing jobs in the world, and when one opens, dozens of applicants queue for attention.

Why? Well, there are all sorts of benefits. Salaries range from $150,000 to close to $1 million a year. Perks include a condominium in either Arizona or Florida for two months, first-class travel including suite accommodations on the road, full medical coverage, time earned on the world's most lavish pension plan, an automobile (at least with most franchises), a cut of baseball's multimillion-dollar merchandise licensing operation, and recognition from millions of sports fans.

But the appeal of managing goes beyond the material reward. Most managers used to be players, many of them at the major-league level. Ask any athlete what he or she misses most in retirement and most will mention the loss of a competitive outlet. Managing provides that high night after night.

There is also the simple, addictive attraction of the game itself. Baseball people are lost without their game. Whether they be managers or players, broadcasters or general managers, public relations directors or groundskeepers, they can rarely escape the hold of the game. And no job more immerses someone in all the game's nuances than managing.

I hope this book will shed a little light on what it's like to manage a major-league team. As a group, managers are the most engaging and enjoyable people in the game. Like high-wire walkers or test pilots, they are members of a most exclusive fraternity who know coming in that sooner or later they will eventually crash and burn.

But few managers regret getting the chance.

Peter Pascarelli
Wayne, Pennsylvania
December 1992

Chapter 1

"Everything Is My Business"

◆ Jim Leyland leaned on a fungo bat, surrounded by some of his coaches and minor-league coaches and instructors as the 1991 Pittsburgh Pirates loosened up for another spring training workout.

They were defending National League East champions, but there was an undercurrent of grumbling over the winter's contract battles in which eight players, including National League Most Valuable Player Barry Bonds, went to salary arbitration. However, it was hard for the Pirates not to be loose and relaxed on this gorgeous Florida morning.

Players were easing into their daily routine. Their stretching exercises were punctuated by the usual raucous insults. Now they were in pairs, playing catch to loosen their arms while a small crowd of onlookers, most of them snowbirds from up north, gaped at the many familiar faces.

Leyland was being kidded for swearing off cigarettes and coffee that spring, only to replace them with a big morning cigar and a mug of black tea. "That's a hell of a health program you're on," said Rich Donnelly, one of the Pirates coaches.

Rocky Bridges, a longtime Pirates minor-league manager, piped in with, "That reminds me of a story." Because Bridges was famous for his stories and his jokes, the group of coaches and instructors gathered around for another tale.

Meanwhile, Bonds and Bobby Bonilla, the Pirates outfield stars, were throwing to each other close to a fence that separated the field from the clubhouse and adjacent to an area where the media watched the workout.

A photographer approached Bonds from behind the fence and started clicking off pictures. Bonds told the photographer to stop, but when he persisted Bonds stopped throwing and said to the cameraman, "I told you to keep the fucking camera out of my face."

The photographer immediately went looking for a Pirates official since there was no club policy prohibiting photos at an open workout. Meanwhile, a photographer who was a friend of Bonds and doing a private project for the outfielder began taking pictures. When the original photographer returned with the then-Pirates publicity man Jim Lachimia, the photographer became even more irate. Lachimia tried to reason with all sides.

"Barry, this guy has as much right to shoot as anyone. The club doesn't grant special favors to the media," said Lachimia.

Bonds stopped throwing and approached Lachimia, getting right into his face. "Look, I decide who takes my picture, not you," said Bonds. "You don't tell me who takes my picture. You don't tell me anything."

By now, the scene was being noticed all over the field as well as by the media, but Lachimia didn't back down. "Barry, we can't have one policy for you and another one for the rest of the team," he said.

Bonds then screamed, "You can kiss my ass. You get that camera out of my face or I'll take care of it myself, do you hear me? You don't decide who takes my picture. Get the fuck away from me."

Lachimia backed off as Rich Donnelly whistled for the players to break down into groups of infielders and outfielders. Leyland, having seen only the end of the scene, thought it was something he could deal with later.

When Bonds sauntered into the outfielder group, he was confronted by Bill Virdon, a longtime major-league manager who annually served as an outfield instructor in spring training and would become a Pirates coach in 1992. Virdon is well known in baseball for his physical strength, his toughness, and a temper that is slow to kindle but highly volatile once ignited. Virdon was seething and quietly said to Bonds, "Why don't you grow up and stop acting like an asshole? How the hell can you treat people like that?" Bonds spit back, "It's none of your fucking business. Who the hell are you anyway?"

Virdon snapped, grabbing for Bonds. Pirates coach Gene Lamont and Triple-A manager Terry Collins held Virdon back as Leyland hurried to the group.

"What the hell is going on?" he screamed. Bonds screamed back, "You stay out of this—this isn't any of your business."

That set off Leyland. "None of my business? I'm the goddamn manager. Everything is my business and I'm not going to have you disrupt the whole fucking ball club, do you hear me?" shouted Leyland. Cameras were clicking and pens flashed across notebooks as the media recorded the ugly scene.

Said Bonds, "He [Virdon] has no business coming at me. This ain't his concern. I have nothing to do with him. I do what I want."

Leyland fired back, "Well, you can just do it somewhere else. I'm sick and tired of this bullshit. I've been kissing your ass for five years and I'm sick and fucking tired of it, do you hear me? If you don't like the way you're treated here or you don't like our rules, then take off the goddamn uniform and get the hell out of here because you're not going to turn this team upside down. If you don't like it here, then get the fuck out of here."

Leyland, as if ranting at an umpire, turned to leave and then came right back at Bonds, who was being calmed down by Bonilla. "You're one guy here and that's it," screamed Leyland. "I don't care who you are. Everybody goes by the same rules here and if you can't handle that, then get off my field. Just get the hell off my field because I don't want you around. You either go with the program or leave. I'm not going to listen to this shit anymore. Do you hear me? Just get off my field."

Bonilla lifted Bonds up and half-carried him away from Leyland, taking him far out into the outfield. Leyland meanwhile turned to his coaches and players and said, "Come on, let's get to work. The show's over, boys."

The Pirates were used to little blowups. Leyland was never afraid to tear into a player in front of other players and the players knew it was never done for effect but rather was genuine anger on Leyland's part. They also knew that such explosions always passed and were never followed by grudges. "When he blows, he blows, but then it's over and he treats you the same as anyone else," said veteran catcher Mike LaValliere.

However, this blowup was something out of the ordinary, coming as it did in full public view of TV cameras and reporters. That evening it would become part of every sportscast in the country. Most analysts suggested that it showed the disintegration of the Pirates, who appeared riddled by dissension and discord.

The incident actually would have the opposite effect. Leyland hadn't planned the March tirade and in truth was embarrassed by it later. "I'll be watching myself making an ass of myself all year now," he moaned later the same day. But the temper tantrum could not have come at a better time.

Pirates players had had their own fill of Bonds's complaining. Like Bonds, they had all either directly or indirectly felt the hard edge of the Pirates' contract negotiations. Although none hesitated to criticize, they also felt it was time to put their displeasure aside and get back to the work of winning another division title.

Bonds had always been hard to take. On the one hand, he was a superbly gifted athlete and a teammate who could be counted on to play his hardest every night out and produce in the most pressurized situations. But his grating personality sometimes wore out his teammates. There were stories that winter about how rude and boorish Bonds acted when part of a touring team in Japan. Said Andy Van Slyke, who had been with Bonds on the tour, "You know, they polled the Japanese people on the three worst days in their country's history. Number 3 was the bombing of Nagasaki. Number 2 was the bombing of Hiroshima. And number 1 was the day Barry Bonds stepped off the plane in Tokyo."

When Leyland finally exploded at Bonds, it seemed as if the whole team exploded with him. The Pirates needed Bonds, but they also needed to let him know that he had to turn down the volume. Leyland said what most of the Pirates would have liked to have said. That's part of what he does for a living.

It is a sign of the times that perhaps the most important job of modern baseball managers is to set the tone for their ball club. Long gone are the days when managers were, in effect, fitness instructors who used spring training to work their players into playing shape. With few exceptions, the modern, wealthy players are in condition year-round. A manager's biggest task is to gauge his team's collective psyche and create the kind of atmosphere that will extract the best preparation and performance.

Leyland has always been his team's weather vane, even in his first year as the Pittsburgh manager when the Pirates were the worst team in baseball. As the talent improved and individuals grew into stars, the Pirates almost unanimously took their cue from the guy they all called Hump.

That's how it was in 1987, when in the final weekend of the season the Pirates swept a series from Philadelphia to ensure they would not finish last for the first time in four years. Leyland proceeded to weep in the clubhouse, and so did many of his players who had been through the horror of the earlier years.

That's how it was during the 1990 season as Leyland steadfastly refused to talk about the pennant race. Instead, he would only discuss that night's game. His team adopted similar tunnel vision in wearing down the New York Mets in the stretch run to win the division title.

Leyland knew on that March morning in 1991 that his team had to stop bitching about contracts and get its head back into the new season. A man loyal to his employers, Leyland was not about to use the "us against them" tactic of making the club's management the enemy. He knew that his veteran team wouldn't buy any talk of being underdogs because his team knew it was too good to be an underdog.

When Bonds pushed Leyland to the breaking point, the resulting incident perfectly served Leyland's purposes. Leyland's tantrum was genuinely spontaneous. But as the year unfolded, it also proved to be the 1991 Pirates' turning point. "We had to get all of the contract junk and all the griping out of the way before we could ever be a good team, because that stuff could have festered all year," said LaValliere. "But the thing you have to remember is that even guys who were unhappy all respected Jim. And what's more, everyone trusted him to do what was right. So when Jim blew up at Barry, we all sort of felt a cloud lift. It was as if we had our argument, we had our family feud, and now it was back to work."

The Pirates would go on to blow away the NL East in 1991 for their second straight NL East title, only to fall short in the league play-offs when Atlanta's pitching shut them out in the last two games in Pittsburgh to win an epic seven-game series.

That play-off disappointment set in motion a series of events that would again challenge Leyland's leadership in 1992.

Leyland and his players had been through a lot together. Three years previously, general manager Syd Thrift was fired in a power struggle with the club's owners. The Pirates annually led the league in acrimonious arbitration cases. There was near mutiny when Larry Doughty, the next GM, ran afoul of baseball's waiver rules and inadvertently lost some top prospects, and then cut even deeper into the club's minor-league depth with a series of trades.

Shortly after the '91 season ended, Doughty himself was fired. The Pirates then lost free agents Bobby Bonilla and Bob Kipper. Also gone was club president Carl Barger, who left the Pirates to oversee the creation of the Florida Marlins expansion club. Barger's departure was especially hard on Leyland. The two had become close friends. They were neighbors in the woodsy Pittsburgh suburbs and frequent golf partners. Barger was a business advisor to Leyland, and they often dined together with each other's families.

Barger's departure sparked rumors that Leyland, whose contract was scheduled to expire after the 1992 season, would follow to Florida. That speculation led the new Pirates management to negotiate a five-year deal with Leyland, worth close to $1 million a year. Ironically enough, on the morning after Leyland signed the new deal, Barger came to Leyland's house for breakfast, became ill, and had to be rushed to the hospital by ambulance. It turned out to be a reaction to medication, although Leyland would later joke that "Carl just couldn't handle Katie's cooking."

Other than losing Bonilla and Kipper, the Pirates had done little in the off-season under new president Mark Sauer and GM Ted Simmons, who joined the club less than a month before spring training. They did re-sign third baseman Steve Buechele to a four-year $14 million contract, but that move was viewed somewhat skeptically. Leyland privately believed the money might have been better spent trying to re-sign pitchers Doug Drabek and John Smiley, both of whom could be free agents after the 1992 season (as could Bonds, who the club felt was unsignable). But Leyland had not yet forged a relationship with the two new executives, so there was little he could do to suggest that. In the old days, Barger would say to Leyland, "Let's get us a ring on our finger," and persuade Douglas Danforth, the club chairman, who held the purse strings, to make a move desired by Leyland.

So Leyland faced an uncertain spring of 1992 with new bosses, tighter budgets, and a lineup that would be minus Bonilla's 100 RBI. He was convinced the Pirates would have to add an outfielder with some offensive skills, so trades were inevitable. He knew that his veteran players would watch the moves closely: If there was any inkling that the Pirates were minding the bottom line more than winning, there would be hell to pay.

Leyland would also open spring training without Gene Lamont, his longtime third-base coach and most trusted lieutenant.
Lamont was named over the winter to be manager of the Chicago
White Sox. His spot at third base would be filled by Rich Donnelly, and his spot on the staff, by Terry Collins, but no one
could replace his closeness with Leyland. However, Leyland did
ask Bill Virdon to join the staff on a full-time basis. Virdon didn't
need a coaching job at this stage in his distinguished career, but
Leyland needed Virdon's solid presence and he needed him as
a sounding board when things went poorly. Virdon would let
Leyland know during spring training.

Despite all that, Leyland approached spring training no differently than he approached spring trainings in the past. Like
most managers, Leyland had meticulously organized the Pirates'
spring training from the first day on which pitchers and catchers
reported right through the exhibition schedule. The workouts
reflected how much had changed in modern baseball. A generation ago, players would come to spring training in order to get
into physical condition for the playing of the long season. Many
players worked off-season jobs and did not have the time or access
to conditioning facilities.

But today's players don't need to find extra work. Most maintain
a year-round workout regimen that keeps them in condition 12
months a year. Few players beyond such publicized ones as Lon-
nie Smith, Kevin Mitchell, and John Kruk arrive in spring training with any significant weight problems.

All this means that spring training is no longer a time for
players to get into condition. But it is still needed to get into
baseball shape. That's especially true with pitchers, who are,
along with the Florida Chamber of Commerce, the people who
benefit most from spring training. Most everyday players are ready
to open the season after a couple of weeks of spring training, but
pitchers need all the time they can get.

Pitchers are the reason why spring training is six weeks long.
They're the reason why so many teams schedule so-called B
games, unofficial exhibition games played in the morning prior

to the real exhibitions. And they're largely the reason why spring training is organized down to the minute.

Leyland gives all of his coaches generous rein, especially during spring training. Once the full squad reports ten days into spring training, batting coach Milt May has some players taking early batting practice in the cage directly outside the Pirates' clubhouse. May and the players set up those sessions themselves; May gives Leyland a list of who's hitting when, but otherwise it's May's show to run. So is the setting of hitting times for the entire club. When a player needs extra at bats, May might coordinate with Leyland a trip to the minor-league complex to take some at bats in a minor-league exhibition.

Leyland gives much of the infield responsibility to Tommy Sandt, who oversees those players getting extra practice as well as the routine infield drills all teams conduct every day during the spring. For example, Jeff King, when his cranky back allowed, was taking several dozen extra ground balls at first and second base in the spring of '92, since Leyland planned on him filling a utility role during the season.

As Lamont did for years with Leyland before going on to manage the White Sox, Donnelly was the general coordinator of all spring training workouts. He set the times for all batting practice groups and work on fundamental drills and oversaw the setting up of extra games, either with other clubs (the B games) or at the minor-league camp. And Donnelly also set up what Leyland called his "All-Star games," which were intersquad games played prior to the opening of the exhibition schedule.

The pitching was in the hands of pitching coach Ray Miller, who was coach of some of this generation's best pitching staffs when he was with the Baltimore Orioles.

Miller kept his own notebook of how long every pitcher threw every day in spring training. He also kept the same information on a giant chart in Leyland's office that mapped out every pitcher's schedule from the first day of camp when the healthy ones throw eight minutes right through the exhibition schedule to the rotation that would start the regular season.

Leyland allows his coaches to have most of the responsibility for their areas. And the coaches appreciate the freedom.

"I know that if I feel something is important to do with one of my pitchers, Jimmy will go along with it," said Miller. "That might sound like a little thing, but when you don't have that freedom, you find out it can be a big thing to overcome. If players think that the coaches are just puppets for the manager, you aren't going to get through to them. But it's all pretty natural here. If I tell one of my pitchers something, he knows that's how it goes, that I have Jimmy's support."

Unlike some managers, Leyland takes no particular extra interest in any one phase of the game. He is more of a personnel director than an instructor. He will often take charge when the club is practicing fundamental drills or might talk one-on-one with a player about some aspect of his play. And he is always the last word concerning playing time, extra work, and discipline. But he has no single specialty he considers his own.

Unlike Leyland, however, several other managers spend the spring concentrating on specific aspects of their team's play. In Plant City, Lou Piniella never hesitated to spend 30 minutes or more working with a specific hitter. A former batting coach and excellent hitter himself, Piniella would often be the coach out early working with a hitter. Tony Perez, the Reds' batting coach, had no problem with the arrangement; Perez in fact welcomed Piniella's involvement, viewing it as another way to get the job done and not as any intrusion into his own authority.

With a new pitching coach in Larry Rothschild, Piniella was also taking a more hands-on approach with his pitchers during the spring of 1992. He did not work with them on pitching intricacies or mechanics, but he wouldn't hesitate to discuss strategy.

In Vero Beach, Tommy Lasorda rarely got involved in individual instruction. Instead, he was his team's lightning rod, someone who would dominate attention and deflect it away from individual players. It was a time-tested strategy that unfortunately may have become outdated. For example, in the spring of 1992, the Dodgers camp was in an uproar after Darryl Strawberry had a press conference to introduce his new book, a tome in which Strawberry, among other things, accused the New York Mets of racism. Nothing Lasorda could do was going to draw attention away from that.

Some managers physically involve themselves in drills. Minnesota's Tom Kelly throws batting practice almost every day, a routine that keeps his club loose and also provides him with an outlet to get away from reporters' questions or any other distractions on a given day. Lasorda throws early batting practice throughout the season to his younger players, both for the physical release and to get a chance to look at some of his organization's younger players in a relatively relaxed setting.

As for Leyland, he often spends batting practice stalking the outfield or infield, talking to players individually. It's a time when he can be alone with a player without an interruption. Often, it's just a casual conversation about the player's family or whatever. For example, early in spring training, Leyland spent a lot of time with Andy Van Slyke, at first due to genuine concern for Van Slyke's three-year-old son, Jared, who accidentally fell into a swimming pool and was pulled to safety by Van Slyke's six-year-old son, Scott. Later, it was concern for Van Slyke's chronically sore back, a problem that Leyland would have to deal with throughout the season.

Van Slyke's wasn't the only physical problem that caused concern during the spring. King's back was also suspect. Bonds was plagued by a sore hamstring. Second baseman Jose Lind was plagued by a sore knee. And Leyland also was concerned about the Pirates' overall depth. So when he read one morning in early March that Kirk Gibson had asked the Kansas City Royals to trade him, Leyland went to GM Ted Simmons. "Look, Ted, he's making a lot of money, but it's only for this year," said Leyland. "I go back 15 years with Gibson. I had him in A ball and he'll go along with the program. If he has anything left, he can help us in a lot of ways. He could give us a little more pop and some speed we could use. And the guy is an animal. He won't hurt in the clubhouse."

Simmons had cursory reports on Gibson's status and dispatched special assignment scout Lenny Yoachim for an in-person look. Simmons knew the Royals needed a left-handed pitcher and the logical candidate was Neal Heaton, who was making $1.1 million and figured again to be in a long relief role for the Pirates. Leyland hated to part with Heaton, who was valuable insurance for the starting rotation, but at the same time he knew that Heaton's salary made him expensive insurance. By trading him for Gibson, the Pirates would be adding only $800,000 to their payroll. The money part of it all didn't concern Leyland; what he did tell Simmons was that Gibson's potential value to the club likely outweighed Heaton's.

So the deal was done on March 10, and Gibson joined the Pirates. The exhibition season had already begun. Pittsburgh somewhat ironically opened against Lamont's White Sox. Chicago's rookie manager was in the middle of one of baseball's most riveting subplots, the anguish over the future of Bo Jackson. And Lamont was also concerned with the condition of Carlton Fisk, while at the same time working in the arrival of his newest big name, George Bell, who had come via a trade with the Cubs.

Leyland and Lamont visited for a while, two friends talking shop, and Leyland was bemused by the situation in which his former coach found himself. "Hell, Geno, here you are in your first year managing worried about Bo Jackson being able to play and wondering if Carlton Fisk would be able to come back from an injury. Man, you got it made if you have to worry about names like that. In my first year with the Pirates, I was worried about whether Bill Almon would be ready to play short. You got it made."

"Well, Hump, the difference is that no one expected you to win 60 games with your first team," said Lamont. "You had a free ride. They're expecting my team to win the division."

Most managers, especially during the first half of the exhibitions, don't take stock in victories. Yes, winning is better than losing, but as long as players are getting in their work, as long as the injuries are held to a minimum, as long as people hustle and play fundamentally sound baseball, the only results that matter are those of rookies seeking to make an impression. For the veterans, all you want to see is effort and good health.

"Hell, for the first three weeks, the starters play five or six innings tops and usually see a different pitcher in every at bat," says Whitey Herzog. "And then in the late innings, you try to get your relievers work and they're usually facing Triple-A hitters who they've never seen and your relievers are working on different pitches and so you can't figure that the results mean anything. I would just want to avoid getting anyone hurt and not embarrass ourselves with how we played. And I always tried to avoid extra innings."

Herzog would try to ensure not having to play extra innings in the spring by always having available what he called his "spring closer." It was a pitcher who was not particularly effective and who could rarely escape a game without letting someone score. When Herzog's Cardinals were tied in the ninth inning of a spring game, especially one on the road, he would have his spring closer ready to go. If his club didn't score in the top of the inning, on would come someone like Joe Boever or Dick Grapenthin, and usually a run would score to end the game, and Herzog would have his team on the bus back to St. Petersburg.

However, spring results can sometimes unnerve a franchise. In 1984, Jim Frey was in his first year managing the Chicago Cubs, who sunk into an amazing Cactus League losing streak. The streak reached 11 games entering a weekend in which the Cubs' owners, the executives of the Tribune Corporation, were in Arizona for their annual spring training visit.

Throughout the streak, Frey remained publicly unconcerned. "Sure, we'd like to be winning some of these games, but the main thing is that we have a plan that we're sticking with and we're getting the job done every day," Frey would tell reporters. When the media left, he'd turn to his friend and third-base coach

Don Zimmer and say, "Donnie, when the hell are we going to win a game? They're going to swallow this plan bullshit only for so long."

With the Tribune's top executives watching, the Cubs took a three-run lead late in an exhibition against San Diego. Taking no chances, Frey called upon his bull-pen ace Lee Smith to finish up the game even though Smith was not definitely scheduled to pitch that day. "What the hell, I figured it might not be a bad idea to win a game with all the bosses watching," recalled Frey.

However, two walks and an error loaded the bases with two outs, and then San Diego's Carmelo Martinez, a former Cub no less, cranked a grand-slam home run to hand the Cubs their 12th loss in a row.

Into Frey's office trooped Tribune chairman of the board Stanton Cook and some aides. Frey said to Cook, "Mr. Cook, I know this must look pretty bad, but let me just tell you that we have a plan here, we worked on it all winter, we think it's a good plan, we're going to stick with it and we're not going to let some exhibition games worry us."

Recalled Frey, "I figured Mr. Cook would give me a little pat on the back and say hang in there."

Instead, Cook listened to Frey and said quietly, "Jim, have you stopped to think that maybe you have yourselves a horseshit plan?"

Said Frey years later, "I about died right there. I figured I'd be the first manager fired in spring training. But then he gave me a little laugh and left. And it all turned out all right in the end." Indeed, that Cubs team went on to win the franchise's first title in 39 years.

Philadelphia manager Nick Leyva began the spring of 1991 on thin ice but hardly in imminent danger. However, throughout the spring, Leyva was unusually critical of his own players. Leyva's bluntness, although admirable from a journalist's point of view, became a growing irritant to GM Lee Thomas, who was uneasy about Leyva's comments largely because he was actively involved in trade talks and did not want his players' value diminished by the criticism of their manager.

The breaking point came late in the spring after an exhibition in Port St. Lucie against the New York Mets. After weeks of wrangling with the Cubs, Thomas had reached tentative agreement for a trade that would send pitchers Bob Scanlan and Chuck McElroy to Chicago in exchange for reliever Mitch Williams. But McElroy that night blew a three-run lead, giving up a game-losing, grand-slam homer to then-Mets outfielder Darren Reed. After the game, Leyva told the Philadelphia writers, "McElroy choked, he just looked scared to death out there."

When informed of Leyva's remark by writers, Thomas went ballistic and threatened to fire him on the spot. Leyva's comment hit the wire services and quickly reached Cubs GM Frey, who just as quickly called Thomas and put the deal back on hold. Ultimately the trade was made ten days later, but Thomas, although deciding against a spring training firing, had made up his mind that Leyva would be gone at first sign of a Phillies slump. And after a 4–9 start, Thomas indeed fired Leyva.

Leyland, of course, faced no such pressure in the spring of 1992. He was secure with his new contract. He was also secure in knowing that his players trusted his judgment.

But by the third week of spring training, he faced a challenge to all the authority and all the trust he had built over the years. He would question whether he had lost his voice within the Pirates' organization. He would also wonder for the first time if he could count on his players' best efforts.

Chapter 2

"We Still Have a Hell of a Club"

◆ Spring training still has loads of charm. Unfortunately, the rickety old ballparks that were once the essence of the Grapefruit and Cactus Leagues are becoming extinct.

Modern complexes abound, especially in Florida, where heretofore sleepy backwater towns like Plant City, Port St. Lucie, Port Charlotte, and Kissimmee have spent millions to build unimaginative concrete stadiums to house major-league teams for six weeks. And in places like Clearwater and Dunedin, the business of spring training has meant the expansion and sterilization of onetime Florida jewels.

But not in Bradenton. The home of the Pittsburgh Pirates remains largely the same as it was when Paul Waner and company frolicked in the Gulf Coast sun. There have been some minor upgrades here and there, but what you see is largely what was there 50 years ago.

Leyland's office at ancient McKechnie Field is a tiny cubicle at the far end of the clubhouse, next to the training room and across from the lunchroom, which is always stocked with crackers, peanut butter, and coffee. Unless something is going on, the office door is almost always open. That's the way Leyland operates. Any player who wanders by will always get a word or two from the manager.

One March morning, the day the NCAA basketball tournament was to begin, was typical. Barry Bonds strode by and Leyland yelled, "Who do you have in the pool?"

"I haven't picked yet," said Bonds. "I'm trying to buy some extra picks."

Leyland and Donnelly shook their heads. "Why is BB buying more picks? He's the luckiest SOB around here," said Donnelly. "He'll reach into the hat and pick Duke, sure as I'm sitting here."

Drabek poked his head in and Leyland yelled his daily refrain: "You better sign. We can't be fooling around here. Get that agent of yours up from Houston and let's get it done." Said Drabek, "Hey, I keep telling you I'm ready. Tell your guys to get going."

Then catcher Don Slaught walked in and said, "That was a nice one you pulled on me." Said Leyland, "You deserved it, Sluggo. You should know by now not to nose around my desk."

It seems that Slaught often wanders into Leyland's office and glances through the legal pad that is always on Leyland's desk. So the day before, Leyland baited his catcher by leaving on the desk a list of names and their likely destination. Beside Slaught's name, Leyland had written, "Trade?"

Such access to a manager is not universal. In Vero Beach, Lasorda will cruise the clubhouse and schmooze with players, but more often than not his office is filled with cronies, not players.

In Plant City, Piniella will often be closeted with his coaches or GM Bob Quinn. Players who visit are usually summoned first.

Rarely is Leyland's door closed. But by 9:30 on March 19, the door was shut.

It had already been a long morning for Leyland. He had put his wife, Katie, and infant son, Patrick, on an early plane back to Pittsburgh. Katie wanted to get their house in order, and she knew that in the final two weeks of spring training her husband would be spending at least 12 hours a day at the ballpark. So it was time to leave the gulf-front rented condo with the swimming pool at every unit and fly home.

Leyland had made plans to go to the dog track that evening. "I'll lose my $50 to $100 and go back home," he said. "I hate going back to the place when it's empty, especially the first night. So, I'll go to the track, go home, and fall asleep."

But sleep wouldn't come easy that night after one of Leyland's longest days as Pirates manager. Upon arriving at McKechnie Field, he was informed that Danforth had instructed Simmons and Sauer to pare down the payroll. And the only place it could be done with any significance was to release veteran relief pitcher Bill Landrum and his $1.7 million price tag.

So Simmons closeted himself with Leyland. And as the coaches took the players outside for their morning stretching exercises, Leyland remained behind closed doors. The door opened once and out came Simmons, but he returned and the door was quickly shut. Then out to make a quick phone call went agent Ed Gilhooly. Then he returned, and the door was shut again. A peek revealed that Landrum was also in the room.

"Oh, boy, here we go," said Bob Walk, a veteran pitcher and one of the many consciences of the Pirates' clubhouse. "This doesn't look good."

An hour later, out rushed an obviously upset Landrum. Paul Meyer and Bob Hertzel, the two Pirates beat writers from the *Pittsburgh Post Gazette* and *Pittsburgh Press*, approached Landrum. They are the only traveling writers around the Pirates. Both are veteran baseball writers who have as good a rapport with the team they cover as any beat writers in the business. But Landrum snapped at them. "Another one bites the dust. I'm fucking released so get away from me for a while, will you?" said Landrum.

Leyland brought his coaches into his office. "They made me swallow this one. What the hell else can I do?" Leyland told them. "I'm going to try not to say anything I shouldn't and I hope you guys try the same thing. But what the hell are we going

to do in the bull pen? Mundo, you're the best, you better think
of something."

Mundo is pitching coach Ray Miller, who indeed is one of
the best pitching coaches in baseball. He was doodling on his
clipboard and looked up to say, "Well, we got to make up for
413 innings that we've lost from last year's staff. That's all, just
413 innings."

The total of 413 innings represented the loss of Landrum,
Neal Heaton, Bob Kipper, and the recent trade of lefty 20-game
winner John Smiley to Minnesota. Leyland was seething; he had
just barely gotten over the Smiley trade. He had known that the
Pirates could not afford to keep all of their potential free agents,
and when asked by Simmons and Sauer whom he would trade if
he had to choose between Smiley and Drabek, Leyland answered
with Smiley. But Leyland was still caught by surprise when the
trade with Minnesota for young pitcher Denny Neagle and Class-
A outfield prospect Midre Cummings had been announced. Leyland knew talks were going on, but he had assumed that Simmons
would confer with him before making any deal final. When the
trade was announced without Leyland's prior knowledge and then
when Simmons told reporters that Vicente Palacios would likely
replace Smiley in the Pittsburgh rotation, Leyland snapped.

A reporter from a Sarasota paper had asked who would replace
Smiley, and Leyland had been noncommittal. Then the reporter
retorted, "Well, Ted Simmons says it's going to be Palacios."
That's when Leyland exploded.

"No one tells me who does what on my team, do you get
that?" screamed Leyland. "I decide who the fuck is on my team
and I ain't even close to knowing who is in the rotation. No one
else decides, is that fucking clear?" Smiley meanwhile was sitting
in a nearby batting cage, tears streaming down his face as shocked
teammates filed by to say good-bye.

Surveying the scene, Van Slyke said, "Welcome to the home
of the defending National League East champions."

On Landrum's release, the outbursts came from the players,

especially when they were told by reporters that Simmons claimed the move was not due to the economics of dropping Landrum's $1.7 million salary. Rather, said Simmons, the move was triggered by the club's desire to keep young pitcher Miguel Batista, who was taken from Montreal in the December Rule 5 draft and thus had to remain on the Pirates' roster all season or be offered back to Montreal through waivers.

Batista was a raw talent. "He's a good Double-A guy," said catcher Mike LaValliere. "But there's no way he can help us this year. Hey, say it was money, at least then they wouldn't be adding a lie on top of a bad decision. Don't tell us it wasn't the money."

Said Bonds, "We aren't a bunch of retards wearing uniforms. Don't tell us it wasn't because of Landrum's salary. Just like they tried to defend the Smiley deal. All we got were minor leaguers. And now we just drop Landrum. You need pitching. If they were position players, you could have a chance to make up for losing them. But they're just giving pitching away because of money. And it seems like they're not going to even give us a chance to win."

Said Van Slyke, "I feel bad for Jim. They're just taking his team away from him. You know he wouldn't go for this if it were up to him."

Leyland heard all the clubhouse grumbling and a lot more from his coaches. Publicly, he held his temper in check. But when he heard Simmons's explanations concerning Batista, that sent him over the edge. "I'm going to have it out with them tomorrow," Leyland told Donnelly. "I'm not going to threaten to quit or anything like that. But he has to know if he makes me take Batista on top of all this, then we might lose the team. These guys aren't stupid."

To the media, Leyland was curt. "I have no comment on it [Landrum's release]," he said. "You guys get it? No comment.

"Batista? He has to make the team like everyone else. I have no idea if he will be on the team. Hopefully he can be a usable pitcher, but I'm not sure about that yet."

Later with his coaches, the mood would be one of dark humor.

"Who can we get cheap?" said Leyland. "Mundo, let's go over to the minor-league camp and look around. Maybe we'll find something."

"If there's no pitching, you can at least get a few stories from Rocky [Bridges, a trusty Pirates instructor]," said Tommy Sandt.

Miller meanwhile said like a mantra, "413 innings, we've lost 413 innings."

Publicity director Jim Trdinich then poked in his head to announce that ex-Steelers coach Chuck Noll would throw out the first ball at the home opener. "Whoop-de-do, I wonder how much we're paying him for that," said Leyland. "This has been one hell of a day. I say good-bye to my family, I'm told to release somebody and kill my bull pen, and I'll lose 100 bucks at the dog track. We're going real good here."

By 7 A.M. the next morning Leyland was reading the papers alone in his condo, puffing a cigarette, drinking coffee, and losing his temper all over again. The more he read Simmons's comments about Landrum's release being the result of the Pirates' desire to keep rookie Batista, the more Leyland seethed. So he jumped into the big white Lincoln Town Car the club leased him for spring training, drove the ten minutes to his McKechnie Field office, and called Simmons. "We've got to talk this morning," said Leyland.

"Come over in a half hour. I'll get Mark in with us," said Simmons, referring to club president Mark Sauer.

It had been an awful week for Simmons. He had been on the job for barely a month and was suddenly presented with situations that any veteran executive would have loathed. Simmons had to pull the trigger on the Smiley deal with Minnesota, which was universally panned. Yet Danforth kept the pressure on, ordering more cuts from the payroll that initiated the Landrum move. As the pressure mounted, Simmons knew he had made some bureaucratic mistakes. The biggest was failing to inform Leyland prior to finalizing the Minnesota deal. Now Leyland was upset all over again, feeling embarrassed by having to defend the Landrum move

and resistant at being told publicly that he would have to keep
Batista, who Leyland felt was no better than a Class-A prospect.

Simmons realized that all could be lost on this March morning
if he and Leyland couldn't get back on the same page.

Leyland's position was unique among major-league managers.
Most managers are at the mercy of their GM or owner, and most
managers are tolerated as necessary evils by their team's fans,
largely ignored when things go well and widely vilified when
things go badly. But not Leyland. He had the security of his new
long-term contract. When Barger was president, Leyland was in
effect a partner of ownership, with more influence than GM
Doughty. When Barger left and rumors flew that Leyland might
go with Barger to Florida or perhaps to Chicago to take the White
Sox job, Danforth instructed Sauer to move quickly to keep
Leyland in town.

Leyland actually had little desire to go anywhere. He had
grown fond of the Pittsburgh area. His wife, Katie, was a Pittsburgh native, and the couple loved their sprawling suburban
house. Leyland didn't disappear in the winter like so many managers who manage one place but live in another; he went to
Steelers games and Pitt basketball games, and he worked the local
charity and luncheon circuit.

He felt pride in how he had helped turn around a franchise
that was nearly extinct when he arrived. "I remember my first
winter with the club," he said. "They came up with the idea of
me and a few other people from the club going downtown and
standing on the street corners handing out ticket information.
I'll never forget standing in 15-degree cold and having people
walk by like I was some kind of nut."

Now Leyland was easily the most popular sports figure in that
football-mad town. It was not lost on the Pirates' owners that
when the club was introduced during the play-offs, the biggest
and most emotional ovation was reserved for Leyland. His decision to forsake managerial free agency and stay with the Pirates
only enhanced his enormous popularity.

Beyond that, he had earned national acclaim as one of the best managers, if not *the* best, in the majors. If the growing tension between Leyland and Simmons spilled into the public arena, Simmons's GM career would be the shortest in baseball history. No one knew that more than Simmons. He didn't want a confrontation and moreover he respected Leyland as much as anyone.

Simmons's office was at Pirates City, a complex of baseball fields and housing for minor-league players in a motellike dormitory that would make your average Motel 6 seem like the Ritz Carlton. Its shabby appearance triggered a grievance from the Players Association a few years ago that forced the Pirates to spruce things up a little.

Leyland arrived in uniform since he would head directly from the meeting to St. Petersburg, where the Pirates were facing the St. Louis Cardinals in an exhibition game that afternoon.

Even before Leyland arrived, Sauer and Simmons got some bad news: Landrum and his agent had filed a grievance through the Players Association, charging the Pirates with an illegal release. A player cannot be released for purely economic reasons, only for performance or conduct detrimental to his club. There was nothing wrong with how Landrum was throwing. He was obviously a better pitcher than Miguel Batista, and he was one of the Pirates' solid citizens. It seemed obvious Landrum was released purely because of money. It was just as obvious to the Players Association. So Simmons knew that Landrum's release wouldn't fade from the newspapers.

Leyland arrived and Simmons said, "Landrum has filed a grievance."

"That's not my business. I don't care one way or another," said Leyland. "All I care about is whether I'm still managing here. If you're going to force Batista on me, then I don't know if I'm managing here or not.

"I mean, Jesus Christ, Ted, how can I sell this to the players? They're not dumb. They know what's going on. And if anything else happens, we don't have a chance. We'll lose them, sure as hell. I wasn't told about this stuff and I feel I deserve that. That hurts a little."

"Jim, this is it, I swear, we don't have to do anything else," said Simmons. "This has been tough on us all and I know a lot of it could have been handled better. But it's over."

"What about Batista?'" asked Leyland. "He can't pitch in the majors. You know that, I know that, everybody on the team knows that. We could have tried to carry him if we had last year's staff. But with what I have left in the bull pen, there's no way I can carry a guy who I know can't help me. We have enough trouble in the bullpen without having to carry a guy who can't help."

Said Simmons, "Look, I want to keep the guy for opening day. If after a while it's clear that it's going to hurt, then we'll look at it again."

Leyland sensed Simmons's stance was softening. He could live with Batista for a few more weeks, wearing down both Simmons and Sauer, and when it became obvious as he knew it would, he could finally convince them to drop the young right-hander. Leyland also realized that Simmons was not being hardheaded about the whole subject.

"Well, I can live with that," said Leyland. "The goddamn thing is that we still have a hell of a club. If I know I can have this club, we have one hell of a club. We have problems in the bull pen but I still like this club. But I have to know that this will be my club, that there'll be no more screwing around. I can sell these guys with what we have now. But if something else happens, we're in trouble."

Simmons and Sauer both were adamant that the major moves were over. With that, Leyland jumped up. "Well, then let's get the hell to work. I'll see you in St. Pete."

Later that day, for the benefit of Meyer and Hertzel, the two Pirates beat reporters, Leyland went into a long discourse about how the storm had passed. However, with a little prodding, Leyland discussed with remarkable candor his relationship with Simmons.

"All the chaos will take its course and we can get back to work," said Leyland. "We all bitched, but now it's over and we can all get on with our business. The bullshit is over—now let's go, let's see what we have to do.

"What did I meet about with Ted? It was a friendly thing. I felt a little hurt and I let him know. But I don't know how to do everybody's job. My job is to manage this team. That's all I want to do. I think Ted Simmons will be a great general manager. So much has happened here so fast. He's done the best he could and I respect that. I like to think that it's mutual. A GM doesn't owe me any explanations. I can say no to something, but it's his decision in the end and I respect that. But I do think I should be asked.

"And I don't think we should try to hide things so much. I was upset the last few days. And I want it out in the open. What the hell, that's part of the game. What the hell sense is it to hide things that you guys in the press already know anyway? We shouldn't have so many secrets in this business so that the real secrets can stay secrets. How's that one? That's a pretty good line, right?

"Look, at this point all I'm going to worry about is that we can get healthy. Andy's back hurts. Chico [Lind] has a knee. Sluggo has a shoulder. Barry has a hamstring. King has a back. That's what's important, not all this other bullshit. We have a hell of a club. I believe that. Yeah, the bull pen is a concern, but if I can put something together out there, we'll have a helluva club. If I can't, then maybe it will be a problem.

"But damn it, I like my team. Everybody is talking about the trouble we're in, but I look around and see Bonds and Van Slyke and [Jay] Bell and Lind and Drabek and [Zane] Smith and all these guys. That ain't too bad."

However, Leyland shrugged off questions about how he would deal with the players. Their mood had remained sullen. Danforth had visited the clubhouse that morning with some business associates and several Pirates made it a point of walking out. Bonds

came into the dugout in St. Petersburg and said to Leyland, "It's
my daughter's birthday and I'm not even there. I should just take
a walk out of here."

"How old is she?" asked Leyland.

"She's one," said Bonds.

"Well, Barry, she's not going to know whether you're there or
not, so let's get to work."

Bonds muttered under his breath and then sauntered off toward
the outfield. Leyland stared after him but said nothing. However,
minutes later, Leyland was slowly making the rounds of the outfield, talking to players individually. The healing had begun.

The next day, things began loosening up. Leyland and Miller
spent the morning at Pirates City, where Batista threw in a game
involving some Pirates reserves and assorted minor leaguers. But
Leyland also wanted to see left-hander Steve Cooke, a Double-
A prospect. The Pirates' big need was another left-hander in the
bull pen and the reports on Cooke were good. Leyland had been
told that Cooke was set to throw. But when he arrived, he was
told by the minor-league staff that Cooke was not throwing. "Jesus
H. Christ, that's great, that helps a lot," said Leyland.

Still the mood was improving. Miller asked if Simmons would
come from his office to watch Batista throw. "He's probably sitting
in there with the shades down," said Leyland.

Among the Pirates reserves was Gary Varsho, who is often on
the receiving end of Leyland's kidding. The day before, because
of injuries, Leyland had changed the schedule of who was to play
in St. Petersburg; Varsho had originally been off and had planned
a trip to Disney World with his wife and baby but had to go to
St. Pete instead. Leyland spotted Varsho's wife and baby near the
field and sauntered over. "So how was Disney World, was it a
nice trip?" said Leyland, talking just loudly enough for Varsho
and the bench to hear.

Varsho just shook his head. "How mad is she, Hump?" said
Varsho.

"Gary, she's a great lady, she's not mad at me. She's mad at
you."

Varsho, a left-handed hitter suddenly fighting for a job with the recent addition of Kirk Gibson, is also notorious for being unable to hit left-handed pitching. The trip to Pirates City was expressly so Leyland could see what left-handers were in the minor-league camp who might help. This didn't bode well for Varsho. "I just hope Ted doesn't come down to watch this, Varsh, or I might not be able to save you," said Leyland.

"Now, Mac, you're another story," he said, addressing Lloyd McClendon. "You haven't got a hit all spring. The trouble is that you've lost too much weight. You have to get fat again so you can hit."

One of the left-handers to throw was Mike Dalton, who was wild but who did retire Varsho with two men on. Next to throw was Sherman Corbett, minor-league pickup out of the California organization. Lo and behold, Varsho stepped up and yanked a single off the left-hander.

"That's enough for me. Are you ready to go, Ray?" said Leyland.

"I've been ready since we got here," said Miller.

So the search for the left-hander would continue. But Leyland still had to grapple with the not-so-small matter of the Pirates' morale. Their public sniping at the organization had quieted. But a clubhouse that had been for years among the most easy-going in baseball was unusually tense.

For example, there was the case of the young left-hander Denny Neagle, who through no fault of his own was suddenly thrust in the uncomfortable position of having to personally justify the trading away of the 20-game winner Smiley. Neagle read the sneering comments of teammates, who dismissed him as "some minor leaguer." And he sensed that Leyland needed to be convinced he belonged.

Neagle's debut with Pittsburgh ironically came against the Twins, and he produced a decent four-inning effort that eased the pressure somewhat. Leyland, as most managers do in spring training, watched the game from a folding chair to the side of the dugout. Next to him was Miller.

Leyland saw that Neagle did not have overpowering stuff. His fastball was in the average range of 85 miles per hour. His breaking ball seemed average as well, although he appeared to have the makings of a good change-up and decent control. "What do you think, Ray, can you help him?" asked Leyland after the second inning.

"Jim, he's got four usable pitches and a smooth delivery," said Miller. "That's a pretty good start. I think he's giving his pitches away, so let me talk to him about something."

An inning later, Miller seemed at least somewhat satisfied. "Well, he listened and changed what I suggested," said Miller. "That's another good sign."

"Well, he looks like a guy who needs to be ahead in the count, because he ain't going to overpower anybody," said Leyland.

"He overstrides a little and we can work with that, which could help the velocity a little," said Miller. "You're right, though, he's not a power pitcher. But he's around the plate and knows a little how to change speeds. If he's a guy that can make adjustments, he might be all right."

Miller later spent time with Neagle, who had barely been introduced to most of his teammates and felt a bit ostracized.

"Look, Denny, these guys are good guys here. "They're just hurt at what's happened around here. It's not you," said Miller. "All you can do is go out and do the best you can. You're not John Smiley and you're not here to replace him, either. You're Denny Neagle and your job is to make Denny Neagle the best pitcher he can be. You're pitching for the best manager in base-ball, you have the best defense in the National League behind you, and I've been around some of the best pitchers in baseball. So use all that, and all this stuff will pass."

Miller left him and Neagle sat quietly for a moment. "I needed that," he said. "And really it felt good just to pitch. I just want to earn a job here."

But the larger problem remained the mood of the Pirates' veteran nucleus. They had been playing listless baseball for ten days. There were assorted nagging injuries. The bull pen was a mess. And opening day was now only two weeks away.

None of the injuries appeared serious. And the bull pen would be a problem that would likely have to be addressed throughout the entire season. But listlessness was something that needed an immediate remedy, which is why Leyland decided it was time for a team meeting to talk about attitude, something he does very rarely.

Now, teams have meetings all the time. Most clubs meet virtually daily in spring training, but these are merely organizational sessions. With so many extra players in camp, especially early in spring training, a daily meeting is needed just to make sure everybody knows where he is supposed to be at the right time.

Virtually every team has some kind of meeting before the first game of each series. They usually meet in groups: The pitchers and catchers go over opposing scouting reports of opposing hitters with the pitching coach and manager, outfielders and infielders meet with other coaches to go over the defensive alignments for opposition hitters, and the hitters usually meet with a coach or a manager to go over the other club's pitchers.

There are meetings in spring training to go over rules, such as whether ties are required on team flights or if there will be curfews, a rarity in modern baseball. There are also meetings late in the season to talk about how to divide postseason money.

At rare times, there are even meetings where the managers and coaches are asked to leave so the players can have their own encounter session among themselves. Most managers don't mind such players-only meetings, unless they start occurring so frequently they become mutinies.

However, the meetings that get the most attention are those in which managers shut the doors and try to inspire or browbeat or scream their team into a better performance. Every manager has a different idea about the wisdom of such sessions.

When Earl Weaver managed the Baltimore Orioles, he rarely

had meetings. One reason was that the Orioles were usually winning so much, there wasn't a need for such things. For another, those Orioles teams had great clubhouse leaders like Brooks Robinson, Frank Robinson, Lee May, Eddie Murray, Mike Flanagan, Jim Palmer, and Mark Belanger. Such players served as policemen for the occasional instances of less than 100 percent effort or any of the other transgressions that trigger managerial meetings. Also, Weaver yelled at his players so much in the course of the daily game that he had little reserved for any meetings. When the Orioles did slump and Weaver would be asked if he might have a meeting, his response was, "What good will a meeting do? What if I have a meeting and we still keep playing lousy? Then what do I do?"

In other words, Weaver's theory was that you'd better pick your right spot because you can't cry wolf too many times. A lot of baseball men of Weaver's generation agree.

"I don't have any game plan other than a meeting on the first day of full spring training and on opening day," says Giants manager Roger Craig. "Otherwise, they just happen spontaneously most other times.

"Heck, when I was playing there was no such thing as managers offering the players any of this motivational stuff. You either pitched good or it was Double-A. That was your motivation, and no one had to spell it out for you.

"I guess kids nowadays are more insecure, not just in baseball but everywhere in society. I said five or six years ago that I thought owners would start going for younger managers because of the difference in eras between my generation and the new one. There has definitely been a change in personality of the players and with these players, you have to relate, communicate, or whatever the right word is.

"But I don't think meetings are the best way to do it. I think the best way is for the manager to be the first to know everything that is going on around his club and with his players. And I want my coaches to make sure I know everything. That way, maybe we can get a guy straightened out before he becomes a problem or before his problem becomes our problem. Yeah, that sure is different from when I played, but it's a fact of life."

When Dallas Green managed the Philadelphia Phillies to the 1980 World Series, he had a different theory on meetings. With a team that included some of the most difficult players in baseball, Green spent a lot of time screaming. He also used the ploy of ripping his team to writers, employing a voice that would carry into the clubhouse and beyond.

However, Green did save one of his most notable closed-door diatribes for a crucial time. The Phillies were in Pittsburgh for an August series in which they would end up getting swept four games. In between games of a Sunday doubleheader, Green tore into his team. "You're all so fucking cool, well, you better get off your butt and beat somebody," screamed Green in a voice loud enough to penetrate the concrete walls and allow him to be heard in the corridor. "You're a good team but you aren't one now. You can't look in the fucking mirror. You just give up. If any of you don't want to play, then go into the fucking office and tell me you don't want to play anymore."

After losing the second game that day to fall seven games out, the Phillies ran off seven straight wins and turned their season around. So maybe that meeting worked. Or maybe it was the meeting held by Phillies GM Paul Owens on Labor Day in San Diego during that same wild 1980 season when he careened into the clubhouse and gave the Phils a tongue-lashing that nearly deafened the swallows on their way to Capistrano. Since Owens and Green were extremely close, the players knew that Owens's explosion was no usurping of Green's power but instead was an extension of it. Coincidentally or not, Philadelphia proceeded to roll through September and on into the play-offs.

Green believes his style would still work now, a dozen years later, but he acknowledges that most teams seem reluctant to go the hard-nosed route. "So many teams are so fundamentally poor," says Green. "And that's not because the players aren't as good athletes, because in most cases they're better. Nor is it necessarily that they haven't been taught because a lot of them come out of big college programs where they get decent instruction, and out of farm systems that have more coaches than they ever did [in the past].

"It comes from lack of discipline. These players don't listen, they don't have the mental toughness it takes to think about the game. So many players don't carry intensity. They instead coast, and what they need now more than ever is discipline, is having someone on their backs constantly. But so many clubs are caught up with trying to keep their players happy. That's bull. Hell, if I saw a couple of sloppy games in a row, I'd let them hear about it."

There are managers who frequently have meetings. One is Lou Piniella, who doesn't hesitate to vent his temper after especially tough losses. He kept up a constant stream of such outbursts in 1990 when the Reds' big first-place lead was being threatened in August by the Giants. Piniella's meetings culminated with a classic session after the Reds were swept in a series in San Francisco. In it, Piniella started acting out the fable of the tortoise and the hare, feigning crawling to show the tortoise and then hopping to demonstrate the hare. Some Reds players literally were gagging trying to keep from exploding into laughter. But the Reds soon stabilized shortly after that meeting and went on to win the World Series.

However, many managers believe that the highly paid modern player has no loyalty to any organization, so such appeals fall on deaf ears. Since most veteran players have financial security, there is little with which to threaten them other than, as Oakland's Tony LaRussa often says, "playing time." Says LaRussa, "The one hammer I have over them is that little lineup card. I decide who plays and who doesn't."

Managers also come to realize that they are dealing with much more sophisticated players, not to mention players who are very set in their ways and less receptive to instruction.

Cubs manager Jim Lefebvre enjoys lecturing his team on various pet nuances. In fact, Lefebvre is so convinced of the importance of such lectures that he has been known to practice them in front of a home video camera.

One such subject is taking pitches. He had his Cubs spend portions of several batting practice sessions in spring training taking pitches, a novel exercise considering his roster included such free swingers as Andre Dawson, Shawon Dunston, Sammy Sosa, and Ryne Sandberg.

Lefebvre also lectured on the art of the 3–1 count, a theory that basically suggests that a hitter's ultimate goal should be to work the count to his favor. However, such established stars as Sandberg and Dawson are notorious first-ball swingers and the lecture was basically ignored, with some veterans loudly tapping their bats on the dugout floor during Lefebvre's enthusiastic recitation of his theory.

But in the last week of March, Leyland wasn't faced with such impudence or lack of effort. Nor was he displeased with his players' work habits. In fact, he was every bit as frustrated by the club's moves as his players were. And he had been every bit as biting in his comments as they had been.

Leyland had managed most of these players for years. All save for veterans like the newly acquired Gibson had had their greatest success with Leyland as their manager. Even with Gibson, there were emotional ties: Leyland had managed Gibson in the minor leagues when both were in the Detroit organization. So there was a lot of mutual loyalty, a lot of shared experience.

Leyland was instead faced with a crisis of spirit. One reason the Pirates had won division titles in 1990 and 1991 was that they believed in their own ability to win. Few experts might have picked them to win in those seasons, but they believed. Now there were doubts about whether they were good enough anymore. They had lost Bonilla. They had lost over 400 innings from the pitching staff, including a 20-game winner. They faced losing Bonds and Drabek after the season.

Leyland knew that a team that felt sorry for itself, that felt it had built-in excuses for not winning, would eventually fold along the way. The bottom line was that Leyland believed that even with all their losses and their various weaknesses, the Pirates were still good enough to fight for another pennant, but they'd never give themselves the chance with the mood that was developing.

So on March 25, 1992, Leyland told his coaches to pass the word that the team would meet in the outfield at 9:15 A.M. prior to its daily 9:30 exercise and stretching period.

The players sat in a circle, with Leyland standing in the middle holding his fungo bat. This was strictly a men-in-uniform production. When Jim Trdinich, the Pirates' media relations director, started walking toward the group, Leyland brusquely waved him away; this was for the ears of players and coaches only.

It was classic Leyland, a mixture of bluntness and cajoling, a blend of baseballese and common sense. "All the stuff that's gone on here has been tough on you, I know that," he began. "It's been tough on me, too. I hate to see this club lose people. And damn it, I have feeling for those guys. I have feeling for Smiley. I've been his only manager in the major leagues. How do you think it felt for me to trade him after he breaks through and wins 20?

"But we all know that this stuff is part of the business. It's the same business that pays us all very, very well. And as long as we're all here in this uniform, we have a responsibility to this team and this organization to put the stuff behind us and get back to work.

"We can't keep this shit going. It just won't work. We keep this going and we just won't give ourselves the chance to do what we're capable of doing. All I ever ask any of you is to just give yourself the chance to do your best. If that means we don't win, then fuck it. If what we're capable of is third place, then fine. If what we're capable of is first place, then fine. But we have to at least give ourselves our best chance.

"That's all I'm asking you now. We can't do anything about free agents. We can't do anything about the finances of the team or about trades. This is the team we have and it's still a damn good team. All we can do is go out and do what we're capable of doing. All we can do is go out and give ourselves the best chance we can. If that means third place, fine. If that means sixth place, fine. If that means first place, fine.

"But we'll never know what we could have done if we start making excuses for ourselves now. All I can do is manage the best I can. And all you guys can do is play the best you can, and then we'll see where it gets us. I've always enjoyed being around you guys. We've been through a lot together and I wouldn't trade any of it. So let's go, let's turn the page and get going. We can't do anything about all that's happened. But let me tell you something, I like this team. Let's go."

There wasn't any request for questions. The Pirates didn't leap to their feet cheering and charge into the new day. Leyland's talk took all of 12 minutes.

But the change in mood was perceptible. For the first time in days, there was baseball talk around the batting cage. For the first time in days, the sarcasm disappeared from players' conversations.

Later Donnelly said to Leyland, "Well, the atmosphere seems a little better."

"Yeah, well, we'll see," said Leyland. "We've got some moves to make before this spring is all over.

"Richie boy, remember in *Hoosiers* when the kid fouls out and Gene Hackman is sitting out the one kid who didn't follow orders so they're down to four players? Then the referee comes over and asks if he has a substitution to make. And Hackman says, 'My team is on the floor.' Well, that's what I'm going to say from now on. 'My team is on the floor.' "

Of course, it wouldn't be the Pirates if this day didn't have its crisis. An hour after Leyland's address, Bonds was schmoozing at the batting cage with Dick Vitale, the ESPN college basketball maven, when a ball came back against the netting where Bonds was standing and struck him in the eye. Bonds went down like he was shot, Leyland and others hovering around him until assistant trainer Dave Tumbas led Bonds away.

"He's okay," Sandt told Leyland. "He just got a little bruise."

Injuries were the bane of any manager in spring training. Before being hit by the foul, Bonds had been nursing a sore hamstring. Leyland never pushed Bonds to return. Trainers always remind managers that of all injuries, pulled hamstrings are the most temperamental. It had become a standard line for managers to say, "We'd rather he miss a couple of weeks than come back too soon and miss a couple of months." For a player like Bonds, whose base stealing and defense depended on sound legs, such concern was especially acute.

Beyond worrying about his hamstring, Leyland was acutely aware of massaging Bonds's fragile psyche. Leyland went out of his way in the final couple of Florida weeks to pump up Bonds in front of the media.

It all started when there was speculation that the Pirates were considering naming a team captain. Leyland quickly squelched the idea. At the same time, he took the opportunity to boost Bonds, who ever since the blowup with Leyland in the spring of '91 had been labeled, unfairly in many ways, a problem player.

Standing near the batting cage during batting practice one morning, with several players well within earshot, Leyland talked about captaincy.

"There ain't gonna be a captain here because I'm the captain around here," said Leyland. "What's a captain do, anyway? Does he pat guys on the ass? Clap his hands? Come to me with other players' problems? That's all bull.

"Every player on this club knows that if he has a problem with me or with the club or with his personal life or with a teammate, he can come to me or he can come to any of my coaches. Why the hell do you need a captain to come to me with all that?

"All this stuff about leadership being communication and clapping hands and cheering is all crap anyway. Do you know what leadership is? Leadership is BB busting his ass every day in left field, stealing a base when we need it in the eighth inning, breaking up a double play, hitting a double with a man on first.

That's leadership. Leadership is Spanky [Mike LaValliere] throwing out a guy at second with the game on the line. Leadership is a guy like McClendon, who doesn't bitch about his playing time, who does his job when we need him, and who helps out the guys in the clubhouse. That's leadership.

"People ask me if Barry is tough to handle, if other people don't like him. That's crap. All I know about Barry Bonds is that when the game starts, he plays his ass off. All I know about Barry Bonds is that when the game is on the line and people are yelling at him, he's going to deliver. That's all a manager or a teammate can ask of someone. Yeah, it's nice if everybody likes everybody else. But you know what I think about stuff like leadership and chemistry? It's nice to have, but I'd rather win. And so would any player worth a damn."

Much of this was deliberately meant for Bonds's ears. Leyland knew that his star left fielder would almost certainly leave after the season via free agency. But Leyland also knew that in his one last season with the Pirates, Bonds could help produce another division title. Leyland was confident, as were the rest of the Pirates, that Bonds was capable of producing big numbers even without Bonilla around him in the lineup. So Leyland wanted Bonds primed for opening day, and Bonds looked ready.

Of more concern was Van Slyke, who was flown to Pittsburgh for tests on his sore back. The examination revealed a degenerative disc condition that was not operable but likely to plague Van Slyke periodically for the rest of his career. "It means that I have a 30-year-old body and a 50-year-old back," said Van Slyke.

Van Slyke's condition meant that Leyland would need to carry someone who could play center field on short notice. Bonds could do it, but Leyland was reluctant to move him out of the left-field position he played better than anybody in baseball. It meant that Cecil Espy, who was on the bubble to make the club, would stick on the opening-day roster. It also meant that the Pirates would be on the lookout at all times for other outfield help.

Lind's sore knee meanwhile improved to the point where he

could play the last dozen exhibitions. Not so fortunate was the catcher Slaught, whose ailing rib cage would land him on the disabled list to open the season.

While waiting for his players to heal, Leyland had pushed Simmons to make a roster addition in the final weeks. The need for another left-handed reliever remained acute since the only lefty Leyland trusted was Bob Patterson. Leyland had operated the last three years with a perfectly balanced relief corps of three left-handers and three right-handers. The flexibility that afforded him usually masked the absence of a genuine closer-type reliever. By "left–righting" teams to death, Leyland often was able to cut into the opposition's bench reserve of pinch hitters and get the percentages in his favor for the final outs of a game.

With Heaton and Kipper gone now, only Patterson remained from the left-handers. Landrum's exit had cut the supply of proven right-handers to Stan Belinda and Roger Mason. Leyland did not have a feel yet for Neagle, who was likely ill-suited for the kind of bull-pen role Leyland loved to employ. And Batista was a nonperson.

A week before opening day, some experienced help materialized. Ironically because of the presence of Heaton, Kansas City had released veteran left-hander Jerry Don Gleaton. Leyland urged Simmons to sign Gleaton quickly. Simmons concurred, and the Pirates picked up the lefty.

Still, Leyland felt he needed to stock up more pitching arms. He had always carried 11 pitchers so he would have the flexibility in any game situation to alternate left-handers and right-handers, batter to batter if necessary, in late-inning situations. With the addition of Gleaton, he had the three bull-pen left-handers he felt necessary, although one was the unproved Neagle.

But because they had to keep Batista, Leyland and Miller talked about keeping 12 pitchers. "Let's face it, we can't use Batista unless it's a blowout, which means if we carry 11 including him, we're really carrying 10 and that's not enough," said Leyland.

"Yeah, but the schedule helps a little," said Miller. "We have three off days in the first two weeks. We don't need a fifth starter until the middle of the third week, which means we can keep Palacios in the bull pen. Then when we need to go to five starters, we can add a pitcher."

So the Pirates decided to open with 11 pitchers including Batista. When they needed to add another pitcher, Leyland and Miller already were leaning toward bringing up veteran Dennis Lamp. Lamp had been signed to a minor-league contract, and in two looks at the minor-league camp, Miller was convinced that Lamp was healthy and able to be a serviceable middle reliever for the Pirates.

Late in the spring, Leyland made it a point finally to see left-hander Steve Cooke. He was a prospect who would need time in the minors, but as Leyland told Simmons, sometime during the season Cooke could help the Pirates. "He has decent stuff and he looks like he has some confidence to him," said Leyland. "So let's watch him, Teddy."

Another left-hander on whom the Pirates would keep tabs was Rosario Rodriguez, who was injured for most of the spring. A talented but erratic pitcher, Rodriguez had probably the best stuff of those left-handers who the Pirates were hoping would surface. But Rodriguez was not known for his dependability. "The thing with him is that he doesn't always know who we're playing against," said Miller. "Sometimes that's all right, I guess. But he's not the kind of guy who ever makes you feel really comfortable."

With Slaught disabled, longtime Pirates farmhand Tom Prince landed on the opening-day roster. Over the spring's last couple of weeks, Sandt had been giving Prince daily early-morning workouts at third base. "He wouldn't kill us down there, so at least he provides Hump with another option if we ever need it," said Sandt.

Also disabled was rookie pitcher Paul Miller, who showed some promise in limited appearances. Among the last cuts were infielders Jeff Richardson and Carlos Garcia, moves that meant the Pirates would not carry a utility infielder.

However, that wasn't as odd as it appeared. For one thing,

Leyland wanted as much flexibility in the outfield as he could find with Van Slyke's back uncertain and right field a likely platoon position. Gibson had to be kept. Leyland wanted to keep Cecil Espy for his pinch hitting and running ability. He also wanted Gary Varsho, who in 1991 was a reliable pinch hitter.

For the short term at least, the Pirates felt themselves covered in the infield. King, once his back improved, had worked out some at short and showed he could play there if Bell needed a one-day rest or the Pirates were caught in extra innings and needed a move. If Bell were injured for any length of time, Garcia could be quickly recalled. Third baseman Steve Buechele could play second, as could King. King, McClendon, and now Prince could all fill in at third if Buechele had to move. With Slaught disabled, McClendon served as a third catcher behind LaValliere and Prince. Leyland also had several players who could play the outfield and also fill in at first base.

Plus, it was not as if there was any anguish over sending out Garcia and Richardson. Garcia was one of the Pirates' most highly regarded young prospects, but he needed to play every day to refine his skills. So it was largely preordained he would open the year with the Buffalo Triple-A club. Richardson was meanwhile a journeyman.

Nevertheless, Leyland spent several minutes with each player individually, explaining why they were going back to the minors. His message to both was similar: "You've worked hard all spring and we appreciate that, and don't think we'll forget about you," said Leyland. "It's a long season and a lot can happen, so go to Buffalo, keep yourself ready, and when we need an infielder, you'll be the first we look at to bring up here."

No manager enjoys cutting players. But as Leyland said, it's a lot harder in the minors when a demotion usually means the end of the major-league dream. "You have kids who think they have a chance and those kids have families and friends back home who all think they have a chance. And when you're an A ball manager and have to tell one of those kids that they're not going to make it, it tears you up because once you're cut in A ball, it usually means that you're going home.

"At least up here, when you send someone back, they've reached a certain level and might still have a chance. Hell, it's never easy. I know how it feels because it was done to me. You just hope you can make it as easy on the guy as possible and leave him with some hope or something."

By spring's end, Leyland had emerged from the firestorm caused by the Smiley–Landrum moves to begin feeling much better about his club. Since making his outfield speech March 25, the Pirates had gone on to win eight straight exhibition games. Leyland was very worried about his bull pen and overall pitching depth, and he was already feeling very uneasy about what he saw of Gibson's deteriorating bat speed. But in spring training's final two weeks, Leyland had developed a better working relationship with Simmons and was growing to respect Sauer, the club president. His top players were rounding into top shape, and Bonds looked primed for a monster season. Katie and Patrick were home in Pittsburgh, waiting for him to return to the house he had bought two years ago.

As Leyland relaxed in a clubhouse in Miami with good friend Carl Barger prior to the next-to-last exhibition, he was ready to go. "Spring training is too long. I was ready to go two weeks ago," Leyland told Barger.

Leyland appeared to have weathered his sometimes tumultuous spring. Meanwhile, other managers had their own tests in the spring of 1992.

Rookie Red Sox manager Butch Hobson had the daunting chore of confronting superstar Roger Clemens when Clemens reported to camp late and explained his tardiness by saying, "I get more work done by myself. If I was in Winter Haven right now, I'd just be standing around in the outfield spitting sunflower seeds."

Hobson went nose to nose with Clemens when the pitcher finally arrived, and the early-season incident was an instant test of Hobson's clubhouse respect. It all blew over, thankfully for Hobson, for whom Clemens would be the least of his problems as the long season unfolded.

Cincinnati manager Lou Piniella had a calm camp until Rob Dibble, his eccentric reliever, went to Vero Beach for an examination of an ailing shoulder. Dibble then told former teammate Eric Davis that he might need rotator cuff surgery, although the injury proved much less serious. Piniella had to spend three days denying Dibble was seriously injured and answering charges that the Reds were involved in a cover-up. Piniella finally brought Dibble into his office and exploded, "When can you learn to just keep your mouth shut? All you do is make a tough situation worse. For Christ's sake, will you just learn to shut up?"

No manager had a more rugged spring than the Mets' Jeff Torborg, whose club was engulfed by gossip columnists when a story broke that Dwight Gooden, Vince Coleman, and Daryl Boston had been named in a rape investigation from a year ago. Subsequently, it was learned that the woman making the complaint, from which there were no charges ultimately filed, had been brought to Florida by Mets pitcher David Cone, who later was mentioned in an unrelated sexual assault case involving another woman.

Mets players found themselves being followed into bars by reporters from the tabloids. Some suspected that their phones were being monitored. When tabloid reporters were then banned from the clubhouse and regular sportswriters were issued special badges, one of the tabloid types wrote that the new badges were handed out "as if they were condoms at an orgy."

Finally, the Mets players voted not to talk to the media for the final eight days of spring training. Torborg and new Mets GM Al Harazin tried to argue them out of the decision. But led by veterans Bobby Bonilla and Eddie Murray, the players were adamant. So Torborg, who took media access to the other extreme, what with his three daily radio shows and his willingness to talk to anyone toting a notebook or microphone, was placed in the position of publicly backing his players' decision and having to submit to all questioning related to the ballclub himself.

By the time the Mets reached Baltimore for their final exhibition, Torborg was exhausted by his effort to be unfailingly accessible and upbeat about the circus that was surrounding his club. "I think they're voting today to start talking when the season starts, which is the reasonable thing to do," said Torborg. "And I have to say that no one will be happier to see them do that than I."

Chapter 3

"A Buck in His Pocket and a Package of Cigarettes"

◆ Three Rivers Stadium was sold out for the April 6 opener, and the big crowd rose to applaud the raising of the 1991 NL East Championship flag.

Then came the introductions, and as was custom, the manager was announced first. The ovation that greeted Leyland dwarfed any of the greetings that followed. Bonds was cheered and so were Van Slyke, Drabek, Bell, Lind, and the others. But the roar for Leyland was something different. He stood alone on the field for several minutes, occasionally tipping his cap, tears running down his face, as the cheers washed over him in a remarkable show of affection.

In some cities, the manager gets booed on opening night. In others, he is politely cheered. In Pittsburgh, there was no question that as the 1992 season opened, the most popular man wearing a Pirates uniform was the manager.

Before a game had been played, Leyland seemed to have it all: a lucrative new contract, an adoring wife and healthy baby boy, the respect of the entire baseball world as one of its best managers, and the undisguised affection of his hometown fans.

However, Leyland was hardly an overnight sensation. His road to domestic bliss and professional stardom was a long and sometimes frustrating journey that took him through the baseball hinterland from which few ever emerge into the Big Show.

Before arriving in Pittsburgh in 1986, Leyland had been a baseball nomad for nearly 20 years. He spent much of that time seemingly buried in the minor leagues, living what seemed to be a lonely existence that was only briefly interrupted by a failed marriage midway in the 1970s.

He grew up in the town of Perrysburg, Ohio, one of seven children of good, hardworking parents. His father, James, was a foreman at a glass factory in nearby Toledo. He introduced his son to baseball, taking Jim to Cleveland for his first major-league game in 1954 when the Indians were the best team in the league. From then on, baseball was the life Jim Leyland wanted to have for himself.

Leyland was signed by the Detroit Tigers upon graduating from Perrysburg High (whose other famous grad is Atlanta Falcons coach Jerry Glanville). A catcher, Leyland never played above the Double-A level in his six seasons from 1964 through 1969. But he had known from the start, when he first reported to the Tigers' minor-league training camp, that he would never play in the majors.

"I had my hopes and dreams like anyone who signs a contract," he said. "But when I took a look at the other players and saw how talented some of those guys were, I knew there was no chance for me. I really had no ability whatsoever."

A lot of young players who come to a similar conclusion quickly lose their baseball dreams. But Leyland loved the game too much, and if he couldn't be a major-league player, then he would become a minor-league player. The Tigers kept him around in their minor-league system for six years, largely because every organization likes to have extra catchers.

"I couldn't hit worth a damn and I tried everything to get better," said Leyland. "I hit four home runs in six years and I can tell you where and when and off whom I hit every darned one of them. Somebody would ask me, 'What's the highest you ever hit?' I'd answer '.279.' And then they'd say, 'Where was that, in the big leagues?' And I said, 'No, my senior year in high school.'

"But I never thought of quitting. Honest to God, I never did. I was doing something I loved. And I tried to learn, I tried to help my teams any way I could. I'd coach a base if they needed someone. Or I'd warm up guys in the bull pen. Heck, I got signed only because they were looking for an extra catcher in spring training and that's the darned truth.

"Money? I wasn't in it to make money and I'm still not. When I signed, I got no bonus when I signed. I got $400 a month and I was glad to get it. I thought I had it made. I bought a new shirt and new pair of pants every two weeks. My father used to say, 'Give that Jimbo a buck in his pocket and a package of cigarettes and he'll be happy.' Now I'm rich beyond any possible dream. And I've still got the same buck in my pocket and a package of cigarettes."

By 1969, he was 25 years old, and the Tigers had younger bodies to hang on in the lower minors. They offered Leyland a job as a coach in Montgomery. He didn't have to think about it for very long. "I figured if I went home, I'd try to go to college and then maybe try to be a baseball coach. And here I had been offered a job as a baseball coach, so I grabbed it."

At 26 years old, he became a manager of a rookie-league team in Bristol, Virginia. He was paid $6,000 that season. And so began 11 seasons of managing in the minors.

Home was his suitcase and his car. "I'd come home after a season and I'd be broke again like always," he said. "My brother Bill would lend me some money. And I'd get some kind of winter job. One year, I worked in the post office. My dad got me a part-time job one winter in the glass factory. I drove a truck, I worked some construction.

"I'd stay in my old room at home and help out Mom and Dad. My brothers and sisters helped out the rest of the year, then the two months I'd be home would be my time. And then it would be back for another season."

Getting married and having a family was not a viable option. "Heck, I didn't have enough money to support myself, so how could I think about supporting a family?" Leyland recalled.

"The thing was that I never wanted anything else but baseball. I had the fever. And I had to be free. When all you have is your car and a pitching machine and one suitcase of clothes, you can throw your stuff in the backseat and be heading south at a minute's notice.

"And that's all I had. I didn't own anything. I'd live in a hotel all year. When we left for a road trip, I'd check out. When we got back home, I'd check back in. And I loved it all. I swear, I loved every place I went. All those towns, Clinton, Lakeland, Montgomery, all of them. I loved it all."

Along the way, he tried to learn how to handle players and manage the game. He'd spend hours in spring training talking baseball with old hands in the Tigers organization, scouts and coaches like Fred Hatfield and Hoot Evers. He would watch the major-league managers when he could and the Tigers' Sparky Anderson or whoever might be playing the Tigers in exhibitions.

But Leyland never thought he was on his way to something else beyond what he was doing.

"I never planned or dreamed 'Here I am, managing in the minors, and someday I'll be managing in the majors.' I just tried to do the best job I could wherever I was in any season. But I never really thought about the big leagues. I didn't think it was possible."

Leyland has become justly renowned for his rapport with players. A big reason why is likely the years of dealing with hundreds of kids, so few of whom would ever reach the big time. He had to release so many of them along the way. He had to tell so many that their dream was dead, that they had to find something else to do with their lives. He had to deal with so many of their problems, counseling kids not much older than himself after a close relative died or a wife had decided to leave or a throwing arm had gone bad.

Leyland once told *Sports Illustrated* how he remembered the first such kid he had to release. He remembered how that kid was from New Jersey and how he started crying and told Leyland that "if I could play baseball for anyone, I'd want to play for you." Leyland remembered how he started crying along with the kid.

Leyland's own struggles to play the game and his years of watching so many others similarly struggle has likely taught him how to understand all the frustrations and insecurities that are part of playing the game, which is why he can so easily relate to players struggling in slumps, just as he can so openly appreciate the greatness of a Barry Bonds.

Just as he loves the game, he also loves the people who play it. "Between the minors and majors, I've probably managed 800 or 900 players," said Leyland. "And in all that time with all those players, I can't think of more than ten players I didn't like as people. That ain't too bad a percentage."

Although Leyland played down his ambition as a minor-league manager, he grew to be frustrated at not being considered for a major-league coaching job with Detroit. "I remember one winter I came home and I was griping that they wouldn't hire me to be bull-pen coach and they wouldn't hire me to coach first base or coach third," said Leyland. "And my mom says, 'Don't worry, maybe they'll ask you to coach second base.' My mom didn't always know a lot about baseball but she sure knew how to stop me from griping."

But Leyland would eventually get to the big leagues. While managing Evansville in 1979 (a year in which he won the American Association championship), Leyland became friendly with LaRussa, who was managing against him for Iowa. They remained friendly, keeping in touch over the next few years after LaRussa had been hired to manage the Chicago White Sox. And in 1982, when LaRussa had an opening for a third-base coach, he hired Leyland.

Leyland was 36 years old and finally in the big leagues for the first time. To this day, he doesn't forget how he felt. "We opened the season in New York because snow wiped out our home opener," he recalled. "Our first game was going to be on a Sunday, and on the Saturday night, Roland Hemond, who was the White Sox's general manager, asked if I wanted to come along to a concert at Carnegie Hall. Hell, Carnegie Hall, it was the second time in my life I had even been to New York.

"Then the next day, I come to the ballpark and I have a brand-new uniform hanging in the locker. My shoes are shined. I'm walking around the outfield and find myself standing next to Yogi Berra."

Leyland coached with LaRussa for four years. After the 1985 season, Syd Thrift was named the new general manager of the Pirates. Once an innovative scout and player development expert, Thrift had been out of baseball for years. However, he had kept in touch with the game. He wanted a young manager to take over a Pirates team that was likely the worst in baseball and in need of a complete overhaul. He had heard about Leyland through Hemond and other contacts. After one interview, Thrift hired Leyland on the spot.

After a 22-year odyssey, Leyland had made it to the top. "I'll never forget my first game in Pittsburgh," he recalled. "They introduce everybody on opening day. And they called my name and I came out to the field. I looked up in the stands and found my father. And I was so proud to have come so far. And I knew he was proud, too."

Leyland's father passed away in 1988. When he tells the story of his first game in Pittsburgh as Pirates manager, as he has periodically been asked to do over the last three years now that he has become a marquee name, Leyland can't help but choke up.

Leyland meanwhile settled down for the first time. Katie O'Connor was working for the Pirates' promotions department. After being named manager, Leyland bought a condominium in Pittsburgh but knew nothing about furnishing it, so he asked Katie to come to the furniture store with him and help him with the purchases. A year later, they got married with Leyland's brother Tom, a priest, performing the ceremony. Katie likes to kid now, "If I had known I would end up having to live with that furniture, I would have picked out some different things."

For someone who was a loner and a vagabond for so long, Leyland, say his closest friends, has never been happier. He and Katie bought a house with a big yard in the beautiful Pittsburgh suburbs and dug into the community. He is visible around town, giving his time to many local charities, such as the Arthritis Foundation and the Epilepsy Foundation, both which have honored Leyland for his work, and serving as Christmas chairman for the Salvation Army.

Yet he and Katie have had their own trials. The couple lost their first baby when it was stillborn in October of 1989. Leyland lived with Katie for four days in the hospital. Amid their grief, they vowed to have another baby as soon as they could. Patrick was born almost two years from the day of the first infant's death.

Leyland has never allowed his success or celebrity to change him, as it has so many others in a similar position. "Things like that happen and you realize that you can't take yourself seriously," he told *Sports Illustrated*.

Leyland's long minor-league background is another reason why he is so unaffected by his success. "I don't know, I guess a lot of it comes from the reason why I still think people play the game," he said. "Everybody nowadays talks about the financial situation in baseball. But the thing that motivates you, no matter at what level you're involved, is the competition. Hey, the money is really nice, but the competition is what makes you tick. It's Barry Bonds against Doc Gooden. It's us against them. And when you look at it, it's no different here in the big leagues than a pickup game when you choose up sides as a kid and say 'Okay, let's beat those other guys.'

"I really believe that. I really get a kick out of competing every night. And I think when you lose that as a player or a manager, you can't do your job no matter how much money you're making.

The competition and the people are why I love managing so much, not just the money."

As much as Leyland's long, slow climb to his managing job is a tale of determination and love of the game, it is hardly the only route to major-league managing. There is no one way to become a major-league manager. For every manager who opened the 1992 season in the majors, there are nearly as many different backgrounds to their jobs.

In recent years, there has been a trend toward hiring managers who, like Leyland, earned their stripes by managing in the minors for years. There has been movement away from the so-called old boys network, which for years saw most managerial openings filled by retread managers who had been fired from other jobs.

A factor in changing that mind-set has been the success of Leyland and of people like LaRussa, who played 16 seasons of professional baseball, with only parts of four of them in the majors, and managed a season and a half in the minors before becoming manager of the Chicago White Sox.

Detroit's Sparky Anderson had a somewhat similar prelude to managing the majors—a ten-year playing career, of which only one season was spent in the big leagues, followed by minor-league managing and then his hiring by the Cincinnati Reds. So did Atlanta's Bobby Cox, Minnesota's Tom Kelly, New York's Buck Showalter, and White Sox manager Gene Lamont. And for that matter, so did many successful managers of the recent past, including pennant winners like Tommy Lasorda and Earl Weaver.

Whether that means that to be a major-league manager the best background is to be a fringe player is open to question. But it is true the large majority of managers barely made a ripple as players.

And it's also true that a remarkably large number of managers were catchers in their playing careers. Leyland, Lamont, Baltimore's Johnny Oates, Seattle's Bill Plummer, California's Buck Rodgers, the Mets' Jeff Torborg, and St. Louis's Joe Torre all were catchers in their playing days.

However, it's also true that there are other managers who were outstanding players, who weren't catchers, and who had little or no managerial experience before being hired to manage major-league teams.

Cincinnati's Lou Piniella, Kansas City's Hal McRae, Toronto's Cito Gaston, Cleveland's Mike Hargrove, the Cubs' Jim Lefebvre, Texas's Bobby Valentine, and Boston's Butch Hobson all were good players in their days. And none had any appreciable managing experience before getting their first managing jobs.

When you look through baseball history, the examples of successful managers who were also great players are virtually nonexistent. The theory has long been that the great player finds the game so much easier than the journeyman player that, as a manager, the great player can't relate to those who struggle. And because the game might have been so much easier for the great player, he might not have had to observe the game as intently as the fringe player, who needs to find any possible extra edge that might help him outwit someone more talented.

That said, there are few managers more tuned in to his players' feelings than the Cardinals' Torre, who was a great player in his time. And few managers were more out of touch or alienated more players in a short time than the Padres' Greg Riddoch, who came from the struggling minor-league background used as a successful springboard for others.

In other words, there is no all-encompassing theory that is 100 percent true when it comes to managing. And there is no one way of managing a baseball team or handling modern players. Everyone has to have his own method of doing the job.

"I ain't no smarter than anyone else, I'm no psychologist or any of that stuff," said Leyland. "But I decided right from the start back in Bristol, Virginia, to do something I learned from watching my father at the glass factory. He supervised men and I watched how he did it. And the main thing he always tried to do was to be honest with all of them.

"And that was the thing I decided I had to do right from the beginning. To me, being honest is the most important thing for a manager. You tell a guy what you really think of him and even if it's something he doesn't want to hear, even if it's something he doesn't like, if he knows you're honest, he at least has to respect you. When you start playing games with people, you end up getting in trouble."

When a club hires a manager nowadays, that amorphous question of how the manager handles players is likely to top any list of criteria. Similarly, a club has to have an idea of how the manager will deal with the media. The question of how a manager operates his game strategy is almost overlooked or at least relegated to secondary consideration. Nowadays, new managers invariably have so-called bench coaches who are usually veterans who know the league and keep an eye out for lineup changes and the like. And judging talent, which should be a primary asset of any manager, is something that a lot of clubs don't even take into consideration.

The bottom line of all this is that there is no one prescription and no one background for hiring the best manager. Just like with scouting players, a lot of it comes down to luck and circumstance.

"I had a good idea of what kind of man Jim Leyland was when I hired him," recalled Thrift. "I knew the kind of reputation he had with the people with whom he worked. I knew that a lot of very good people who I respected thought very highly of him. And when I met him, I knew he had the kind of personality who could handle what were going to be a few tough years before we got the club in shape. And I thought he had a chance to become the contender.

"But I'd be lying if I told you that I knew right when we hired him that he'd become one of the greatest managers in the game. There's no sure fire way for hiring a manager. You just try to do your homework and rely on your instincts when you talk to the man. And then you hope for some good luck."

Luck or not, the Pirates found themselves with the rare manager who had become the symbol of his franchise. In a profession where instability is a given, Leyland was in his seventh season with Pittsburgh and armed with a five-year contract. He had become the one constant on a club riddled with the changes and stresses of baseball's modern economics. He had made the long journey from minor-league obscurity to the status of a true star.

The Pirates opened the 1992 season with a starting rotation uncertain beyond Doug Drabek, Zane Smith, and Randy Tomlin. The bull pen looked like a mess with no proven closer and minus three important veteran arms. There was no proven first baseman. Right field was missing the 100-RBI bat of Bobby Bonilla with a platoon of bit players looming as his replacement. No one knew who would be the leadoff hitter. No one knew for sure how Barry Bonds, the team's biggest star, might react in his free-agent season if the Pirates struggled out of the gate. Andy Van Slyke, the teams' other star, was playing with a back condition that was a threat to sideline him at any time.

Few people were picking the Pirates to contend in the NL East, where the Mets, who had spent off-season millions; the Cubs; and St. Louis all looked more solid than Pittsburgh.

But if there was consolation for the Pirates, it was that few people picked them to win in 1990 or 1991. And there was Leyland. In the Pirates' minds, he represented an edge no one could match in the NL East. "Jim thinks we can win and so do we," said Mike LaValliere. "If we stay healthy, we'll hang in there, and if we stay close, we always figure Jim will think of something."

Chapter 4

"Ain't This a Great Business?"

◆ By the end of April, the Pirates were making the early-season doubters look silly. Following a shutout win over Houston on a Saturday night in the Astrodome, their record stood at 16–6. It was the best start in the major leagues, quickly putting Pittsburgh in control of the National League East and giving the Pirates an amazing streak of 11 straight baseball months that ended with them in first place.

Pittsburgh was doing it all, getting great starting pitching, big hits from Barry Bonds, and assorted contributions from every man on the roster.

It was the kind of start managers dream of. But Leyland was hardly resting easy hours after the Pirates' 22nd game of the season. He retreated to the Westin Galleria, the hotel where the Pirates and every other National League club stays in Houston. The hotel sits amid one of the country's largest shopping centers, at the hub of which sits a rather incongruous skating rink.

Leyland is not one of those managers who drowns his sorrows in hotel bars. If he wants a postgame pop, he will usually have his coaches up to his suite, where they won't run into any players and thus can avoid any delicate situations.

Years ago, managers like Earl Weaver would put the hotel bar off limits. His theory was, "I have this bar, they can have the rest of the city." But in recent years, most managers allow, and obliquely encourage, their team to imbibe in-house. "Hell, they can get in trouble when they hit the streets. At least they're under the roof when they stay in the hotel," said Whitey Herzog when he managed the Cardinals.

With Leyland, as with most modern managers, there are no such things as curfews or off-limit establishments. "Hell, they're adults. Some of them make millions," said Leyland. "I ain't gonna tell them what they can do. They know we expect them to handle themselves professionally and if what they do off the field affects their job, then we'll find out. But we don't have any trouble with this group." Indeed, the Pirates are a rather docile group. A big night is a pizza delivered to the room and a couple of hours with a Nintendo Game Boy.

On this Saturday night, Leyland wants to unwind. So he has his coaches up to the suite for a few drinks and a lot of talk. The conversation was serious. A major roster move was imminent, and the decision would be one of Leyland's toughest.

After a stretch in which off days allowed the pitching staff to remain well rested, the schedule was about to toughen. As a result, Pittsburgh needed to add a real 11th pitcher. That part of the equation was easy; the pitcher to be added was rookie Paul Miller, who was ready to come off the disabled list. But the question was how to make room for Miller. The Pirates would have to drop a position player and there were no easy choices for Leyland, his coaches, or GM Simmons.

Nervously pacing with a 7-iron in his hand (he had brought his golf bag back to his room after playing with Donnelly and Collins that morning), Leyland thought out loud as he bounced around all the options he would end up discussing with Simmons when the club returned home Monday.

The most obvious move was to shuttle third catcher Tom

Prince back to the Triple-A team in Buffalo. But Leyland resisted that easy choice.

"I talked it over with Teddy and we could lose him if we send him down," said Leyland. "We'd have to put him on waivers to send him down and Teddy doesn't think he'd clear. And I'm afraid to lose him.

"Hell, Sluggo [Don Slaught] can get hurt any time. We don't have anyone in Buffalo who could catch up here. And if we lose a catcher in the expansion draft, we're stuck. So it ain't gonna be Prince."

Said Donnelly, "Well, I guess it could be Espy or Varsho."

"How can I tell Espy or Varsho that they don't deserve to be here?" said Leyland. "They bust their ass when I need them. They don't cause no trouble. They got some big hits for me last year and they've got some big hits this year. There ain't no way I can tell either of them that they don't belong here."

Leyland kept pacing with the 7-iron as the room got silent. Finally, Donnelly spoke. "Well, Jim, that leaves only one guy as far as I can see it."

"Yeah, ain't that a bitch," said Leyland. "It comes down to one guy. It comes down to Gibson. I gotta recommend to the general manager and the club president that we eat about a million and a half bucks worth of salary. And I then gotta tell a guy I helped break into baseball years ago that he can't cut it anymore. Ain't this a great business?"

The room was silent. Everyone knew the feeling Leyland had for many of his players, especially ones like Gibson, who go back years with him.

"Hey, Richie, get a few balls out of my bag," Leyland said suddenly. "Watch this. Open the patio doors there."

Leyland pulled open the curtains, dropped a golf ball on the shag carpet, and addressed the ball with his 7-iron.

"Watch how good I'm swinging, boys," said Leyland, as he proceeded to hit the ball through the open doors, over the patio, and out into the dark, empty parking lot below.

Leyland cranked out a dozen shots. And one can only guess

how Sunday shoppers the next morning reacted to the sight of golf balls littering the parking lot.

Leyland kept his decision to himself through Sunday, an endless day because the game was ESPN's "Sunday Night Game of the Week," after which the Pirates would fly immediately home for a game the next evening.

He deflected questions about the imminent roster move. Actually, the rumor of the day was that Drabek was close to signing a new contract. However, Leyland wasn't holding his breath. He sat in the tiny Astrodome visiting manager's office with Miller, who reported, "Well, Dougie doesn't know what's going on. He talked to his agent and he said they were talking, but that's it."

Said Leyland, "Well if it happens, great, but there's nothing I can do about it. We've gone through this before last year with Bonilla. You keep hearing all these stories and in the end, what happens is going to happen. Mundo, it ain't gonna change how we play tonight."

"No, you're right there, but it would make life a little easier if we kept one of these guys," sighed Miller.

After a 1–0 loss, the Pirates slept their way home on the charter flight. Before leaving the airport, Gibson asked Milt May to include him in a small group scheduled to have extra batting practice early the next afternoon prior to the game against Cincinnati.

Gibson had started the season auspiciously, homering in successive games in Montreal. But after that series, he went 2 for 25, and it was noticeable to all that he could not catch up with an average major-league fastball. Gibson worked constantly with batting coach May, but in recent at bats, he had begun struggling just to make contact at the plate. Leyland had hoped Gibson might come around, and he kept telling his coaches that even a shell of the former Gibson could help. "The guy's a presence in that room. That means something," Leyland kept saying.

But now it was time to do what needed to be done. Leyland arrived at the ballpark shortly after noon and closeted himself with both Simmons and club president Mark Sauer. Leyland had half-expected some resistance to his decision to release Gibson. The Pirates would have to eat over $1 million in salary, assuming that no other club would claim Gibson on waivers. And the Pirates had spent the spring making wrenching decisions to cut salaries.

But Simmons was immediately supportive. "Let's face it, Jim, if Gibson was a 22-year-old kid, we would have made this move weeks ago," said Simmons. "He's not catching up on any pitches. I agree with you that this is the way we have to go. Do you want me to tell him?"

"No, this has to be mine alone," said Leyland. "This one is tough. Just make sure it's not announced until after I talk to him. I don't want the guy embarrassed."

Leyland went down to the clubhouse and was told by May that Gibson was on his way in for hitting. "Before he dresses, Miltie, get him in here," said Leyland. "I want to get this done early. The press and TV will be here in a few hours when they announce this, so I want him to know as soon as possible."

Within minutes, Gibson was in the clubhouse and was summoned to Leyland's office, which sits at the far right end of the Pirates' clubhouse, past the trainer's room and the lounge and next to the equipment room. Like most managers' offices, Leyland's is hardly a threat to be featured in *Better Homes and Gardens.* It includes a desk, Leyland's wooden rocking chair, and assorted couches and Naugahyde chairs. Leyland's shower and closet are to one side. The dominant wall hanging is a collage of memories from Leyland's stay in San Francisco during the 1989 earthquake. On his desk are two new pictures of Katie and Patrick.

Gibson grabbed a cup of coffee and made himself comfortable next to Leyland. Gibson sensed what was coming. He had for days been quietly resigned to the possibility that he would be released, a move that likely would mean the end of his career. Gibson knew full well how poorly he was playing. He also was savvy enough to know that few teams would be interested in him if the Pirates did not want his services.

Worn down by years of injuries and frustrated by his eroding skills, Gibson wasn't crushed by the thought that his playing days were over. A proud, intense competitor, Gibson was hardly the type to want to simply hang on. His many physical problems had robbed him of much of his prime playing years. He could no longer run with abandon or turn on fastballs with awesome power.

With his children growing up, Gibson had begun warming to the idea of being home in Michigan, fishing and watching the kids play ball while overseeing his burgeoning business interests in real estate development. So when Gibson saw Leyland close the office door and looked at the grim look on Leyland's face, he said, "Well, Hump, I guess it's me, isn't it?"

Tears immediately started streaming down Leyland's face. He had thought for days about how he would react to axing Gibson. The two went back to 1978 when Leyland was manager of the Class-A Lakeland farm club of the Detroit Tigers and Gibson was a much ballyhooed rookie out of Michigan State, where he also starred as a football wide receiver.

The next year Leyland and Gibson went together to Triple-A Evansville, and Gibson reached the majors late in the '79 season. "The guy was one of the greatest athletes I've ever seen," recalled Leyland. "He could do everything. And what with all the publicity he got, he still worked his head off all the time. When Kirk Gibson was healthy, he was a superstar."

The two remained close, frequently talking by phone. Gibson called Leyland shortly after the 1984 World Series when Gibson's two homers sealed the Tigers' fifth-game, Series-ending victory. And Leyland was one of the first people who got in touch with Gibson after the memorable first game of the 1988 World Series.

Now, Leyland wept, and Gibson would later say that the hardest thing about being released was having to console Leyland. "Jeez, Gibby, I wish this could have worked out, I wish this could have been different," said Leyland. "I couldn't wait to manage you again. But I have to make this move and I want you to know that this is one of the toughest things I've ever had to do."

"Hump, don't take it personally," said Gibson. "We both know this is a business and this is the decision you have to make. Whatever playing time I'm getting is hurting other guys who deserve to be playing. Heck, you gotta get Merced in there. He deserves to play more.

"You gotta hell of a club here, Hump. It would have been great to be with you right into the Series. But it didn't work out. So don't feel so goddamned bad. I'll be fine. The only thing I regret is that I never got a chance to play for you when I was in my prime. I would have liked to have given you some of those years."

Leyland and Gibson then embraced. "Just remember what you mean to me," said Leyland, his voice still choked.

Such emotion, such loyalty is rare in these days of big contracts, free agency, and managerial instability. Few managers get a chance to manage anyone long enough to develop any real ties. Many managers try to avoid developing emotional loyalty to players anyway, fearing it will cloud their decision making.

However, some of the very best managers develop deep feeling for players who produce for them over the years. Earl Weaver to this day bears the image of an umpire-baiting, irascible genius. But no manager had deeper loyalties to his players than Weaver.

One of his favorites was Lee May, a dependable RBI-producing first baseman and designated hitter for years in Baltimore after many distinguished seasons in Houston and Cincinnati. "Mo" was one of the Orioles' leaders, a no-nonsense type to the media but a genuinely funny and hugely respected presence in the Baltimore clubhouse, who taught players like Eddie Murray and Ken Singleton how to conduct themselves as professionals.

By the time Murray had emerged as a genuine star at first base, May was a designated hitter. When his production began sagging, Weaver sat May occasionally against tougher right-handed pitching. But despite evidence to the contrary, Weaver resisted the urgings of his coaches and some of the media that May would have to be relegated to a part-time role. Weaver would not even pinch-hit for May in the most obvious of situations. "I don't care what anyone says. He's always been a guy who comes through when it matters and I ain't gonna bury him," Weaver would fume.

But it became obvious even to Weaver that May was irreversibly on the down side of his career. And it crystallized one night in Kansas City. The Orioles were down by a run in the eighth inning. With a runner on second and Royals reliever Dan Quisenberry on the mound, May was scheduled to bat. Quisenberry was death to most right-handed batters, and Weaver's trusty index cards on which he had recorded what each of his hitters had done lifetime against the other teams' pitchers showed that May was 0 for 8 lifetime versus Quisenberry.

Weaver put his two index fingers in his mouth and whistled, a skill that could make him heard during the running of the Indy 500. May turned from the on-deck circle, and Weaver motioned him over. "I've got to hit for you here, Mo, I gotta send up a left-hander," said Weaver, his head down as he was unable to even look May in the eye.

Players on the Orioles bench held their breath and watched. A proud veteran like May could well be expected to show some temper. But May simply put his bat back in the rack and said. "Okay, Skip," as he walked to the other end of the dugout. It was the first time since he was rookie 15 years ago that May had left a game for a pinch hitter.

The pinch hitter was Dan Graham, a reserve catcher who was running in from the bull pen where he had been warming up pitchers. Graham proceeded to deliver a single that tied the game. Weaver was busy looking at his lineup card for other moves when Orioles coach Frank Robinson tapped him on the shoulder. "Earl, look at this," said Robinson, his own voice cracking.

Lee May was grabbing a catcher's mitt from the top step of the dugout and trotting toward the Orioles' bull pen in left field. With the game tied, the Orioles' bull pen needed to get busy; with Graham in the game as well as Rick Dempsey, the other catcher, the bull pen needed help warming up pitchers. And May, although out of the game, could help the club by helping out in the bull pen.

Weaver quickly ducked into the dugout runway, a place where he usually hid to puff cigarettes. But this time, he ducked into the runway to cry. Hours after the game, he still couldn't shake himself of his emotions. "All you assholes in the press wonder why I stick with people like Lee May for so long," said Weaver. "Well, tonight you found out."

The other extreme of all this might be Tommy Lasorda, who professes undying devotion to players he might have managed for only a month.

Such a player in the 1992 season's early days was Eric Davis. The Dodgers were off to a sluggish start and so was Davis, who was hampered by a herniated disc in his first four weeks with the club. But he had somehow become a Lasorda favorite. When Davis would walk into the clubhouse every day, Lasorda would give him an effusive greeting. With visitors, Lasorda would make a point of giving Davis a huge buildup. "This is a great man, right here," said Lasorda one day. "He's banged up and he still goes out there and plays as hard as he can all the time. A guy like him, who can be a free agent after this season, you'd expect him to be careful. But this guy plays hard.

"And he would do anything in the world for you. Hey, Eric, come here. Eric, I'm short some money, can you lend me a grand?"

Davis dug into his pocket, came out with a roll of bills, peeled off ten $100 bills, and handed them to Lasorda without saying a world. "Isn't this guy something?" said Lasorda. "Eric, keep the money. I was just making a point."

However, Lasorda could add a sharp edge to his public schmoozing. Almost a year ago, he had a similar mutual admiration society going with Darryl Strawberry, who got off to a wretched start in his first season with the Dodgers. Publicly, Lasorda stroked Strawberry, but privately he seethed at what he perceived to be Strawberry's passive reaction to his slump. Over the winter, Strawberry had undergone a well-publicized religious awakening and he would often make religious allusions when talking about his on-field slump.

Lasorda finally had enough. He had Strawberry into his office one day in Philadelphia and unloaded, trying to goad Strawberry into showing some emotion. "Don't you care about the game anymore?" Lasorda screamed.

"Sure, I care, but I've put it in perspective," said Strawberry.

"Perspective? What the hell is perspective?" said Lasorda. "Don't you get mad anymore? Don't you want to compete anymore?"

"Temper is something I'm trying to conquer," said Strawberry.

"Yeah, well, don't you think that Jesus Christ lost his temper once in a while?" said Lasorda. "Don't you think that when He was being scorned and mocked, He got mad? Don't you think He used that anger to His own benefit? If Jesus could get mad, why the hell can't you get mad when you strike out?"

This ecclesiastical discussion eventually fizzled out. Strawberry eventually turned around his season. But Lasorda noticeably toned down his expressions of devotion to Strawberry.

However, loyalty only goes so far, even for Leyland. On the one hand, he will back players who had produced for him over the years. But like most managers, Leyland is not likely to change his mind about a player once he's reached the conclusion that the player can't help him win.

Such was the case with Miguel Batista, the young pitcher taken in the Rule 5 draft whom the front office forced Leyland to keep on the roster. With fewer than 200 professional innings in his career, Leyland and pitching coach Miller were convinced that Batista, whatever potential he might have, could not help. Instead, he was taking up a needed roster spot. Having one unusable pitcher disrupted the delicate balance of the entire Pirates' staff. Few things are more important to the success of the Pirates than Leyland's ability to handle his pitching.

There is no part of any manager's job more difficult than pitching strategy. Few managers do it better than Leyland.

He works in close tandem with pitching coach Miller, as do most managers with their pitching coaches. Few managers hold total sway over their pitching staffs, one particular exception being

San Francisco's Roger Craig, a former pitching coach himself. However, on most clubs, pitching coaches have powerful influence. Coaches like Miller and Oakland's Dave Duncan are given wide berth and receive deserved credit for their team's pitching success.

Even an autocrat like Earl Weaver surrounded himself with two of the best pitching coaches of the last 25 years, George Bamberger and later Ray Miller. But that didn't keep Weaver from hearing criticism, especially from Jim Palmer, Weaver's best pitcher for many years. Palmer would often say about Weaver that "the only thing Earl knows about pitching is that he couldn't hit it." Considering that Weaver averaged over 90 wins a year through his long career, that's an indication of the sensitivity involved in handling pitching.

Managing a pitching staff is a multilayered challenge. There is the first whole matter of dealing with the fragile psyche of pitchers. Pitching coaches invariably serve as buffers between their pitchers and the manager. That can be a chore when dealing with volatile managers. Weaver would constantly scream at his pitchers to throw strikes, and the constant yelling from the dugout caused shell shock in some young pitchers until they became conditioned to the treatment.

Cincinnati's Lou Piniella never hesitates to step over his pitching coach and tongue-lash one of his pitchers. In a nationally televised 1990 game, Piniella came to the mound to counsel rookie Chris Hammond and started screaming in Hammond's face in full view of the stadium and TV audience.

Piniella was involved in a 1992 incident that underscored the need for candor between a manager, his pitchers, and the pitching coach. Prior to a late-season game, Piniella was led to believe by reliever Rob Dibble and pitching coach Larry Rothschild that Dibble had some shoulder stiffness. During the game, Piniella then used rookie Steve Foster to save the game and when asked why later, Piniella related that Dibble said his shoulder was sore.

Dibble then denied to reporters that he had a sore shoulder. When Piniella was informed of Dibble's remarks, he screamed,

"No one calls me a liar," and charged into the clubhouse for his soon-to-become-famous wrestling match with Dibble. It was an extreme incident, but it also illustrated why managers and pitching coaches constantly monitor the physical and mental status of their pitchers.

Meanwhile, the mechanics of pitching strategy are just as complex. Setting the starting rotation is one of the basics. Choosing who starts and in what order can be an uncomplicated process until someone gets hurt or there's a rainout or two. Then juggling the rotation so that everyone gets proper rest and no one sits out too long between starts can become a complex chore.

Infinitely more finesse is needed to handle a bull pen. Miller appreciates Leyland's skill in manipulating his relievers.

"No one I've ever seen handles a bull pen like Jim. He's the best," said Miller. "He will never burn out anyone. If it means that he might have to take a beating in one game in order to keep the bull pen fresh down the line, he's willing to take that risk.

"We try as much as possible never to use a reliever more than two days in a row. He is careful about trying to use someone after he warms them up. He tries not to let a pitcher go too long without getting to face at least a few batters.

"We've never had that 35- or 40-save guy, an Eckersley or a Lee Smith. So that has made the job even tougher. We have a lot of games where we might use three guys to get the last five or six outs. The teams with the big closer know that guy is going to get the last three outs, so it makes everything a lot easier.

"And because of that, we've needed 11 pitchers in order to make sure we always have someone fresh out there. That's a tough way to manage, but Jim does it as well as anyone."

It doesn't take too much misuse to tire out a bull pen. And it's not just the number of games in which a pitcher actually appears; if a reliever is asked to warm up two or three times a night for three or four straight nights, that takes just as much of a toll as pitching every night. Burning out a pitching staff is the quickest way for a manager to kill his own pennant chances.

Most pitching coaches keep track of how many times their pitchers warm up, and sometimes the figures can be stupefying. There was one year in Baltimore when Tippy Martinez was the Orioles' only left-handed reliever for most of the season. And in that season, Weaver had Martinez warm up 323 times.

In the Red Sox clubhouse after the third game of the 1990 American League play-offs was a graphic tableau of what happens when a manager burns out his bull pen. Boston's Joe Morgan was notorious for getting his relievers up virtually every night, although not always actually using them in games. There in the Red Sox clubhouse on this afternoon in Oakland were three Red Sox relievers sitting in front of their lockers with ice packs strapped to their pitching shoulders. The interesting thing was that none of them had pitched that day.

Other strategic challenges faced by managers are the in-game decisions involving changing pitchers, the kind of pitches used for particular batters, and whether or not to intentionally walk or pitch to a particular hitter in late-inning situations. There is no "right" way for a manager to make those decisions; it often comes down to feel and intuition.

"I'll never forget one of my first games in my first year of managing in A-ball," said Leyland. "One of the veteran Tigers scouts was with me in the dugout, and the game got to a point where I felt I had to make a move. I asked the scout what I should do, and he told me, 'You're the manager, it has to be your call from now on.' And I swallowed hard and went out to change pitchers. It's one of the toughest things a manager has to learn."

Leyland, like most managers, will rarely come to the mound for visits, leaving that chore to Miller, his pitching coach. Leyland will only come to the mound to remove a pitcher. Leyland maintains, as do most veteran managers, that when he comes to the mound, he has already made up his mind to change pitchers and will not be swayed by anything his pitcher might say.

The more secure managers say they similarly will not allow themselves to be talked out of a decision to intentionally walk a hitter. "You take what a pitcher thinks into account, maybe, but you always have to remember that these guys are competitors and they usually think they can get anyone out," says Miller. "And a manager has to take that decision out of his pitcher's hands, especially in the late innings when the game is on the line and the pressure has the adrenaline flowing."

One of the most famous instances of a manager waffling came in the fifth game of the 1984 World Series. The Padres were trailing by a run in the eighth inning when the Tigers put runners on second and third. With Rich Gossage pitching and Kirk Gibson, who had already homered, at bat, San Diego manager Dick Williams signaled to his catcher Terry Kennedy for Gossage to intentionally walk Gibson in order to pitch to right-handed hitter Lance Parrish. However, Gossage resisted the decision, and finally Williams came running from the dugout. Gossage continued to state his case, and Williams, one of the most intimidating managers who ever lived, allowed Gossage to get his way. So Gossage pitched to Gibson, who hit his third pitch into the right-field upper deck for a three-run homer that virtually clinched the Series for the Tigers.

As for calling pitches, Leyland and Miller will usually sit side by side and both flash a constant stream of signs to whoever is catching. The majority of these signs are decoys. But in pressure situations, there will invariably be signs for specific pitches as well as for pitchouts or throws to first base. Such orchestration has become common to most clubs, adding to the complexity and uncertainty of managing pitching.

There was no such indecision involving Batista. Leyland and the Pirates were convinced he could not help them. Beyond mere pitching maturity, Batista was unwittingly a symbol to Leyland of all the front-office moves in the off-season that had left him with a shaky pitching staff. Leyland made no effort to hide his feelings from anyone, including Batista. Leyland didn't want Batista. Over the season's first two weeks, Batista made only one appearance, a two-inning stint in a blowout game with Philadelphia.

By April 20, Pittsburgh needed to make roster space for catcher Don Slaught, who was ready to come off the disabled list, and someone had to leave to make room on the roster. The usual suspects were considered—Prince, Espy, Varsho, etc. But as would happen later when Gibson was dropped, Leyland resisted dropping any of his proven bench players.

So the obvious man became Batista. As a Rule-5 player, he would have to be put on waivers, then offered back to Montreal. The Expos has already made it clear that they would take Batista back.

Leyland's conversation with Simmons didn't last long. "Look, Teddy, I'm not going to use the guy so by keeping him, it means that we're actually short a pitcher and short another man on the roster," said Leyland. "I know he has some ability, but it might be two years before he's ready and we have to win now."

Simmons grudgingly went along. As he would say later, "No one uses a roster better than Jim. We get credit for having a flexible team, but the real issue is that we have a manager intelligent enough to involve all his players and brave enough not to fear what contributions all those nonregulars make.

"If we had one of these managers who play the same nine guys every day, I might have tried harder to keep Batista. With Jim, I knew that keeping Batista would rob Jim of a possible move, and no one makes moves better than he does."

So the moves were put in motion to drop Batista. However, because he was a Rule-5 player, the process was complicated. And it ended up creating one added bit of tension. The Pirates first had to put Batista on waivers for 72 hours. He cleared without being claimed. Then, per the stipulations of the Rule-5 draft, they were required to offer him back to Montreal.

Here's where things got interesting. The rules stipulate that the Expos had a 72-hour waiting period before they had to make their intentions official. The Pirates happened to be in Montreal when all this was going on. So although the Expos had long ago made up their minds about taking Batista back, they invoked the 72-hour waiting period. In the process, they prevented the Pirates

from activating Slaught while they were playing the Expos, keeping Batista officially on the Pittsburgh roster for the three additional days.

Leyland blew up at Simmons. "What the hell, can't we get
the goddamn rules straight?" said Leyland. "We get screwed for
three days because we don't know the rules."

Simmons shot back. "Jim, I know the rules," he said. "Montreal is the one screwing us. Their GM [Dan Duquette] told us
twice that they would take Batista back as soon as he cleared
waivers. Then when Batista cleared, Duquette comes back and
tells me they would wait the 72 hours. It's bullshit, we look like
assholes, but we gotta live with it."

Leyland fumed throughout the whole series in Montreal while
Slaught sat idle and slightly amused by the whole affair. "I don't
know why anyone would want to keep me out of the lineup. I
haven't played a game in a month," he said.

Within a week, there was another stir in the Pirates' organization. Douglas Danforth announced that he was stepping down
as the club's chairman of the board and putting all the club's
major decisions in the hands of club president Mark Sauer. Danforth said that his resignation had been planned all along, that
he had merely waited to give Sauer time to settle in with the
Pirates' organization.

However, the Pittsburgh clubhouse had a different impression.
The word was that Danforth had refused to go along with a
tentative contract settlement with Drabek and resigned rather than
take the heat. That was denied by all sides, but the whole affair
just added more intrigue. However, Leyland kept his distance
this time. When Danforth made his announcement, Leyland
brought his coaches into his office. "I'm staying out of this one,"
he said. "This one is none of my business. I don't know about
the contract stuff or any of that. All I know is that Sauer's a good
man. This shouldn't hurt. We'll be all right."

Chapter 5

"I'm Just Another Guy, Working Hard"

◆ The pitch to Gary Redus, the first pitch of a May 12 game in Atlanta, appeared to be slightly outside. However, umpire Mark Hirschbeck called it strike one. Redus, who is one of the quietest Pirates players and is rarely known to argue, did not say anything.

When the next pitch appeared even more outside and Hirschbeck again called it a strike, Redus briefly stepped out of the batter's box and looked at Hirschbeck. However, Redus still did not speak to Hirschbeck.

The third pitch to Redus was the most clearly outside of them all. But Hirschbeck punched his right arm into the air and signaled Redus out on strikes. Redus whirled and said, "That was the worst one of them all, that was way outside."

As is the style of many modern umpires, Hirschbeck took off his mask and got right back in Redus's face, screaming at the player to "shut up and get back to the dugout." Redus yelled back, and Hirschbeck ejected him before Leyland could run from the dugout and get between his player and the umpire. Said Leyland, "Damn it, those pitches were all outside. You can't run my player for your mistake. Get with it—he didn't show you up, you blew three pitches." Hirschbeck yelled at Leyland to get his "ass back in the dugout." Leyland briefly stopped to yell some more and then returned to the dugout.

Leyland and the Pirates rarely have problems with umpires. "We probably yell less than any club in the league," said Leyland. However, this night in Atlanta was different.

Pirates players and coaches were on Hirschbeck all night, questioning his pitch calls throughout the game. On a couple of occasions, Hirschbeck peered into the dugout as if looking for someone to confront. When he'd turn away, the Pirates would shout, "What are you looking at? Keep your head in the game and don't blow any more calls."

It was all out of character for the Pirates, who even umpires agree are among the easiest clubs to deal with. But the Pittsburgh dugout felt Redus was run without a reason by an umpire who they felt had a short fuse and was looking for trouble.

The night passed without further incident. But the tension would spill over into the next game.

An umpire who is behind the plate for one game rotates the next day to third base. In Atlanta, the visiting dugout is on the third-base side, so Hirschbeck was easily within earshot of the Pirates' bench. For the first few innings, he seemed to be baiting the Pittsburgh players. He would hear a comment and stare in the dugout, looking for whoever was riding him. As the Pirates built a six-run early-inning lead, Hirschbeck's "rabbit ears" did not go unnoticed.

Then the situation became volatile. With the Pirates in the field, Bob Walk came to the far end of the dugout, which was nearest to third base, and started yelling at Hirschbeck. Walk kept asking, "Who are you looking for? Why don't you watch the game instead of looking for trouble in here? You blew enough calls last night by looking in here."

Leyland had meanwhile moved to that end of the dugout to get a drink of water when he heard Hirschbeck yell to Walk, "If you think those pitches were outside last night, wait until the next time I get you guys behind the plate."

That set Leyland off. It's one thing for an umpire to go after one of his players. But Hirschbeck crossed a line when he suggested that his calls would change because of some disagreement with the Pirates.

Leyland ran onto the field, screaming at Hirschbeck. The umpire rushed at Leyland at the same time and the two bumped into each other. Hirschbeck immediately signaled that Leyland was thrown out of the game, but that just caused the manager's temper to rise another octave, screaming something about Hirschbeck being "a bush-leaguer."

Hirschbeck again threatened Leyland, shouting back, "Just wait until I get you guys behind the plate again." Leyland appeared ready to physically charge Hirschbeck when third baseman Steve Buechele got to him, as did Rich Donnelly, who had run from the dugout to pull Leyland away. Bonds ran in from left field also to try to calm Leyland down. However, Hirschbeck was out of control himself. He started stalking Leyland, screaming at the Pirates' manager until umpire Charlie Williams ran over to pull Hirschbeck away.

Leyland finally left the field. But before Leyland had left for the clubhouse, leaving the bench in the hands of Virdon and Donnelly, Hirschbeck again came striding toward the dugout, this time yelling at Walk, who was still yelling at him. Williams came running in from second again to quiet Hirschbeck down while Walk was led away by Ray Miller, and the game, which would eventually become an 11–10 Pirates squeaker, was allowed to proceed.

After the game, Leyland was not apologetic about his own behavior. "I'm glad I did it," he said. "I'm sick and tired of everyone backing off from umpires. When a guy like that does something like that, they shouldn't get off without being called on it. That was a disgrace."

When asked about whether he might face suspension from NL president Bill White for apparently bumping Hirschbeck, Leyland replied, "I'll appeal anything. The guy was wrong with what he said and what he did and I'll fight anything. That was a disgrace. In fact, I intend to talk to Bill White about this whole thing, no matter what happens."

In the end, Leyland was not penalized further, and he never ended up discussing the Hirschbeck incident with White. Ironically, Hirschbeck's umpiring crew was in Pittsburgh the weekend following the series in Atlanta, and there was a controversial call involving a wild pitch that appeared to score two Pirates runners but was then reversed by Williams. In the ensuing argument, Hirschbeck stayed well away from Leyland and the Pirates.

From the Pirates' point of view, the whole situation was allowed to die without further incident. It was Leyland's one significant altercation with an umpire in 1992, and one of the most volatile he ever experienced in his managerial career. But such wars have been the norm for managers throughout baseball history.

Arguing with umpires is as much a part of baseball tradition as chewing tobacco. From John McGraw to Leo Durocher to Casey Stengel to Billy Martin, managers have been as much known for their arguments with umps as they have for peerless strategy. No one in modern times was known more for such confrontations than Earl Weaver.

Weaver's showmanship raised arguments to the level of an art form. He combined his own volatile and coarse temper with a comic flair that became as much a part of the Weaver legend as his succession of 90-win seasons. Weaver was ejected over 100 times in his Orioles managing career. He was ejected before games even started. He was ejected from a World Series game. He was even ejected from an exhibition game in spring training.

Some umps, bruised by years of being the target of Weaver's sharp tongue, claimed, particularly toward the end of Weaver's career, that he staged his histrionics in order to keep himself in the spotlight. However, the fact is that guerilla theater was part of Weaver's modus operandi long before he even reached the major leagues.

He had memorable blowups with umpires when he was managing deep in the minor leagues. Former players like Dean Chance and Bob Belinsky, hardly shrinking violets themselves, still tell stories of their days being managed by Weaver in Class-A. They love to relate how one night Weaver got thrown out of a game after some wild dispute. He walked out of the ballpark and around to center field, where he proceeded to climb the flagpole to protest his ejection and to watch the rest of the game. The problem was that after the game was over Weaver couldn't get down the flagpole. Long after the lights had been turned off and the crowd had departed, a local fire department was called to assist his descent.

Weaver didn't climb any flagpoles once he reached Baltimore. But his relationships with umpires sparked countless shows. There was the night in Oakland when Weaver was ejected by umpire Jim Evans. Now, the dugouts in Oakland do not directly connect with the clubhouse. You have to walk behind the backstop and up stairs under the grandstand. On this night following Weaver's ejection, the umpires began to notice that Orioles coaches seemed to be standing suspiciously still in one corner of the dugout. Evans also realized that he had not actually seen Weaver walk behind the backstop.

So Evans approached the dugout. Coaches Frank Robinson and Jim Frey stood still in the corner and Evans told them to move. Behind them was a small door behind which was a dugout rest room. Evans flung open the door, and there was Weaver, crouched, smoking a cigarette. Evans screamed for him to go to the clubhouse, and after the game he called Weaver, "the Son of Sam of baseball."

Although Weaver would never hesitate to play to a crowd, he was ultimately motivated by trying to gain a winning edge. One of his best shows came one night in Cleveland when a tiny crowd of around 4,000 were treated to a Weaverian tour de force. Among the umpires that night was Bill Haller, considered the best AL ump of his time. A dour sort, he was also Weaver's biggest nemesis. No umpire ejected Weaver more times than Haller. Although many of Weaver's umpiring foes actually were amused at times with his antics, there was no love lost between Weaver and Haller.

In Cleveland, Haller made an interference call on a throw up the first baseline that gave the Orioles an out and a man on first instead of second and third and none out. The resulting argument raged on for minutes, Haller at one point folding his arms and staring down at the shorter Weaver and sarcastically shaking his head at Weaver's yelling.

Suddenly, Weaver held up his hand as if to say "wait a minute." He then ran into the dugout and came back on the field brandishing a rule book, which he opened to the interference page, held it in front of Haller's face, and began to demonstratively point at the page.

Haller quickly thumbed Weaver, whereupon the Orioles manager began tearing pages from the rule book and throwing them at Haller one by one. Paper soon littered the area between the first baseline and the pitcher's mound. Weaver finally got to the end of the book, and as he walked from the field he tossed the remains into the stands. The small crowd rose to give Weaver a standing ovation for his show, whereupon he raised both arms and gave the crowd a Nixonesque V for victory salute.

There was the summer when Weaver was suspended for three games by AL president Lee MacPhail for protesting a game in Chicago on the grounds of "umpire integrity," a slap at umpire Ron Luciano, with whom Weaver constantly warred. Weaver didn't appeal the suspension; instead, he openly disdained MacPhail by announcing that he was taking "three days' vacation." Weaver spent his "vacation" sitting ten rows behind home plate in Metropolitan Stadium in Bloomington, Minnesota, flanked by a pair of Orioles scouts, watching the Orioles play a weekend series with the Twins and openly flashing signs to his dugout.

There was the summer when MacPhail handed Weaver another suspension after Weaver's cap poked umpire Rich Garcia in the eye as they went face-to-face in an argument. Well, the next time Garcia had an Orioles game was during a momentous five-game series with the Yankees. Baltimore and New York were separated by two games and the series drew 250,000 to Baltimore.

A dispute arose over a play at the plate and out stormed Weaver to argue.

Weaver played Memorial Stadium like Elvis played Vegas, and the sight of Weaver racing from the Orioles' dugout to argue elicited the same sort of delighted screeches that greeted the first strains of "Jailhouse Rock." So when he raced to the plate on this humid Saturday night, the crowd erupted. But the sound exploded when Weaver quickly stopped in front of Garcia and elaborately, with the timing of Olivier, slowly turned his cap around backward so as not to shove the bill into Garcia's face again. After the inevitable ejection, Weaver waved his hat in Garcia's face and then flung it into the air, an act he repeated three times before kicking dirt all over home plate and finally retreating to the dugout runway to thunderous applause.

Then there was the March day in West Palm Beach when a spring training crowd that would have been happy just to see Eddie Murray play three innings instead was treated to a vintage Weaver performance when National League umpire Joe West called a balk on an Orioles pitcher and Weaver went ballistic. He got ejected and then refused to leave the field for at least ten minutes while the crowd howled and players sat in the outfield grass.

Weaver's behavior was certainly often extreme, but his coaches always insisted that it was rarely premeditated. "Earl would come back to the dugout after one of those displays and his chest would be heaving, his face would be red, and you'd swear he was ready for a heart attack," said Jim Frey. "You can't plan or fake that kind of stuff."

However, there were specific instances when Weaver would stage arguments. He had been tossed one night for openly smoking in the dugout, and when he carried the lineup to home plate the next evening, he had what appeared to be a cigarette in his mouth. When the umpire started to eject him, Weaver started eating what turned out to be a chocolate cigarette.

The bottom line was that there was a purpose to Weaver's constant baiting of umpires, that he was always looking for an edge. He would start complaining about pitches from the first inning, even though his own eyesight wasn't the sharpest. But Weaver plainly believed that if he kept the umpires on edge, he might get a borderline call in his favor at another point in the game.

Some of Weaver's players felt his constant berating of the umpires was counterproductive. "Pitching for Earl was never really relaxing," recalled Steve Stone, who had a career year, his 25-win 1980 Cy Young Award season for Weaver. "If you threw ball one, he'd scream at the umpire no matter where the pitch was, and as a pitcher you'd wonder sometimes if umps stuck it to us just to get back at Earl. On the other hand, he'd scream at us to throw strikes just as much as he'd scream at the umpires, so who knows?"

It was also no coincidence that Weaver saved some of his most vociferous moments for times when the Orioles were struggling or were in a pressure situation. Such was the case with Garcia the night with the cap. The Orioles at the time were in danger of slipping back in the race. Weaver's explosion shifted much of the postgame attention away from his players and onto himself. And it got the Baltimore crowd worked up at a time when the place was getting somber over the team's position.

Weaver as well as other managers would use umpires the way many basketball coaches will go after a referee and take a technical foul in hopes of waking up their team or the home crowd. For example, during the 1990 pennant race, Lou Piniella ignited a Cincinnati crowd and his own slumping team with a wild argument that ended with him pulling second base out of the ground and tossing it into the outfield.

But those aren't the only types of ploys managers can use to twist the umpire's role to their advantage. One of the more common is constantly asking an umpire to check the baseballs being thrown by a pitcher suspected of scuffing the ball or throwing some kind of illegal pitch. Some managers try to persuade an umpire to check the pitcher's glove to see if he's concealing any illegal substance. Toronto's Cito Gaston caused one such brouhaha in the 1989 play-offs when he asked umpires to check balls thrown by Oakland relief ace Dennis Eckersley. Such tactics aren't necessarily aimed at actually exposing a cheater; rather, they are designed to disrupt the pitcher's concentration.

Conversely, managers and coaches often complain to umpires about illegal pickoff moves. Such complaining might not necessarily rattle the pitcher, but it could plant a seed in the umpire's mind and perhaps result in a balk call later in the game.

Managers have also been known to alter their pitching plans upon learning who will be the home-plate umpire on a given night. "Say you've brought up a young pitcher who is a breaking-ball pitcher and you have one of the umpires in our league who just won't give a breaking-ball pitcher a strike," explained La-Russa. "Well, in that situation, I'll probably try to put off that young pitcher's start a day if it makes sense with the rest of the rotation. The fact of the matter is that the way some umpires call balls and strikes can seriously hamper certain pitchers' ability to get their best results. So it's a factor you have to stay aware of a lot of times."

LaRussa is also a stickler for making sure umpires are made aware of any indication that a pitcher might deliberately be throwing at Oakland hitters. LaRussa had to be corralled by the umpires at one point in 1992 when he seemed on the verge of coming to blows with Yankees manager Buck Showalter, who came rushing from the dugout to protest LaRussa's claims that Yankees pitchers might be head-hunting. Later in the season, LaRussa also helped initiate the ejection of two Kansas City pitchers in beanball incidents, simply by his vociferous protests after an A's batter was hit by a Royals pitch.

Despite all the arguments and confrontational umpires, few actual feuds last very long between teams and individual umps. Philadelphia had a running battle for a while with NL umpire Joe West, one of the cockier umps in the game, after they protested West's actions during a bench-clearing brawl with the New York Mets. West grabbed and flipped to the ground a Phillies player in what Philadelphia viewed as an overly exuberant manner. They complained to the league office, and the resulting grudge escalated to the point where the Phillies just assumed they would have an ejection in every game of theirs that West umpired.

But such feuds are rare. As much confrontation as there might appear to be nowadays, the bottom line of any umpire–manager relationship is consistency. Umpires appreciate managers who will only argue when they feel they have a legitimate beef and avoid arguments for show. Umpires particularly appreciate managers who don't yell cheap shots from the dugouts of which only the umpires are aware.

Managers on the other hand just hope for umpiring consistency. Both players and managers like to feel confident that a borderline pitch on the outside corner that is called a strike in the second inning is still a strike in the eighth inning. Players and managers like to know that a pitcher's move that is called a balk for one team is also called for another. Managers like to think that umpires are bearing down on their jobs.

Indeed, in the seventh game of the 1992 NL play-offs, in what would be the Pirates' darkest hour, one of the turning points would be a borderline call by home-plate umpire Randy Marsh that resulted in a walk to Atlanta's Damon Berryhill. On television, the pitch looked like a strike instead of ball three.

But the Pirates didn't argue it at the time, and they didn't complain about it later in the emotional aftermath of that seventh game. The reason was that they had genuine respect for Marsh's work ethic.

"If it had been another guy, we probably would have yelled like hell," said Ray Miller. "But Randy Marsh is a real professional. You know that he is always bearing down and trying his best to make the right call in any situation. If he missed the pitch, then he missed the pitch through honest effort. You can't yell about that because he's a guy you know tries his best to do a good professional job. And that's all you can ask out of any umpire, just an effort to do a good professional job."

By mid-May, the Pirates were the talk of baseball. After 33 games, they were 23–10. Leyland, already a full-fledged celebrity in Pittsburgh, was becoming a national item, hailed everywhere as one of the game's best managers.

Such notoriety is a way of life for someone like Tommy Lasorda, who relishes the attention. Lasorda has transcended being just a baseball celebrity. Through his friendships with entertainers and his frequent TV appearances and commercial associations, most notably with Slim-Fast, Lasorda is a celebrity beyond baseball and has been for years.

Managers like Lou Piniella and Hal McRae, who were top major-league players for years, already were used to being celebrities years before they became managers. But handling such attention can be difficult for managers like Leyland, Buck Showalter in New York, or Johnny Oates in Baltimore. Leyland and Showalter never played in the majors and worked their way to the Show along the laborious ladder of minor-league managing. Although Oates played several years in the majors, he was never more than a fringe player.

It is a huge adjustment to cope with being a big man in town along with all the other pressures, stresses, and demands of managing. And many managers end up becoming too taken with the fame. Oates found himself falling into that trap in the weeks after he became Orioles manager in 1991. In 1992 he became a commodity when his Orioles became not only one of the year's surprise teams but also one of the game's glamour franchises because of their gorgeous new stadium and huge home attendance.

"I've been in the game for 25 years but I never was a big-name guy," recalled Oates while sitting in his plush, ultramodern office in Camden Yards. "I've always been happy that I have a lot of friends. And I've been finding out this year what with all the ticket requests I get that I have even more friends than I thought. But after becoming manager, I suddenly had thousands of people who knew my name, recognized my face, and were calling me by name.

"And that's very flattering. I admit that I liked that a lot. I mean, I'm a guy who changed his autograph to make it more legible because people used to ask me who I was after I signed it. But I became manager and people knew who I was. I had a dozen reporters writing down everything I said. I'd walk into restaurants and people would recognize me, shake my hand, offer to buy me a drink. I thought I was pretty cool. There's no question that it all went to my head."

Oates said that the celebrity and the demands of managing quickly consumed him. A month into the job in 1991, Oates acknowledged that he was living his job 24 hours a day, enjoying every minute and losing perspective at the same time.

"My family noticed it right away," said Oates. "Throughout my career, I never liked to see guys who were taken with themselves. I never wanted to be that way, but here I was doing just that.

"It really hit bottom late last season. My wife, Gloria, and I went out for lunch on our 24th wedding anniversary. I had planned to set aside one whole hour to just be with her, and 30 minutes into it I was thinking about that night's lineup. I mean, I was spending 20 hours a day on baseball. I was trying to answer every letter, do every radio show, sit for every interview, return every phone call, and prepare for every game. And in the process, my family life suffered greatly.

"We had a rough winter. We had a lot of time to talk about how I failed as a husband and a father after I became manager. Gloria wants me to spend time at my job and so do the kids. They're my biggest supporters. But they had a rough summer in 1991 being around me. And realizing that finally, hopefully, helped me land on my feet and has taught me to handle all the attention and everything a lot better.

"I respect Sparky Anderson as much as anyone in the business. And he took me aside this spring and told me, 'John, there are going to be times when you have to say no. There are times when you're going to have to turn it off and stop thinking about the lineup or your hair will be as white as mine.' He told me that the job and all the attention can kill you if you let it.

"There are nights when we talk baseball at the dinner table.

But I've made sure that there's also time to talk about how my son Andy is doing in baseball."

Anderson has become something of a father confessor for many young managers. It was only a few years ago that he took a leave of absence because the stress of the job and family concerns were becoming too much to handle. He has returned in recent seasons with a new outlook on the job and the fame it brings.

"When I was younger I never thought about stuff like celebrity or stress," said Anderson. "Then a few years went by and I started questioning it all. I'd wake up and start asking what it all means. I was running around, doing all this stuff and not knowing why.

"And then my wife one day said to me, 'If it ended right this second, you'd have had a career far greater than you ever could have thought.' And she was right. I would have never thought of that. And it made me realize that I had been doing a lot of things I didn't like.

"For one thing, I realized that I didn't like the whole celebrity thing. I would do all these things I didn't really like doing because I didn't want people to think I was above them. But it didn't make me very happy. And now, I do nothing unless it involves children. I work hard on two events every winter back in Thousand Oaks that help kids, and that's about it. Otherwise, my time is spent with my family and friends.

"Younger guys who become managers find it hard to shrug off the celebrity stuff. Getting a managing job is usually a dream come true and guys can get swallowed up by the whole thing. And let's face it, some guys just aren't ready or just don't have what it takes. I talk to them all if they want to talk to me and sometimes, you can tell by just a look in their eyes if they've become too taken with being a celebrity or whatever. It's a real important part of all this. I've been lucky to have a wife who is the biggest reason for getting me through. Some other guys aren't so lucky."

Showalter demonstrated a remarkable ability to handle the New York media crunch through his first season as Yankees manager. For one thing, he didn't have to deal with George Steinbrenner. For another, Showalter has the kind of self-effacing personality that allows him to view the circus with a bemused detachment.

One summer night in Chicago, Showalter was making out his lineup card in between trips to the bathroom. He had been ill for over 24 hours with a virus and looked miserable. When a visitor asked how he was doing, he laughed. "I'm doing great. I feel like I've just had another meeting with the commissioner.

"You know I was thinking last night about how glamorous this job of mine really is. You know, people think of managing the Yankees as being something like being a celebrity or a movie star. I thought about all that last night. Here we are losing a game. I'm so sick that I have to come into the office here and watch the game on television. Here I am listening to Hawk Harrelson and Tom Paciorek yelling 'Yes!' every time the White Sox score a run in between my running to the bathroom because my stomach felt like it was falling apart.

"And I thought to myself that all those people who think it's great to be a celebrity, who think it's glamorous to manage the Yankees, should see me now."

As for Leyland, the demands and attention were on another plateau. With the Pirates off to their great start, columnists were lining up in every city the Pirates visited to write the praises of Leyland. Autograph seekers went after his signature nearly as much as they coveted Bonds's or Van Slyke's. Leyland was recognized in airports, and in Pittsburgh he drew a crowd no matter were he went.

But Leyland is remarkably unimpressed with the whole matter of celebrity. "I like the idea that the people of Pittsburgh appreciate how hard we've worked to make this franchise a winner," said Leyland. "And I like to think that whatever popularity I might have is because they recognize that I'm just another guy, working hard at his job.

"But I try not to kid myself. They can give me a standing ovation on opening night and don't get me wrong, that meant an awful lot to me. But if I make a pitching change that those same fans don't like, they're going to boo and they have every right to do that because that's the way the game has always been.

"That stuff about being a celebrity is pretty much bull. I like the feeling of being known in the community and I try to do what I can with charities and all the rest. But when you're managing a baseball team, the most important thing is making sure your team puts out an effort every night. I never promise we'll win, but I always promise that we're working to the best of our ability.

"And let's face it. I'm no celebrity if we'd been losing the last couple of years. I'd be a coach for someone or managing somewhere in the minors. I'm not kidding myself about all that.

"When we lose, it's my fault as much as anyone else's. I always include myself because when we lose, I have to manage better. I have to make some contributions when we're not winning. You feel that somewhere along the line, I could have pushed a little here or there and we could have gotten the one more run that would have let us win. I try to be as hard on myself as I am on anybody else."

Leyland soon had plenty of opportunity to be hard on himself. After raising their record to 23–10, without any warning they collapsed into the worst stretch a Pittsburgh team had played in four years.

The Pirates lost 11 of their next 12 games, nine of them coming on a 1–8 West Coast trip. However, the tone for the whole swoon was set in the final game at home prior to traveling to California. Any chance of coming back in the game was largely killed by one of Leyland's rare strategical mistakes. What could have been an uplifting victory to send the Pirates off on the road instead turned into a gnawing loss.

The Pirates were three runs down in the bottom of the ninth inning to San Diego in Pittsburgh when Tom Prince led off the inning with a single. One of the slowest Pirates players, Prince was hardly expecting to get any kind of sign to run, especially since the Padres' catcher was Benito Santiago, who might have the best catcher's throwing arm since the retirement of Johnny Bench.

However, Leyland inadvertently flashed a steal sign for Prince, and Prince dutifully took off. Santiago gunned him down at second by 15 feet. The next two batters reached base, and Jay Bell delivered a two-run double that would have tied the score if Prince hadn't been caught stealing. Instead, it brought the Pirates to within a run. And that's how the game ended, as Van Slyke and Bonds could not get Bell home from second.

Immediately after the game, Prince tried to take the blame. "I've got to know better not to go, no matter what I see," he said. "It's a situation where if I don't go, I look like a fool because the sign's on. There's 50 things going through my mind in that situation. I can only do what I see and that's that."

However, Leyland would have none of that. "I'm too upset with myself to talk about anything else," said Leyland. "I can't talk about any players. I messed it up totally. Tommy did exactly what he's supposed to do.

"It was totally my fault, my mistake. I can only remember doing that one other time. But that's no excuse. People give me credit a lot around here. Well, I ain't no genius and I proved that today. The guys battled their rear ends off and I messed the game up."

After the media left the room, Donnelly, who had been quietly sitting nearby, asked Leyland, "I want to make sure this wasn't my fault. You did give the steal sign, didn't you?"

Leyland said, "Yeah, why the hell didn't you ignore me?"

Said Donnelly, "Well, how'd I know this wasn't one of your hunches?"

"Aw, the hell with it, I messed up," said Leyland. "It ain't the first time. Only this time, it was out there for everybody to see."

Leyland's mistake didn't cause much of a ripple in the Pirates' clubhouse. His game strategy was always impeccable. Leyland rarely was outmaneuvered by another manager. His strategy might not always work, but he could invariably bend the percentages in his favor.

He was also a master at educated hunches. Leyland ended an early-season game in Chicago with one of those guesses. With two outs, he sensed through the Cubs' signs and body movements that they'd try a steal. So Leyland signaled to LaValliere to call a pitchout. The runner indeed was running. Leyland had guessed right and LaValliere threw the runner out by ten feet for the final out of the game.

Such successes made the Pirates entirely comfortable with Leyland's strategic handling of games. And Leyland's rapport with his players was so good that when he did make a mistake, it resulted not in skepticism from his players but humor. So even after the San Diego mishap, some of the veterans kidded Leyland for a few days, asking him if he wanted to review the signs. Leyland would feign anger and tell the player to get lost.

Too much is often made about a manager's strategy. Veteran managers like Whitey Herzog, long known as one of the game's very best, downplayed the significance of a manager's moves. "Coming into any season, there are 50 or so games you're going to lose no matter what and 50 or so others you're going to win no matter what," said Herzog. "Those other 50 or so are the one- and two-run games that can go either way. And of those, who knows, maybe a dozen or so can be directly decided by a manager's strategy."

Many managerial moves are obvious to fans and even sportswriters. The "book" on most strategic moves is a part of baseball's history. You go for the tie at home and the win on the road, you bunt a leadoff runner into scoring position, you play left–right percentages with your pitching in close games, and so on.

There are also vastly different managerial styles. Few managers in history have been more revered for strategic acumen than Gene Mauch. Starting with his managing the Philadelphia Phillies during their infamous 1964 collapse and on through his years with Montreal, Minnesota, and California, Mauch built a reputation as a master strategist who would bunt in the first inning, call for hit and run plays at unconventional times, and never allow himself to be outmaneuvered by another manager.

Meanwhile, a manager like Weaver abhored the sacrifice bunt ("It's giving away an out and you only have 27 in a game," was his theory) and would invariably wait for a big inning. Pitching and three-run homers constituted Weaver's basic strategic philosophy.

However, the real difference between a Mauch and a Weaver was often the result of their personnel. No one ever managed more games without winning a pennant than Mauch, whereas Weaver was a perennial winner. Strategy had something to do with it, perhaps, but the biggest reason was players.

The parameters of a home ballpark can also dictate a manager's basic strategy and the makeup of his team. Herzog will forever be known for the Cardinals teams he built around stolen bases and team speed. But it was largely the result of spacious Busch Stadium. "When I got to St. Louis and managed in that big ballpark with the artificial turf a year, I decided right away we needed to build a team that had speed and defense," said Herzog. "Hell, if I had been in Fenway Park, I would have built a different team."

But no matter what their style, managers like Herzog, Mauch, and Weaver did not make many mistakes. And those managers who make frequent mistakes quickly lose credibility both in the clubhouse and with the media.

In 1991, Cubs manager Jim Essian lost most of his club and greased his own skids toward dismissal with a series of misfiring strategic moves. The worst might have been with Mark Grace, one of the Cubs' best hitters, at the plate and runners on first and third in a close game. Essian signaled for a gimmick play in which the runner on first base pretends to stumble on the baseline, drawing a throw by a pitcher and thus allowing the runner on third to sprint home.

It is hardly a new play. Teams have been trying it in various permutations for 40 years. Earl Weaver used to spend an hour every spring going over the play on what he called "the little diamond," which was a spare practice infield tucked behind the third-base grandstand at ancient Miami Stadium. Orioles veterans would always complain about practicing the play every spring. But invariably, Weaver would use it once or twice a year to steal a run—or in the case of a 0–0 game with the White Sox, steal a game with an eighth-inning use of the play with the unlikely duo of Eddie Murray on third and Doug DeCinces at first.

However, Weaver used the play with weak-hitting Lenn Sakata at bat, not his number three hitter, as Essian did with Grace. So when the play backfired and the Cubs runner at third was tagged out, Grace wheeled in the batter's box and in full view of the intrusive cameras of WGN, screamed, "Why the hell don't we play baseball here?"

Players aren't necessarily great students of the game. However, they notice when their manager gets consistently overmatched, and they will quickly turn on a manager when his luck starts running out. For example, the Giants' Roger Craig was known as a master of the unconventional, calling for pitchouts at unlikely times and having them thwart a stolen base or hit and run. Some thought he was stealing signs; others thought he just had a well-honed ability for the good guess. Whatever, he had a huge success ratio for a number of years. But in 1991 and 1992, as the Giants collapsed in many areas, so did Craig's run of luck. Pitchouts were made with nothing going on, in the process just moving counts in the batter's favor. As a result, many of the same players who marveled at Craig's prescience just a couple of years ago now questioned his managerial ability behind his back and eroded much of his authority in the process.

When Joe Morgan managed the Red Sox, Boston players would kid that they didn't need any signs because Morgan would never push any buttons after running out the starting lineup.

Back in the late 1970s, Seattle players quickly turned on manager Maury Wills after Wills fouled up a succession of strategic moves such as mistakenly coming to the mound twice in an inning and thus being forced to remove a pitcher he actually wanted to keep in the game.

But a manager's real in-game strategy begins with his lineup. And strategy has a far better chance of being accepted if players feel comfortable with their own playing time. So the occasional mistake by Leyland was overlooked by the Pirates players because they had long since accepted whatever lineup moves he elected to make. For example, Leyland platooned players at three positions—catcher, first base, and right field. None of the players involved complained about the intermittent playing time because Leyland was absolutely consistent in his use of them in their given roles. And bench players who were largely used in pinchhit situations accepted their roles because Leyland always tried to keep them as sharp as possible through occasional starts.

Keeping his bench ready was an art Leyland learned from his years coaching with LaRussa. "It never had made sense to me how on the one hand you ask a pinch hitter to produce in what is almost always a critical game situation, and on the other hand that key hitter might not have had an at bat for a week," said LaRussa. "How can you expect a guy to come through when he sees a pitcher once a week? That's a big reason why it's important to try and keep everybody sharp any way you can."

Weaver would consult his trusty index cards (nowadays managers have computer printouts) that listed what his hitters had done against any given pitcher. And Orioles players quickly got used to being benched on a night when their stats suffered against a given pitcher. Players would look at the lineup card, and when they were benched, the byword became "the index cards got me again."

However, the other side of those benchings was that someone else was getting playing time and staying sharp against a pitcher with whom the player had likely had some career success. Rarely do winning managers get by with using the same players all the time. Especially in these days of record-high numbers of disabled list assignments, a useful group of reserve players is a virtual necessity.

And as LaValliere said of Leyland, echoing the words of players who have played for the Weavers and Herzogs and others, "What Jim does so well is putting his players in situations where they have the greatest chance of succeeding. You might want to play more than he lets you. But after a while you acquire total confidence in Jim's moves.

"You know that whatever he does usually ends up being the best thing for the team. If he does screw up, it's no big deal because you know it's not going to happen very often. The whole effect of that is giving the team a really secure feeling that when we're in a tight spot, Jim is going to think of something that will help. And we can see the other side of all that sometimes. Another manager will screw up or Jim will outmove him and we can see right away that the other team gets deflated. And all that gives us an edge, no question about it."

Chapter 6

"I Gotta Sit and Answer the Stuff"

◆ Sitting at the desk in the cheerless bunker that passes for a visiting manager's office in Philadelphia's Veterans Stadium, Leyland was on the phone doing a radio interview. It was an interview that was not likely to win a Peabody Award.

"Yeah? Well I don't want to say anything until I see it," was Leyland's first answer. "It's hard for me to answer something like that," was his second answer. "That's about all I can say," was his third and final answer, whereupon he slammed down the receiver, got out of his chair, kicked the chair once against the closet door, and then kicked it a second time into the closet, where it came to rest on a pair of freshly polished baseball shoes.

"Do you believe this crap about Bonilla?" said Leyland, slamming shut his office door so that his tirade didn't spill out into the clubhouse. "Now he's saying crap about our organization. He's saying that we didn't support him and weren't up front with him.

"I'll tell you what, if he says anything about this club, about this organization, or about how I or anyone else treated him, I'll nail him. I swear to God that I'll nail him. I don't have to take that. I've got stuff on him that I've never told anyone. I have a pocket full of bullets and I'm going to use them if I have to, I swear to God I'll do it."

By the second week of June, the Pirates seemed to have survived their first crisis of the 1992 season. They had rebounded from their 1–11 skid to win seven of their next ten in Pittsburgh, including three out of four from the Mets, who remained their most feared competitor. However, the series with the Mets was a stormy one.

Bonilla had returned to Pittsburgh for the first time in a Mets uniform. Objects were thrown at him by some upper-deck fans during the first night's game, and Bonilla was roundly booed throughout the weekend. Leyland himself had tried to help calm the first-night incident by picking up the dugout phone and screaming at the stadium security personnel to get to the upper deck and arrest the unruly individuals.

Bonilla's comments weren't the only words to set off Leyland's temper. Barry Bonds defended his friend Bonilla and hinted that Pittsburgh fans were being motivated by racism in their treatment. "When Sid Bream came back for the first time after he left as a free agent, they gave him a standing ovation," said Bonds. "When Bobby came back, they threw things at him and booed."

Bream indeed is white and Bonilla indeed is black. But another difference between the two is that Bream remains a Pittsburgh resident who is very active in several community organizations despite being a member of the Atlanta Braves. Additionally, Bream publicly anguished about leaving Pittsburgh and made the decision only because the Braves gave him an extra guaranteed year beyond what the Pirates felt they could offer. For a player with a history of serious knee problems, that extra guaranteed season was a critical factor. Many Pirates fans meanwhile felt that Bonilla was never interested in staying in Pittsburgh at any price, especially after he rejected the club's four-year $18.5 million offer made back in 1991.

Later in the same weekend, Bonds upped the ante when he somehow connected the Bonilla incident to teammate Andy Van

Slyke. "Andy Van Slyke is the White Hope in Pittsburgh," said Bonds. "They gave him a new contract but let Bobby go. That's because Andy is Mr. Pittsburgh. The surest way to get sent out of this organization is to mess with Mr. Pittsburgh."

So by the time the Pirates got to Philadelphia following the series with the Mets, Leyland was sputtering at his coaches. "How dumb can Barry get? I mean, what possible connection is there between what happened with Bonilla and Andy?" said Leyland. "This is a joke."

"Well, Hump, at least we don't have to worry about it all being in the newspapers," said Donnelly. "They'd be keeping this alive for weeks if they were publishing."

The Pittsburgh newspapers had been shut down by a strike that began just prior to the disastrous West Coast trip. As a result, two of the club's darkest moments—the losing streak and the Bonilla–Bonds controversy—were not being analyzed in the local newspapers.

Such an absence of local newspapers would be a welcome relief to many clubs. But the media atmosphere around the Pirates is far less frenetic or adversarial than in other cities. Most of the players and coaches had good working relationships with Hertzel and Meyer, who were both tough and fair in their reporting on the club, as well as the city's columnists. The reporters remained around the club much of the time because the *Press* and *Post-Gazette* were producing fax newspapers and telephone reports via a 900 number, but it wasn't the same for anyone. The club itself quickly felt the effects of the strike on their attendance.

"Some of those columnists would be tough to take right now with all this crap," acknowledged Leyland. "But you know what? I miss the guys. I like shooting the shit with Hertzel and Meyer. And most of the columnists are all right. I've never had much of a problem with any of them.

"And I miss having the paper to read. I always like starting the day with coffee and the paper and reading what the local writers have to say. I miss that. I don't think the strike is good for the club at all."

The most famous newspaper strike in recent baseball history came in 1978, when the New York papers were shut down during the heat of the Yankees' memorable race with the Boston Red Sox. Those Yankees reeked with constant controversy created by personalities like George Steinbrenner, Billy Martin, Reggie Jackson, Graig Nettles, Thurman Munson, and Sparky Lyle. The absence of reporters had a calming effect on that club.

"I always have got along with most of the writers, both as a player and as a manager," says Reds manager Lou Piniella, a member of the '78 Yankees. "But with that club, with all that went on around us, not having the press around to stir things up or keep stuff alive probably helped us concentrate a little better on the pennant race. If we had to be reading all the time about controversy, it might have created just enough distraction to keep us from catching Boston in the end and forcing the play-off."

Even without any local press around, Leyland still felt it necessary to talk to his club about the whole Bonilla thing. Criticizing the Pirates organization was something he would not let pass.

"Even if this isn't a big deal because there ain't no press doesn't mean I can let it go," said Leyland. "I still have to talk to the boys because this stuff has got to stop. Richie, tell the clubbie to get everyone because we're having a short meeting."

Leyland's message to his players was short and sweet. "You guys can say anything you want, you know that," he said. "But you better be careful when you say things that reflect on how this organization treats people because when you do that, you're wrong.

"I ain't talking about contracts. Contracts aren't my business. I'm talking about how you're treated as men. And if any of you says that one of you has been treated differently than someone else, you better come to me because that just ain't true and every one of you knows it. This organization has treated every one of you the same way and as far as I'm concerned, none of you has a beef.

"You're treated well because we're proud to have you here. That's the fact. So whatever's been going on the last few days, let it die because you're getting into an area where you're gonna be off base. That's all I got to say."

The meeting didn't cool off Leyland's anger. "I just don't get Bonilla," he said. "This club did things for him that people will never know about. Here you are as a manager and you're with these guys all the time and you see them do stuff that you never talk about. Instead, all the time, you try to put your players in a good light and not bury them when you have a chance.

"And this is how they thank you. Well, if he says anything else, I'll bury him. I swear I will."

There is so much more media work for most managers than the public realizes. Hours before the game, they meet with the various writers covering the club, who can range in number from as many as a dozen in cities like New York, Los Angeles, Philadelphia, and San Francisco to as few as one as in St. Louis, a one-newspaper city.

Occasionally, news is made in these pregame sessions. A player might be put on the disabled list or a change made in the upcoming pitching rotation. At the very least, the manager is often the focal point for the early stories required of East Coast writers, who must fill space for early editions that go to press before the completion of night games. The manager is usually the source for much of the information in the "notes" columns which most reporters write in addition to their daily game stories.

After games, managers face the gauntlet of newspaper reporters and radio–TV crews anxious for comments on the night's events and in a hurry to meet deadlines. Most managers receive requests for local TV interviews prior to games, and virtually every manager has a radio show that usually consists of one of the team's play-by-play announcers asking him a few questions before the game.

The Mets' Jeff Torborg adopted a unique extension of the radio show forum in 1992 by agreeing to a lucrative deal with WFAN, the all-sports station and New York flagship station for Mets baseball. Torborg not only had his pregame show but also appeared daily in drive time with "Mike and the Mad Dog," the highly rated talk-show duo of Mike Franscesa and Chris Russo. Torborg also had a postgame show as well.

Radio shows became an issue with the Mets in 1991 when then-manager Buddy Harrelson bailed out on his radio show because of what he perceived to be overly critical questioning by cohost Howie Rose. Harrelson's refusal to do his own show helped grease the skids for his eventual dismissal. Rose, a well-prepared, aggressive professional, ended up being replaced in 1992 as host of the Mets' pregame radio show; the club obviously felt that it wanted to have more control over its message, so the messenger was changed.

The Mets are sensitive to the need to make their personnel more adept at handling the media. Like several other organizations, the Mets employ an outside firm to train players and front-office personnel in dealing with the media. Torborg and others went through several sessions in the off-season at which they faced mock press conferences and then were critiqued on how they handled their answers.

Since Torborg had always been appreciated by the media for his accessibility and good nature, the Mets obviously thought that the radio blitz strategy would serve to, in effect, send the club's message above the heads of the media and directly to the fans. But the Mets didn't count on losing. And they didn't count on Mike and the Mad Dog and other WFAN broadcasters actually asking Torborg tough questions.

Torborg, who had professional broadcasting equipment installed in his Shea Stadium office, found himself spending an inordinate amount of time preparing for his broadcasts so as not to be caught off guard. But his preoccupation with his radio show didn't help to avoid trouble.

Controversy brewed when Torborg said during one of his shows that he thought reliever John Franco was not 100 percent physically. Since he hadn't broached the subject with Franco, the veteran reliever took exception when Torborg's radio remark became news.

Then there was the whole affair concerning whether Bobby Bonilla called an official scorer during a game. Torborg said on his postgame show that Bonilla merely was calling the press box to inquire after the health of Mets public relations director Jay Horwitz, who had a cold. But that story didn't bear up to scrutiny, and on his next show Torborg admitted that maybe he shouldn't have commented at all on Bonilla.

Finally, there were assorted confrontations between Torborg and Russo, who during one show pressed Torborg on a strategic point, whereupon the mild-mannered Mets manager snapped, "I've been in this game for 30 years and I think I know a lot more about how it's played than some guy like you who's never worn a uniform in your life. I'm the one who's the professional in this game, not you."

All this, mind you, on a show for which Torborg was being paid an estimated $250,000 last season.

Torborg's situation was extreme, but even the routine daily media ritual inevitably produces tensions between most managers and some members of the media. Sportswriters don't hesitate to criticize managers' moves or get players to do the dirty work. Second guessing of managers is part of the game and is to be expected. But what usually sets off a manager is either a question he considers uninformed or a player criticism that is allowed to be printed unanswered in the newspaper.

There are still underground tapes of legendary eruptions from various managers. Lasorda produced a classic several years ago. After Dave Kingman hit three home runs and drove in eight runs against the Dodgers, a postgame radio interviewer inquired, "What's your opinion of Kingman's performance?"

This rather innocuous, albeit simple-minded, query produced an obscenity-laced eruption from Mount Lasorda. The gist of the diatribe went something like this: "What did I think of Kingman? The mother-bleeper hit three bleeping home runs and you want to know what the bleep I thought of bleeping Kingman? He hit three bleeping home runs. What the bleep kind of stupid bleeping question is that? What the bleep did I bleeping think of bleeping Kingman? How the bleep can any bleeper ask a bleeping question like that?"

Lasorda is notoriously sensitive to second guesses. Although usually charming to many writers, especially those from national publications and not the traveling LA press corps, with whom he has a sometimes frosty relationship, Lasorda erupts at what he perceives to be erroneous reports or personal criticism.

He had such an incident during the nightmarish 1992 season for the Dodgers. He arrived in Philadelphia, his hometown, to read in a *Philadelphia Daily News* column that he didn't want either Juan Samuel or Kal Daniels on his opening-day roster and was unhappy when they weren't traded or released prior to the season.

"Where the hell did this come from, who the bleep would write something like that without first talking to me?" said Lasorda.

The writer was Paul Hagen, a longtime beat writer covering the Phillies and one of the more professional writers in the business. His information was a generally accepted fact within baseball. Lasorda indeed didn't want Samuel or Daniels on his team, but he had never said so publicly.

At any rate, Lasorda stewed and stormed about the story prior to the game that day. And in the fourth inning of the game, the press box phone rang and the call was for Hagen. "Paul Hagen, this is Tom Lasorda. I'd like you to come to my office after the game so you can explain how you write something like that without talking to me first," was the sound coming through the receiver.

Hagen looked into the Dodgers' dugout and there was Lasorda on the phone. "I want to see you after the game and we can talk about your story," said Lasorda. The two met and actually parted amicably; indeed, much of Lasorda's show of anger was meant for his own players, not for the writer.

Such confrontational tactics are hardly unprecedented. Many

managers have been known to try and initimidate inexperienced reporters, partly to test their mettle but also possibly to scare away any potential trouble.

Earl Weaver was a master at testing new reporters. There was the day when a new beat writer reported to spring training in Miami to cover the Orioles. He nervously introduced himself to Weaver, who greeted him thusly: "First of all, that pad you're carrying is too big. The real reporters have those little pads that you can stick in your back pocket, so get rid of that big dumb pad and get one of those little pads that make you look like a professional.

"The next thing is that you're dressed like a jerk. Don't come around here dressed like a jerk. And the last thing is that you don't know shit, so don't ask me any questions until you know what the hell is going on around here. Just stay out of my way because I ain't gonna answer any dumb questions from a new guy who doesn't even know what kind of pad to use."

A reporter in that kind of situation immediately thinks that his only choices are to quit, be totally shattered, or try to hang on and hopefully get into Weaver's good graces. Fortunately, the Orioles of those days were one of the most intelligent, easy-to-deal-with clubs in recent baseball history. Players and coaches went out of their way to tell a new reporter that Weaver was merely putting the reporter through a form of initiation.

And within days, Weaver would treat the new guy like anyone else. He was a master at dealing with the press. On a dull day, he would invariably have a one-liner or comment that would make news. He understood the give and take of a reporter's job. He might explode at a question he perceived as a second guess, but by the next day, the explosion was ancient history. He saved his grudges for writers who either broke confidence by printing something he said was off the record or who wrote something he construed as being personal.

Weaver would go so far as to offer his beat writers "if" quotes when the club was playing in another time zone and deadlines were tight. He'd say before the game, "If the thing goes long and we win, you can write that I said, 'It was a good one to win, it was a game we needed, Palmer gave us just the kind of pitching the staff needed tonight.' And if we lose, you can write, 'This is the kind of game we have to win if we're going to go all the way. Palmer just didn't have it again and you'll have to ask him what was wrong.' That about covers it, doesn't it?"

Journalistically, "if" quotes were in a gray area, but the whole exercise underscored Weaver's appreciation for the reporters' jobs. However, like all managers, Weaver would lose patience at some point with the endless questions, especially the ones he perceived as being less than thought out. And woe to the writer who might have recently written criticism of Weaver from a player.

Such was the case one day when a story came out quoting Orioles shortstop Mark Belanger was wondering about Weaver's moves in a recent loss. Two days later, a reporter asked Weaver why he didn't bunt in a certain situation.

"Why don't you go out there and ask your friend Belanger why I didn't bunt," said Weaver, reaching for an ashtray from his desk and firing it at the wall. "Your bleeping pal Belanger has all the answers. Go ask him and while you're at it, you can ask him about the pitching rotation and any other bleeping thing you want because I ain't answering any of your questions.

"Wait a minute! You asked why didn't I bunt? Well that question is dumb. Dumb. Dumb. Dumb. That's dumb, D-U-M-B. Dumb, dumb, dumb. Now go ask your bleeping pal Belanger what he thinks of me not bunting. He has all the bleeping answers."

Such an outburst was aimed as much at Belanger, a hard-bitten veteran who was always at odds with Weaver, as it was at the unsuspecting reporter who actually felt as if he had done a good professional job by getting Belanger to criticize Weaver. But such an incident underscored the volatile nature of the media—manager relationship, not just with Weaver but with most major-league managers.

Some managers play favorites between writers or play competing reporters against each other. Such strategy invariably makes an enemy of somebody, and in today's tabloid atmosphere an enemy in the press can do a lot of damage to a manager.

That is why several newer managers, notably the Yankees' Buck Showalter, are careful to meet with all the reporters at once before and after the game so that everyone gets the same material. Showalter will let his guard down with a select few, but he rarely indulges in off-the-cuff chatter unless he is sure whom he is talking with. When Doug Rader managed the Texas Rangers, beat writers and Rader rarely spoke at all, which seems like a solution but actually caused both sides all kinds of headaches.

As for Leyland, he has an easygoing relationship with Meyer and Hertzel, his two traveling writers. He is also almost always available to anyone else wanting his time for interviews. Still, he loses his patience at times.

"I try to be as available as I can to everyone because I know they all have a job to do," he said toward the end of the season. "But sometimes, I really have to hold back and not chew them the hell out for some of the dumb stuff some of them ask.

"A guy comes in after a game in July and wonders about the play-off pitching rotation. I mean, what the hell is he talking about? Somebody wants to know why I didn't bunt Van Slyke in a game. The guy is second in the league in the hitting and even if I do bunt him, which I wouldn't, then they'd walk Bonds, which they do about once a series anyway. I mean, it doesn't take a lot of intelligence to figure that out. But I gotta sit and answer the stuff. That drives me nuts."

LaRussa becomes similarly frustrated by what he perceives as being unknowledgeable questions. Beat writers from the Bay Area who cover him regularly often become irritated at what they perceive as LaRussa talking down to them. LaRussa is rarely relaxed around the ballpark; his intense approach to his job limits the amount of small talk or off-the-record chatter he's willing to indulge in. And LaRussa will often answer questions with an acerbic response that might begin, "Well, for those who were watching the game closely, they would have noticed such and

such." The game is serious business to LaRussa and he rarely is
relaxed when he's being asked about it.

But like Leyland, who is less tightly wound prior to games,
LaRussa is also accessible and rarely has serious confrontations
with the press. LaRussa's most serious incident occurred in 1990.
A's catcher Terry Steinbach was hit in the face by a Chicago
White Sox pitch after there had been some prior brushback
pitches. LaRussa, whose in-game explosions related to knock-
down pitches are legendary, charged the mound and later threw
a bat to the backstop after being ejected.

After the game, LaRussa said he would not talk about the
incident. A Chicago-based stringer for a wire service pressed him
twice about discussing the incident, and LaRussa went ballistic.
With cameras rolling, LaRussa started screaming at the reporter.
"A player almost got killed out there," screamed LaRussa. "I'll
talk about what I talk about, you got it?" The reporter muttered
something about LaRussa not getting out of hand and LaRussa
screamed, "Get out of my bleeping clubhouse, get the hell out
of here." LaRussa then advanced on the reporter who was yelling
back, and finally A's coaches Rene Lachemann and Dave Duncan, along with A's pitcher Dave Stewart, ushered the reporter
out of the clubhouse as LaRussa retreated to his office and
slammed the door.

The incident made headlines for a few days, but LaRussa was
not remorseful. He felt the reporter had tried to bait him at an
emotional time when LaRussa's concern was for Steinbach, who
was rushed to a hospital where fortunately the injuries were not
too serious.

Reporters themselves acknowledge that stupid questions by
those in their business can hurt everybody. On the other hand,
as Meyer jokingly said to Leyland when the Pirates manager was
complaining about someone else's question, "You know, Hump,
some of the best quotes you've given me have come in answer
to dumb questions."

Although reporters have an obligation to be reasonably informed in their questioning, they feel justified in requiring managers to at least be available for answers. Even if the answers are evasive or hostile, reporters feel they at least should be given the courtesy of some managerial reaction.

That is why many Cincinnati reporters felt let down by Piniella during the heat of the 1992 pennant race. The Reds were trying to hang on in the NL West in late August when they lost three in a row to the Mets. On a Sunday night, Tim Belcher pitched Cincinnati to a two-run lead entering the ninth, retiring 22 straight batters after allowing a first-inning run.

Piniella replaced Belcher with Rob Dibble to open the ninth, and Dibble proceeded to issue two walks prior to Bobby Bonilla's game-winning three-run homer.

Piniella knocked over a water cooler in the Red's dugout and then screamed at Dibble all the way up the runway to the Cincinnati clubhouse, where chairs were smashed. Piniella retreated to his office and slammed the door shut.

When the media arrived, Piniella was still behind closed doors. Such a cooling-off period is understood in such a crucial game. But then the Cincinnati writers were told that Piniella would not be available for questions.

The reporters plainly felt betrayed. Part of managing is standing up and explaining your moves, good and bad. Even if Piniella had screamed at the inevitable question of why was Belcher lifted, it would have been okay. But not to be available to answer questions about strategy in a game that would in retrospect be the game that might have finished off the Reds' pennant chances was against the code by which managers and writers coexist.

Perhaps Piniella in a way made it up to the reporters weeks later when he fought Dibble in full view of cameras and reporters after Dibble denied telling Piniella his arm was stiff. Certainly, the sight of a manager tackling one of his players was a treat rarely granted the press.

Leyland meanwhile had his own confrontation with the media late in August as well. The Village Voice, of all places, quoted him as saying that the Mets' Vince Coleman was "a living, breathing mistake." Rod Beaton, a baseball writer for USA Today, used the line in one of his notes columns without getting corroboration from Leyland.

Leyland was stunned to read the quote. For one thing, he never said it. For another, it undercut one of his most firmly held tenets, namely, never to talk ill about another team's players.

"I don't even know what the hell is The Village Voice, and for another thing I never said a goddamn thing about Vince Coleman," said Leyland. "How could Beaton write something like that without talking to me first? He's been in my clubhouse dozens of times. I've never done anything to him. I've always cooperated with him just like anyone else. I've known him for years. Why would he do that to me?"

Leyland then summoned Jim Trdinich, the Pirates' publicity director. "Jim, I want you to know that from now on, Beaton's not allowed in my clubhouse ever again," said Leyland. "I don't want him to set foot in here. If he come in here, I want him put out the door. He never talks to me or my players ever again, do you hear me? I don't care what the league says, I don't care what you say, he doesn't come in here as long as I'm manager."

A day later, Leyland was told that The Village Voice reporter said that he thought he heard Leyland say something about Coleman to a group of "guys in suits who I thought were Pittsburgh reporters."

Leyland started laughing. "Now I know the guy is lying, " he said. "For one thing, the newspapers are on strike. And for another, anyone who's been around our club knows that if the guys he saw me talking to were wearing suits, the last people they could have been were Pittsburgh reporters. Hasn't anyone seen how Hertzel and Meyer dress?

"And anyway, that don't excuse Beaton. How can you pick up something someone else writes and put your own name on it without checking it first? That's bullshit."

Beaton appealed Leyland's ban to both the Pirates and the NL office. He also called Leyland at home, only to have Katie Leyland give him an earful about the whole incident.

"Reporters call Jim at home a lot and he is usually available to them" said Katie. "And I don't mind because most of them are polite and always apologize for bothering us at home. It really isn't a bother.

"I know how Jim tries to be fair with everyone, which is why something like this made me so mad."

Beaton also called Leyland and asked if he would accept his apology, saying the two had known each other for six years. Leyland refused. "The fact that I have known him for six years is the reason why I can't understand why he'd do something like that," said Leyland.

In the end, Leyland didn't block Beaton from being allowed in the Pirates clubhouse, but he also did not talk to him. When Beaton did appear for the first time after the incident, he was talking to Van Slyke when Leyland walked by. "Hey, Skip, look who's here," said Van Slyke, holding on to Beaton. Leyland just walked by without turning.

Leyland was sensitive about the incident. He had developed good relationships with all aspects of the media, and such an incident, as discredited and largely insignificant as it might have appeared on the outside, wounded Leyland's sense of fair play. "I always try to cooperate and then something like this happens and you wonder why the hell I wasted my time," he said.

"I realize that it is just one thing and I shouldn't carry it over to affect how I deal with everybody. But I can't help but feel a little wounded by it all."

Indeed, the incident underscored one of the big problems in sports reporting. Over the last decade, there has been a proliferation of the so-called notes columns, which in many cases are the product of a group of writers pooling information among themselves. Hypothetically, all the information should be reliable if all those involved are doing a professional job. Indeed, when the so-called notes networks began years ago, there was a high degree of reliability.

But there is the risk that in the telling of the same stories, the facts start getting changed the farther away they travel from the original sources. There is also the whole question of journalistic ethics and the loss of exclusivity for the newspapers that employ the various reporters.

In most cases, those concerns are recognized and not abused. But things can fall through the cracks, as happened in the case involving Leyland.

It is such incidents that aggravate the already tenuous relationship between the media and athletes. Such incidents allow those who are uncooperative to make the point that, indeed, the reporters will take things out of context, that indeed they are always looking for the controversial, that indeed they are not to be trusted.

Such an atmosphere existed all spring around the New York Mets when tabloid reporters descended on the Mets in the wake of a rape accusation that mentioned some New York players. Although those reporters were not the ones regularly assigned to the team, the atmosphere for all was poisoned and made Torborg's already tough job nearly impossible.

The final irony of all this was that although the Mets ended up being abject failures on the field, it was Torborg, after trying to be all things to all parts of the media, who ended up getting scorched for a variety of strategic foul-ups. In his very first game as Mets manager, Torborg had used all but one of his position players after nine innings. He was criticized for allowing pitcher David Cone to throw 166 pitches in a July game. He was questioned for his endless use of the sacrifice bunt and all sorts of player moves.

Torborg's defense was that his offense was so bad, he had to adopt a conservative approach that necessitated bunting. And because so many of his players were either failures or injured, he was forced into a lot of moves he might normally not have considered.

Torborg, an intelligent and congenial individual, was hardly caught unawares by the New York media coverage. He had been a coach with the Yankees for several years, watching firsthand the kind of media scrutiny unique to New York and also building up some solid relationships with many of the city's reporters.

But there were huge expectations surrounding the 1992 Mets, and when the team collapsed, Torborg was not prepared for being the focal point of so much second guessing. He had several caustic exchanges with writers from midseason on, and his relationships with several writers and broadcasters deteriorated. He admitted to his coaches well into the season that his decision to do the frequent radio shows was a mistake and something he would not repeat in 1993.

Although the media pressure might not have been the sole reason, the frustration of the Mets' awful season combined with the media scrutiny likely contributed to Torborg's public blowups with some of his players, the most explosive being a shoving and shouting match with outfielder Vince Coleman, whose frequent absences due to injuries were a constant source of frustration to the Mets.

Torborg's experience ended up being an object lesson in how media perceptions can greatly influence a manager's perspective. If the media had generally taken the opinion that Torborg should not be blamed for the Mets' collapse and that his 1992 performance, if not winning, was basically a laudable example of applying tireless energy to a hopeless cause, then that opinion, coupled with the fact that he has served only one year of a four-year contract, would likely have allowed Torborg to open the 1993 season with just the normal pressure that accompanies any new season.

But because much of the New York media took the view that Torborg's managerial performance in 1992 revealed serious flaws and insecurities that raise questions about his ability to lead the Mets to a title, he enters the '93 season with a serious need to win right away or face real questions about his future in New York.

That said, what kind of influence the media has over a manager is a matter of some debate. Although the public perception may be different, the fact is that few managers are run out of town by the press. The large majority of writers assigned to cover teams maintain good relationships with the managers they cover. The two sides need each other, the writers requiring managerial access to be kept apprised on the daily grind of newsy notes generated by every club, and few managers being secure enough to withstand the pounding they get if they go out of their way to antagonize the beat writers.

Outsiders don't realize how much contact beat writers have with the manager. They are likely to have some conversation virtually every day from the first day of spring training in mid-February to the last day of the season in early October. That's eight months of daily contact, and inevitably some kind of closeness has to develop.

Writers and managers who have decent relationships use each other, and if both sides are savvy enough, they both know when and how. For example, a manager might tell a writer something that is not meant for publication but is told to prove a manager right or perhaps guide a writer one way or another. Such a nugget might make one juicy story, but if written, the one story might jeopardize months of other stories that the writer might need from the manager. So the writer ends up being used in the one instance but in the end gets paid off with perhaps another insight down the road that can be used for an exclusive story.

The whole media equation is further complicated by the electronic media. Many managers have had difficulty balancing the sometimes conflicting demands of the press and the electronic media. Postgame interview sessions can be especially ticklish.

"I'll be sitting there waiting to be asked a question and it will be five minutes of silence," said Leyland. "The print guys don't want to ask a question because whatever answer they get will be taped by the radio and TV guys. And the radio and TV guys don't ask a question because most of them aren't around the club very much and don't know what to ask. So I gotta sit there like a dummy waiting for someone to ask a question."

The print–electronic conflict has often resulted in shouting matches in clubhouses between writers and microphone wielders, arguments that embarrass everyone else and often have to be quieted by managers or players. However, it has become a fact of life that players and managers are far more cooperative with television or radio than with the press. Many players and managers distrust the press, and they have become savvy enough basically to dictate what they say electronically.

Still, many managers enjoy the give and take with the written press, who are usually around the club on a far more regular basis. Whitey Herzog as a manager was a witty, informative raconteur to the many writers with whom he felt comfortable. He was so at ease with writers that during the 1987 World Series, when clubhouses and managers' offices are off limits, Herzog would hold court anyway, admittance gained by a "secret knock" on the back door of his Busch Stadium office.

But Herzog could also be an impossibly rude interview for those who rubbed him the wrong way. There was the time when Herzog was mentioned as being a possible NL president after Bart Giamatti was elevated to commissioner. NBC's Marv Albert kiddingly suggested that, instead, Herzog might run for president of Yale University. Herzog didn't take the joke well, sputtering on camera, "I don't know what the hell that means. If that's a joke, it ain't funny." And Herzog thereupon unplugged his earpiece and walked off camera.

And writers in attendance won't forget a day during the 1984 NL play-offs. Cubs manager Jim Frey, one of the best all-time storytellers, was entertaining several writers prior to the third game of the League Championship Series with the San Diego Padres. Frey was interrupted in midsentence by a blow-dried hairdo with a microphone who declared, "Jim, we're going to go live so we want you on camera."

Frey barely looked up, saying, "And what am I supposed to do, tell all these guys right here to go to hell, that they're nothing but pieces of shit, just so I can go talk on your camera for 30 seconds? Am I supposed to tell these guys that your 30 seconds is more important than all their jobs? Is that what you want me to do?"

The blow-dried hairdo sulked away. However, the same talking head had his moment two days later following the Cubs' crushing fifth-game loss that sent the Padres on their way to a World Series thumping at the hands of the Detroit Tigers.

Frey was sitting quietly in the visiting manager's office, downcast and barely audible as he answered some questions from the last wave of media. The talking head arrived with his camera, stuck a microphone on Frey's face, and asked, "Jim, do you think your club choked?"

Frey looked up, looked at the questioner, and then looked into the camera and declared, "Go bleep yourself."

And people wonder why managers and the media have such a stormy relationship.

Years ago, there were fewer microphones, and many beat writers were virtual "housemen" who never tried to rock the boat, who would basically write the party line dished out by the manager and gladly broke bread and sipped cocktails on the manager's expense account just to feel part of the team.

However, there is little of that nowadays, since beat writers are younger, are rarely on the job more than a few years in succession, and rarely know or want to know many of baseball's on- or off-field intricacies. The baseball beat job was once the most coveted in sports journalism. Now, it is increasingly seen as a family-straining, backbreaking grind of constant deadlines made worse by surly players and managers who have their own radio shows.

As a result, many of the new writers go to the other extreme. No longer housemen, they become equally journalistically suspect hit men who see lying and subterfuge in every move made by a club, who seek out the negative quote from a player or the mistake by the manager that gains a headline or exploits a weak spot.

But even in the new atmosphere, writers can seldom claim

that they indeed toppled a managerial reign. Writers don't fire managers. Losses fire managers. Writers, even the self-absorbed ones who think of themselves as poets, baseball gurus, or press box Woodwards and Bernsteins, don't make a team lose. They might make teams miserable or uptight, but they ultimately don't make teams lose.

Chapter 7

"I Knew by How They Avoided Looking at Me"

◆ Tommy Lasorda arrived at Candlestick Park, driven by the son of a longtime friend and accompanied by the owner of a North Beach Italian restaurant that had been a Lasorda favorite for 20 years.

An elderly woman wearing a Giants jacket who is a familiar figure outside the clubhouse entrance greeted Lasorda with a hug. The clubhouse guard shook his hand and asked for an autograph.

Meanwhile, the restaurant owner was bringing in shopping bags full of goodies. There were two containers of tortellini in alfredo sauce, one of linguini in clam sauce, another containing fried calamari. There were two containers of grated cheese and two of red pepper. There were three loaves of crusty bread.

While the food was being arrayed on Lasorda's desk in the visiting clubhouse, another friend arrived. He happened to be a liquor distributor and brought in three bottles of wine wrapped in towels, along with a bottle of scotch, another of vodka, and a third of gin, all for consumption on the postgame flight.

Lasorda's coaches went about their business without blinking an eye. Such feasts were commonplace around the Dodgers. Lasorda himself has been dieting for years, remaining slender because of his much-publicized Slim-Fast diet and steady regimen of walking and swimming.

But Lasorda still had loyal friends in virtually every NL city, and those friends just happened often to be in the restaurant business, so the food always arrived for the benefit of Dodgers coaches and their traveling party, assorted players, clubhouse visitors, and even sportswriters.

In Philadelphia, Lasorda's brother would bring in hoagies and *pasta e fagiola* and Italian greens, which were then offered to such visitors as Rollie Massimino, then the Villanova and now Nevada–Las Vegas basketball coach, or perhaps a celebrity like Perry Como, if he was appearing in nearby Atlantic City.

In St. Louis, it was Tony Gitto, the owner of a popular downtown restarant, who would arrive with the fettucini. In Chicago, it might be deep-dish pizzas from a company for which Lasorda used to do commercials. At home in Los Angeles, the food might come from an assortment of Lasorda haunts. In New York, the menu might change; instead of the usual Italian delicacies, Lasorda would often introduce new Slim-Fast products such as ice cream bars and popcorn snacks.

So this San Francisco feast was hardly out of the ordinary. And Lasorda enjoyed playing maître d'. "Here, try this tortellini, this is outstanding," he said as he prepared a plate for pitching coach Ron Perranoski.

"Jay, come here, try this calamari," handing a plate to Jay Lucas, the Dodgers' publicity director.

"Who wants bread? You can't find bread like this in Los Angeles," said Lasorda. "You know, maybe it's the air there or the water or something. But all these years I've lived in Los Angeles and I still can't find good bread. Look at this crust, look at this. You just can't get this in LA."

Bruce Connal, the producer of ESPN's "Sunday Night Game of the Week," walked in. Connal's father is Scotty Connal, the longtime producer of baseball with NBC and one of the original founders of ESPN. "Bruce, whatever you want, take, and whatever I can do, ask me, because your father is one of the great people in this business," said Lasorda. "Here, have some calamari, this stuff is outstanding.

"Hell, I used to do interviews with ESPN when it just started and at the end of the interview, I'd say, 'The only reason I'm doing this is because of Scotty Connal.' I'd make sure they'd get that tape to him.

"Here, Bruce, have some bread with that calamari. You can't find bread like that anywhere. That bread is just outstanding."

The clubhouse grazing made it feel like old times around Lasorda. But the 1992 season had been a nightmare. By June, the Dodgers were obviously not going to be contenders. Injuries had crippled Darryl Strawberry and Eric Davis, the teams' two stars and Los Angeles buddies who had been reunited for what they had thought would be a triumphant season. Instead, they were virtually nonfactors all season. Mike Scioscia, the dependable veteran catcher, suddenly showed his age after 12 hard-nosed years. The pitching staff, for generations the foundation of every Dodgers club, was still competent, but it could not carry alone a team that ultimately would finish last in runs, last in home runs, and last in fielding. All the pitching staff accomplished was to keep a lot of losses close.

Dodgers GM Fred Claire soon decided that the rest of the season would be used to gradually audition players from the Dodgers' farm system. The influx of overmatched kids, combined with the existing mediocrity, meant that for most of the '92 season, Lasorda was managing the worst team in baseball.

So the food, although always the best his friends could buy, became a reminder of the glory days of not so long ago. And the losing took a toll on Lasorda. He is a proud man who craves the spotlight. And it's hard to be a marquee figure when you're managing a team that averages more than an error a game.

The Southern California media, with which Lasorda had mixed relations, began sniping with rumors he might step down after the season. There were other rumors, one of which had him going to St. Petersburg to the Giants should a Florida group in which Lasorda's friend Vince Piazza (whose son Mike is a top Dodgers catching prospect and Lasorda's godson) was a major investor succeed in purchasing and moving the club.

There were even whispers that the entire Dodgers organization would undergo a massive restructuring, that owner Peter O'Malley did not like losing 350,000 customers, and that heads, even Lasorda's, would roll.

In other organizations, such palace intrigue was routine, with managerial firings as commonplace as Bat Day promotions. This season would actually be a slow one for firings, with only three coming in-season.

The first to go in early June was Montreal's Tom Runnells. His demise was widely assumed since spring training. Runnells had shown up at the first workout of the spring wearing a drill sergeant's uniform as a publicity stunt that was widely mocked by Expos players and proved an embarrassment. Later in the spring, Runnells loudly proclaimed before the fourth exhibition game that this was a game "we simply had to win."

Runnells's standing with his players had been already eroded by similar high-schoolish stuff. Several players felt that Runnells's word could not be trusted. After Montreal drifted through the first two months, GM Dan Duquette did the inevitable by replacing Runnells with Felipe Alou.

Later in the season, San Diego's Greg Riddoch was fired. He ironically was a Greeley, Colorado, neighbor of Runnells's. He had been widely assumed to be on thin ice since opening day. Also fired in 1992 was Texas's Bobby Valentine, who had the distinction of owning the longest uninterrupted tenure of any manager who had never won a division title. He had endured for a number of reasons: Valentine had a close relationship with Rangers GM Tom Grieve, the Rangers had contended a few times, and Valentine tirelessly sold the Rangers and baseball in the Dallas–Ft. Worth area.

However, Valentine's self-assuredness grated on many people. His Rangers club, although possessing abundant talent, always was near the league lead in sloppy areas like errors and wild pitches. With a new stadium under construction, the Rangers franchise was beginning to market luxury boxes and their losing team was not helping to generate interest. When Texas slipped far out of contention, Grieve, who had helped Valentine weather crisis after crisis in the past, couldn't save him anymore and replaced him with Rangers coach Toby Harrah. Valentine in turn held a bitter postmortem press conference in which he ripped members of the local media.

Most managers are well aware of the cliché that they are hired to be fired. But nothing really prepares someone for the moment when he is told that his services are not wanted.

In many cases, managers do have a sense of when the axe is about to fall. When he managed the Cubs, Jim Frey knew he had to win in 1986. When the Cubs struggled toward midseason, Frey could sense he was in imminent danger one morning on the road when he walked into the hotel coffee shop and GM Dallas Green and his wife, Sylvia, pointedly did not ask Frey to join them. "I knew by how they avoided looking at me that I was going to get it," recalled Frey.

"After a while, you get to know people really well. And when you're on borrowed time, you can feel people sort of shying away from you like you're sick or something. And that's what it was like that morning. Three days later, I was right. They got me."

The pressure to win right away is more prevalent than ever in these days of huge payrolls. The other cliché about it being easier to fire one manager than 25 players has never been truer in these days of $40 million payrolls and corporate ownership groups that know little about baseball and are propelled by marketing strategies and bottom lines.

In many cases, though, there is nothing Machiavellian about a manager being fired. He can be axed for the simple reason that he has worn out his welcome in one place and management simply wants a change. Such managers aren't usually surprised. They can usually see the news coming.

They might ask their GM to make an obvious personnel move

and have the GM suggest they wait a few days for no apparent reason. Or a manager might get wind of players going behind his back to complain to the front office. When he complains and gets no reciprocal support, the manager usually knows his days are numbered. The press might start speculating about a manager's future. If the response from the GM or owner has any equivocation, then a manager should get ready for the inevitable.

When a manager of the same team for a number of years is not given any long-term security and is forced to fight for various decisions, he knows he'd better win or face the music.

Such was the case with Whitey Herzog in Kansas City. As Herzog recalled in his book *White Rat*, he knew he would be fired by the Royals after a second-place finish in 1979 that followed three straight division titles. He had long sparred with Royals owner Ewing Kauffman despite the team's success. Herzog recounted one incident when for two years he had told the Royals to get rid of troublesome first baseman John Mayberry, saying it was either "him or me."

Herzog recalled, "When they finally did sell Mayberry to Toronto and he came back to Kansas City for the first time, Ewing stood up in his box and gave John a standing ovation. He showed me up in front of the fans."

Kauffman continually gave Herzog one-year contracts despite the string of division titles because "I didn't win in the play-offs." After the '79 season, Herzog knew it was only a matter of time.

"Ewing Kauffman finally had the excuse he needed to get rid of me. By then, if ownership didn't want me, didn't appreciate what I'd done, to hell with them. I'd had it with Kauffman and [GM Joe] Burke anyway. In all the years I worked there, they'd never once invited Mary Lou [Herzog's wife] to sit in their warm, enclosed boxes. She'd be out there in the rain and the cold and they'd be sitting up there acting as though we weren't good enough for them. So when they called me in like I knew they would and said they wanted to make a change, I said adios and that was it."

Herzog's matter-of-fact acceptance of his Kansas City firing is the exception. Most managers, no matter how many years they had been in the game, are usually bowled over by the news.

"How does it feel to get fired?" said Frey, who was also fired as manager of the Royals. "It feels like you got kicked in the stomach. No matter how much you tell yourself that you knew it was coming, it doesn't prepare you for how you feel when it actually happens. You always think that if you get another week, things will turn around. You think that if one player had done better, you'd still be there. You think that if one guy hadn't got hurt, you could have kept it going.

"It can drive you nuts for weeks, trying to deal with the what-ifs and trying to figure who might have knifed you in the organization. Don't let anyone kid you when they say they were relieved to be fired or they knew it was coming so they were prepared. It hurts like hell and it takes a while for you to get over it."

When a manager gets fired, it can often mean that his coaches face the same fate. For example, third-base coach Don Zimmer was fired by the Cubs on the same day Frey was as Cubs manager. Zimmer recalls how after getting the news that day from club officials he returned home to his teary wife who said, "Don, isn't it awful, they fired Jimmy Frey." Said Zimmer, "The hell with Jimmy Frey, they got me, too. Pack your bags, because it was a quinella."

Years later as Cubs GM, Frey was pressured by the Tribune Corporation executives who own the Cubs to fire Zimmer, a high-school teammate and one of his best friends. Zimmer had been through the drill three other times so he was somewhat toughened to the process, but getting fired still hurt.

"I was all right, but you never get used to that feeling of being told you're out," Zimmer said. "The thing that gets you is that a team has to be going bad for a manager to get fired. And usually when a team is going bad it's because players aren't going so good. Managers can't make bad players play good.

"For someone like me who's been in the game so long, I had friends calling me to ask if I was OK. That helps. And when people tell you that they'd want you when they have an opening, that helps too. But it still hurts, no question about it."

The firings that especially hurt are the ones that are totally unexpected. That happened to Lee Elia in Philadelphia when he was fired in the last weekend of the 1988 season. Just two months earlier, GM Lee Thomas had extended Elia's contract through the 1989 season, making the announcement to the team's beat writers in a wood-paneled Ritz Carlton suite in Atlanta, complete with wine and cheese.

But with days left in the season, Thomas decided to make a change and Elia was floored. "It came out of nowhere. Heck, just a few days before, he [Thomas] and I were talking over player moves we wanted to make in the off-season. We were talking about which kids we'd be watching in the Instructional League, what free agents we might want to pursue.

"I have to believe he had it in his mind to bang me even then and was just picking my brain before letting me go. But that was something that took me a long, long time to get over because I still don't fully understand it. I felt double-crossed. But most of all I felt stunned. I was in shock."

As for Lasorda, he had rarely had to endure any speculation about his own future during his long reign with the Dodgers. All his Dodger Blue schmaltz aside, he had been part of the organization for a lifetime. The hallmark of being a Dodger was loyalty and stability. And those qualities were as much a part of Lasorda's life as pasta.

However, for the last few years, the tensions had grown within the Dodgers organization. Ever since Al Campanis resigned as GM following his unfortunate dissembling in the face of Ted Koppel's questions concerning baseball's racial history, a division had developed between the longtime Dodgers baseball men of which Lasorda was the titular head and the regime created by new GM Fred Claire, a courtly and decent man who had been the club's longtime vice president for marketing and public relations.

Even before Claire took over the Dodgers, the talent had been dwindling throughout the organization. A series of disastrous amateur drafts had seriously diminished the reservoir of prospects in what had historically been baseball's most bountiful farm system. Scouting mistakes were made, and although Claire's operatives grumbled that Lasorda mishandled young players, Lasorda privately fumed that the talent simply wasn't there.

Lasorda's baseball acumen had long been overshadowed by his show-biz flair. Over the years, he has become far more known for his hugging and his celebrity friends, for his clubhouse spaghetti and diet drink, for his Stengelese oratory and appearances on network TV, for his tireless charitable work and endless round of speaking engagements, than for his considerable abilities in uniform.

As a result, Lasorda has never gotten the credit he deserves. He's won two World Series, four pennants, and six division titles and missed a seventh by losing a one-game play-off with Houston in 1980. Only Sparky Anderson among active managers has more victories. And no one since Walter Alston, Lasorda's predecessor, has managed the same team for longer than Lasorda has managed the Dodgers.

Luck has played a part in Lasorda's managing ability going relatively unappreciated. He won pennants in his first two seasons as Dodgers manager but was twice beaten in the World Series by the great Yankee clubs led by Reggie Jackson, Thurman Munson, Graig Nettles, etc. When Lasorda finally did win a World Series, it was in the 1981 season that will forever be known for being the strike-shortened campaign that bastardized all that was accomplished within it.

Lasorda's Dodgers won division titles in 1983 and 1985 but play-off losses diminished the accomplishment. The '85 defeat to St. Louis will long be remembered for Lasorda's questionable decision to allow Tom Niedenfuer to pitch to Jack Clark instead of having Niedenfuer intentionally walk him. Clark homered to seal the Cardinals' sixth-game, series-clinching victory.

In 1988, Lasorda perhaps did his most masterful managing job in taking an injury-riddled Dodgers club to a scintillating play-off triumph over the Mets and then a stunning five-game World Series blitz of the heavily favored Oakland A's.

But the ultimate victory will forever be viewed as something of a freak by baseball purists. Ladorda's juggling throughout the season got overshadowed by Orel Hershiser's record-breaking strikeout streak of 59 innings. The play-offs then turned on an implausible Scioscia home run in the fourth game off Dwight Gooden. And the World Series will be forever known for Kirk Gibson's pinch-hit, game-winning home run in the opener.

Since '88, the Dodgers have not been back in the play-offs. They finished a distant second in 1990 and were knocked out of the 1991 race in the final weekend.

Now, in 1992, they were the laughingstock of baseball. Lasorda's bitterness spilled near the surface. He had felt for years that his advice fell on the deaf ears of much of the Dodgers' new hierarchy. And as he reviewed this day's lineup with hitting coach Ben Hines, the frustration came out without warning.

Lasorda looked at the lineup drafted by Hines and asked, "Where's Ashley?" referring to Billy Ashley, a raw 6-foot-7 power prospect. Said Hines, "Tommy, Brantley is pitching and the kid will be overmatched against that breaking ball."

"Overmatched? Hell, he's overmatched against everybody right now, but we gotta keep running him out there," said Lasorda. "Who's catching?"

"Well, Mike is asking when he can get some time," said Hines, referring to Scioscia.

(In fact, Scioscia had come into the manager's office prior to Lasorda's arrival and asked to see a lineup. "I only have San Francisco's so far," said Hines. Said Scioscia, "Yeah, well, maybe you can get me into theirs because I'm having trouble getting into ours.")

Lasorda, however, seemed determined to run the Dodgers rookies out every day per Claire's intention. "Well, let's play the kid [Mike Piazza] again," he said.

He then leaned back in his chair and briefly closed his eyes.

"This is so tough to have to go through," said Lasorda. "I sit here every day and see all you coaches working your asses off, trying to help these players improve. I see these kids out there trying their best, putting out the best effort every night and getting beat all the time. I see the trainers working all the time, never giving up, never losing one bit of their professionalism.

"I feel sorry for all of them. And I feel sorry for the fans. We're not giving them what they should be getting."

"Well, Tommy," said the son of the friend who was hanging nearby. "It's just one of those years."

"One of those years, hell, we're just not good enough," snapped Lasorda, quickly losing the staged persona usually seen by the public. "A lot of this could have been avoided. I'll tell you what. I know one thing and that is that I'm a damned good judge of the talent. I'm one of the best judges of talent you can find in this business.

"I said over the winter after we got Eric Davis that we should try and move guys like Daniels and Samuel while they had value. I told them that with the kind of club we were going to have, we needed to make sure we could put on the field a decent defensive club.

"I'd go to these meetings and the minor-league people would tell me we had all these prospects who were ready for the majors. And I'd ask them how do they know, have they seen them play against major leaguers? And they'd look at me like I was from another planet.

"Some of these guys never seen anything but minor-league baseball. They don't see major-league fastballs. They don't see major-league throwing arms. Just because a guy hits some home runs in Bakersfield doesn't mean he's going to hit them in Los Angeles.

"But when I say that, they tell me that I don't like young players. I love young players if they can play. Who was it who brought a whole young infield to the majors and hung with them? It was me, and the reason was that their names were Garvey,

Lopes, Russell, and Cey. Who was it who pushed to bring up a young left-hander from Mexico? It was me and his name was Valenzuela.

"These kids we have now are good kids. They're trying their hardest. They're giving me total effort. But they just can't play up here yet. Someday, maybe some of them will. Right now, they can't."

Lasorda's frustration with the Dodgers' talent remarkably remained contained for much of the awful 1992 season. But his feelings have been well known around baseball for years. For someone with Lasorda's unique credentials and longevity, it seemed odd that the club's hierarchy had stopped listening to many of his talent assessments. Lasorda had been bluntly telling the Claire regime for years that the talent was simply not there in the Dodgers' organization. He had pushed the club into much of its recent free-agent and trade activity because he did not see any home-grown players ready to help anytime in the near future.

But now, with the Dodgers struggling, with attendance down at Dodger Stadium and with O'Malley for the first time instituting major cuts in spending, the push was being made with the young players. Lasorda and his remaining allies within the Dodgers' organization were skeptical. They did not see any light at the end of the tunnel because they felt the best of the Dodgers' kids were either average players or still years away from being factors in the major leagues.

Lasorda would often go back through recent Dodger history and point to the mistakes he had warned the club against or the successes that were the result of his input. One of the most recent successes appeared to be the young catcher Piazza.

Lasorda had watched the kid play in high school as a favor to Piazza's father. Lasorda saw that Piazza had exceptional power for a youngster, and when the Piazzas visited California, Lasorda brought him to Dodger Stadium and pitched him batting practice.

With then-Dodgers scouting director Ben Wade watching, Piazza ripped several balls into the bleachers. Lasorda asked Wade what he thought. Wade shrugged and said, "Tom, we really don't have any reports on him."

"Reports? What would you recommend if you saw a kid with power like that who is also a catcher?" said Lasorda.

Wade responded, "I'd recommend we draft him."

"Well, this kid *is* a catcher," said Lasorda.

The Dodgers ended up taking Piazza in the 62d round of the 1988 draft, and he has become one of the best dozen prospects in all of baseball.

Lasorda relished such stories because they underscored what he believed to be his eye for talent.

Such an eye is necessary for any successful manager. Anyone can spot the superstars who can run the fastest or hit the ball the farthest or throw the ball the hardest. But what can set managers apart is the ability to look at players and be able to plug them into roles where they have the optimal chance for success. In Baltimore's glory years, Weaver was a master at extracting maximum performances from his bit players. One of the best examples was use of platoons at several positions, most notably in left field where for years players like John Lowenstein, Gary Roenicke, Jim Dwyer, and Benny Ayala were juggled in and out of the lineup and combined for whopping bottom-line totals at their position.

The best managers might recognize a talent either within their organization or with another team and be able to persuade his front office that the player can make a difference. When Davey Johnson managed the Mets, he pushed the organization against its will to bring to the majors a teenage kid named Gooden much ahead of the schedule the minor-league department had set for the pitcher. Gooden became baseball's greatest pitcher two years earlier than the Mets had projected, largely because Johnson had watched Gooden in spring training and realized that no more seasoning, either physical or mental, was needed.

Johnson also pushed the Mets into keeping players he had

managed in the farm system who were not otherwise in favor. One in particular was Wally Backman, who became a key role player in New York's glory years of the middle 1980s.

Sparky Anderson has long been the butt of media jokes because he invariably overstates the potential of young Tigers prospects. He once compared Mike Laga to power hitters like Willie McCovey. He threatened to move Lou Whitaker, one of the great second basemen of this generation, to third base to make room for Chris Pittaro. He once proclaimed that "if you don't like [left-handed reliever] David Rucker, you don't like ice cream."

But Anderson wasn't necessarily guilty of having no eye for talent. He would often use such hyperbole to deflect attention from other areas of his teams. He has also been a master at finding good use for marginal pitchers, extracting career seasons from people like Jerry Don Gleaton, Paul Gibson, and Mark Leiter. And Anderson is by nature an optimist who can't resist projecting players' potential sometimes, perhaps, beyond reality.

The point is that every successful manager has to know how to recognize and use talent. In particular, they have to delineate between the successful minor leaguers without top major-league skills and those minor-league players who can handle a major-league fastball or throw one past a major-league hitter.

No one in baseball would deny that Lasorda had such an eye for talent assessment. But that wisdom seemed to be used less and less within the Dodgers' organization.

And so Lasorda would sadly limp home with the 1992 Dodgers entrenched in last place. For the first time in his 43-year career with the Dodgers' organization, he faced an uncertain future because, for the first time, he was forced to manage a team of bad players. And that's something no manager—anywhere or ever—can overcome.

Chapter 8

"He's a Good Guy, but We Can Replace Him"

◆ It was nearly four hours before game time. Leyland, wearing a dress shirt, suit pants, and stocking feet, was snoring while lying on a couch in the visitor's clubhouse at the Vet in Philadelphia.

Donnelly sat in one of the nearby chairs reading a newspaper. Miller sat in the adjacent coaches' clubhouse smoking a cigarette and going through his overflowing notebook of charts, scouting reports, and his own notations.

The other Pirates coaches kept coming in and out of the office, sometimes checking to see if a lineup was written yet. After a while, Sandt quietly asked Donnelly, "When should we wake him up?"

A growl came from the couch. "I am awake," said Leyland. "Hell, you guys keep walking in and out so much, no one could still be asleep in here."

Leyland opened his eyes while remaining on the couch. Donnelly arose and asked if Leyland wanted some tea. "Yeah, and get me one of those Tastykake things, the ones that have the chocolate cake with the cream inside," said Leyland.

Occasionally, on trips to Philadelphia Leyland and his coaches make sojourns to nearby Atlantic City. They would arrive with the team, rent a limo, and head for the casinos. None of them were big gamblers in terms of money; if anyone lost a couple of hundred dollars, he would be kidded unmercifully. But like most sports professionals, they loved the action, the competition. And it was a way to break up a road trip.

So a visitor asked if Leyland was napping because of a late night at the casinos.

"Naw, we came in this morning," said Leyland. "I was up most of the night with Patrick. He has a cough and Katie and I were up with him a lot."

It had been a short mid-June night for Leyland. The Pirates had played at home the night before. Virtually every road trip for baseball clubs begins immediately after the last game at home so as to get to the road city the night before the next game. However, because of the short trip from Pittsburgh to Philadelphia, Greg Johnson, the Pirates' crack travel director, had decided to give the team an extra night at home and scheduled them on a rare commercial flight (virtually every flight by all clubs is a charter) leaving in the morning.

So Leyland had returned home after the game, spent a sleepless night with his infant son, and then arose at around 7 to get packed for the Pirates' midmorning departure. It was the kind of harried pace that is very typical of a baseball season.

Baseball as a profession is brutal on family life. There are long separations due to road trips. The hours are those of night-shift workers, which means wives are home alone in the evening and husbands often sleep until noon, eat a meal, and head back to the ballpark—when they're home at all. There is more time spent with teammates than with family members.

Compounding the difficult family life is the fact that most players and managers were married at a very young age, many of them during their minor-league careers. Upon reaching the majors, the temptations of big money and the celebrity it brings become readily available, with predictably damaging results.

In the case of managers, the pressure and isolation of the job have often resulted in managers drowning themselves in cocktails to ease the load. Hotel bars have often served as a manager's psychiatrist's couch, a place where, oiled by a few pops, he can vent his frustration to those coaches closest to him or perhaps to a sportswriter or broadcaster. Those legendary barroom battles involving the late Billy Martin received a lot of publicity, but although Martin's fistfights with players and marshmallow salesmen might have been extreme, such late-night inebriation was hardly an aberration among managers of all generations.

Such a life-style obviously exacerbates the family tension that is inherent in the job anyway. Nowhere do people literally live their jobs more than in baseball. And as a result, divorces and separations litter every organization. Certainly, there are many strong unions that endure the rigors of baseball, but it is also true that failed marriages are one of the few things left in the modern million-dollar world of baseball that unite managers, coaches, players, umpires, executives, and journalists.

But Leyland was one of the lucky ones. In this profession so brutal on family life, Leyland reveled in the novelty of being a father and a husband. Indeed, he would often show up at home games wearing a sweatshirt that read "I'm Patrick Leyland's Dad."

Patrick's birth was a very public event. Katie gave birth during the 1991 play-off series, on the off day between games two and three. CBS televised a hospital-room interview with her prior to game four during which Leyland was hooked in from Atlanta. Predictably to those who are close to him, Leyland was so choked up that his eyes filled and he could hardly croak out an "I love you" to her at the end of the interview.

But on this afternoon, there was more on Leyland's mind than just Patrick's sleepless night. For as the Pirates headed toward the All-Star break, he knew more than anyone else that the team was in trouble. Bonds would be sidelined for 18 games with a pulled rib cage muscle suffered on June 14. And though still hanging on to first place, the Pirates had hit a stretch in which they lost 13 out of 20.

Bonds's absence was certainly a factor in the slump. But the

Pirates were seriously short in other key areas. The fact that they were still in first place was due more to the overall weakness of the NL East than to their own performance. Since getting off to their 15–5 start in April, the Pirates had played .500 in May and June combined.

Even with Bonds, the offense had been sluggish all season. Opposing pitchers had only Bonds and Van Slyke to worry about, so they were being constantly pitched around. Orlando Merced was slumping, Jeff King was a first-half bust, and Jay Bell was not the kind of power threat to ease the burden on Van Slyke and Bonds. And the Pirates sorely lacked a legitimate leadoff hitter; Leyland used eight different batters in the top spot in the first 75 games and none fit the bill.

But an even bigger worry was Pittsburgh's starting pitching. The club had never adequately replaced the innings lost when Smiley was traded to Minnesota during spring training. Drabek, Zane Smith, and Randy Tomlin all had been inconsistent, but they were reasonably dependable. But Bob Walk was again sidelined by a chronic groin pull, and the fourth and fifth starters became veteran journeyman Jeff Robinson and rookie Victor Cole. Robinson had some decent efforts but then was shelled in three straight starts. Although Cole has physical potential, he wasn't ready to be a major-league starting pitcher.

The result was that Leyland was using up his bull pen in at least two of every five starts. For the first time in three years, a Pirates reliever, Roger Mason, pitched three straight days. "It's time to do something, Skip," said Miller. "We can't go much longer the way we're going. The bull pen just won't hold up."

It was apparent to Leyland and Simmons that the club needed to make some dramatic moves. They met toward the end of June in Pittsburgh after the Pirates had lost three out of four to the surging Montreal Expos.

"Teddy, we just aren't going to win with this pitching, it's as simple as that," said Leyland. "We're too short. Even when Walky comes back, who knows when he [will get] hurt again? We need a starter who can give us some innings."

The two were puffing on cigarettes in Simmons's office, which smelled like a tobacco store. "Well, before we get to the pitcher, I think I can get us someone to try in the leadoff spot," said Simmons. "Remember I told you about Alex Cole a few weeks ago? Well, Cleveland isn't playing him at all and they'll give him up for prospects and they don't have to be any of our keepers. They just want something for Cole.

"You know how much the guy intrigues me. I remember when he was going to be *the* guy in St. Louis. He can fly; he's a leadoff hitter. He can at least give you some more options. And Lenny Yoachim gave me a really good report on him, too."

"Well, I've never seen him play, but hell, his stats show that he can obviously run. So let's get him. What the hell. Now what about the pitcher?"

Simmons sighed. "You know it won't be easy," he said. "It's going to cost us, we're going to have shop some real people to get anyone who can help."

Both Leyland and Simmons agreed that the two front liners who could be shopped were Jose Lind and Steve Buechele. Lind's defensive contribution was huge, but he was a marginal offensive player who was making $2 million. The Pirates could hope to replace him with a variety of options, including minor-league prospect Carlos Garcia or King.

Buechele was a solid third baseman who supplied occasional punch but not with the consistency the Pirates had hoped. He was in the first year of a four-year $11 million contract to which Simmons never would have signed him. And Pittsburgh had King, John Wehner, or prospect Kevin Young in the wings to play third.

Simmons pointed out that one club he felt would be definitely interested in Buechele was the Chicago Cubs. Although it's rare for a club to trade with another contender in its own division, both Simmons and Leyland didn't believe Buechele would tip the balance of power Chicago's way.

So Simmons talked with Chicago GM Larry Himes to see if there was indeed a possible fit. Himes was interested, and in talking about pitching he mentioned left-hander Danny Jackson. Jackson had been a free-agent bust for the Cubs, winning only five games in a season and a half, and he had a history of physical problems. But in years when he was healthy, Jackson had the ability to be a dominant pitcher.

Jackson was healthy in 1992, and Simmons wanted to see how he was throwing. So he dispatched scout Len Yoachim for a look at two starts and took in a third himself when he was in St. Louis visiting his family at a time that coincidentally coincided with a trip by the Cubs.

Simmons reported back to Leyland. "He's healthy, that's for sure. He's throwing back up to 92, 93 consistently, and he has that big-time slider back," said Simmons. "He's still getting too much of the plate and needs to find a better change-up. But he sure as hell is healthy."

Said Leyland, "Well, Ray can get him the change-up, we know that. If he's healthy, Ray can help him."

Leyland secretly called Cubs pitching coach Billy Connors, whom he knew well largely because of his closeness to former Cubs manager Don Zimmer. Connors told Leyland that Jackson over the last month was throwing increasingly better and was on the verge of turning around his long losing spell.

This being Pittsburgh, the deal could not be final until Simmons and Sauer scrutinized the money. Jackson had two years remaining on a contract that was paying him $2.6 million a year, virtually the same sum being paid Buechele. So financially, the Pirates would come out slightly ahead on the trade since they would have to pay Jackson for just two years beyond 1992, while Buechele was under contract for three more seasons.

Every team has to mind some kind of budget when it makes moves, but few organizations were forced to have tighter purse strings than the Pirates. They were a classic case study of baseball's biggest problem—the plight of the small-market team. Their fan base was limited and they were in an area of the country especially hard hit by the recession. Their revenue from local television and radio was near the bottom of all major-league teams. They had a rocky relationship with the city government, not to mention one of the least advantageous lease arrangements of any club playing in a civicly owned facility.

Because of their difficulty in competing financially with larger-market clubs, the Pirates had already lost Bream, Bonilla, Smiley, and Landrum, among others, and they faced losing Bonds and Drabek after the season. Whereas a team like Toronto or the Cubs can go out and add reinforcements without worrying about the price tag, the Pirates could not make a move without fitting it into their tight budget.

Compounding the situation was that Pirates attendance is notoriously poor, especially considering the team's success. Players privately said they were embarrassed by the thousands of empty seats at play-off games in both 1990 and 1991. And attendance in 1992 lagged behind the '91 pace, when the club drew 2.08 million, an unremarkable total by most franchise standards but a club record for the Pirates.

Leyland, seething after getting swept by Cincinnati in a four-game July 4th weekend series at Three Rivers Stadium, erupted in a rare criticism of the Pirates fans. The series with the then-first-place Reds drew only 95,000 total.

Leyland erupted after the final game of the series. With local TV cameras taping and tape recorders rolling, he called the fan support "a disgrace. There's no other word for it. Here you have a series between two first-place teams and there's more empty seats than there are fans. It's a bleeping disgrace.

"I'm concerned where the hell this is leading to. This isn't something you can laugh off. It's not a damn joke. When I see this kind of support, I worry about the Pirates surviving here."

The phone lines to the local talk shows lit up with a mixed reaction to Leyland's comments. When confronted a day later, Leyland did not back down.

"I ain't retracting one word," he declared. "I'm not mad at the fans; my concern is why aren't there more of them. Where the hell is everybody? They drew 40,000, 40,000, 30,000 over the same weekend in Cleveland. We had 45,000 in St. Louis a few weeks ago for a Wednesday afternoon game. What makes Pittsburgh so damn different?

"I'm not mad at the fans. I just wish those who are mad at me would grab a buddy and come out here."

Leyland's outburst was genuine. He felt a real attachment to the Pittsburgh area, and by signing his five-year contract he had basically put his money where his mouth is, as he admitted to his coaches and others that he could have gotten more money elsewhere if he had made himself available to the open market.

"I signed to stay here because I like Pittsburgh and I want to be here," he told Paul Meyer. "It wasn't just money. There's more money elsewhere, believe me. But I committed here and I want this to work here.

"But there's obviously something wrong and it has me concerned. We have to find out what it is. Is it the economy? Do people think we make too much money? Are we doing something that turns people off? What is it?

"That's what I'm saying. Let's find out what we're doing wrong and try to correct it. Look, we traded John Smiley because we didn't have the money to pay him. Let's be honest about it. We don't have Bobby Bonilla because of the financial reasons. I'm concerned about the future here.

"Hell, I'm not mad at anybody. I appreciate the people who come out. I just wish there were more of them. That's all I'm saying. I am not criticizing our fans."

Few managers are ever in a secure enough position to so openly discuss their team's fans or their franchise's future. Managers are careful to avoid discussions about fans because it is an issue on which they can only lose. Lee Elia, one of the most decent men ever to manage in the majors, never recovered from a temper tantrum he had one afternoon in Chicago, where his Cubs were subjected to some rough treatment by a relatively small Wrigley Field crowd.

"Why don't they get bleeping jobs?" Elia screamed. "They

don't have anything else to do so they come out here and get on my team."

Elia's tantrum went on for several minutes, duly recorded by Chicago radio stations. Despite the fact that he did a solid job of managing a changing team at the time, and despite the fact that he was close to then-Cubs GM Dallas Green (who could appreciate a good temper tantrum), Elia's days were numbered after the outburst, which the Cubs' fans never let him forget.

But Elia was the exception. Leyland's willingness to so frankly discuss his fans and his city was perhaps largely an extension of the fact that he was the rare major-league manager who could speak as one of the area's residents, not just a hired hand who stayed in the city during the baseball season and then left.

The large majority of managers are just passing through. They rent homes or apartments in their club's city but make their winter home somewhere else. Some, perhaps symbolizing the job's inherent insecurity, go so far as to live in a hotel during the season and don't even invest in a six-month apartment lease. Many managers bring their families to their cities only for occasional stays, preferring to keep children in the same schools rather than uprooting everyone for what in many cases is a one- or two-year tenure before the inevitable firing.

So most managers barely make a niche in the community where they work. They might go to a few favorite restaurants or a local racetrack, but their exposure to their community is basically confined to their temporary home, the ballpark, and the airport. During the off-season, they might come to the area for fan caravans and some local banquets, but then they stay in a hotel for a few days before returning to wherever they really call home.

But Leyland was now a Pittsburgh guy and as a Pittsburgh guy, the fans didn't land on him as they might have with the typical carpetbagging manager. And without newspapers to analyze it all, the fan crisis passed.

However, the July 4th weekend was newsworthy beyond all

that. Simmons finalized the deal for Alex Cole, sending two second-echelon prospects to Cleveland. Cole joined the club on July 4. The deal itself was not a blockbuster, but how the Pirates made room for Cole on the roster was something of a stunner.

Both Leyland and Simmons were restless with how the laid-back Jeff King continued to struggle. He had proved versatile in the field, starting at five different positions, but he was hitting just .187 and was in the midst of a 1-for-23 swoon. King had been trudging out for extra hitting with Milt May, but he sunk deeper and deeper into a funk. "His confidence is shot," May told Leyland earlier that week. "He's so down on himself that no matter how much we work mechanically, it just doesn't help."

Leyland was a believer in King's ability. He often said that King had the talent to eventually be someone who could hit 20 to 25 home runs a year. But King had overall been a disappointment in the Pirates' organization ever since they made him the first player taken in the amateur draft of 1986. He had been plagued by back problems, and his best year was 1990 when he hit 14 home runs.

So when Leyland and Simmons discussed whom to drop to make room for Cole, they both talked about sending King to the minors.

"He ain't doing us any good right now with the way he's going," said Leyland. "I've given him as much an opportunity as I can to straighten things out. And Teddy, I still think the guy can be a player. But we can't go on with him like he is right now. Let's face it, this is a production business and we're not getting much production out of him. It might help him to go to Buffalo and get himself straightened out."

Simmons was a big believer in sending players a message, something that is done rarely in these days of fragile psyches and big contracts. As Simmons said later, "In the old days, guys would be sent to the minors all the time just to wake them up. Today, there's so much concern for how the player feels and how he'll react. But there comes a time when it has to be done. If not, there can be irreparable harm done to a player you're trying to develop."

So Simmons was also in favor of sending King to Triple-A. He also had another reason for making the move: The talks with the Cubs concerning Buechele were getting closer to fruition, and if Buechele was going to be dealt, getting King untracked would go a long way toward filling the hole left at third.

So Leyland brought King into his office, ready for King to be upset. Instead, Leyland was pleasantly surprised by the player's reaction. As King told Meyer later that July 4th day, "I'm taking all the extra hitting but everything is going wrong and I don't know why. All I know is that I have been flat-out stinking. I don't have the confidence I should have."

Leyland stayed upbeat with King. "I'm in your corner, I always have been," he said. "Work down there to get your swing together and when you're ready, you'll be right back here. You can still be a helluva player. We all know that."

So King went off to Buffalo and Cole arrived. Leyland would play him against right-handed pitching, bat him leadoff, and see if he could supply any top-of-the-order juice.

Bonds was also on the way back, so the Pirates' lineup was beginning to take on a better shape. But less than a week after the tumultuous July 4th weekend, Pittsburgh made their bigger move.

The Cubs and Pirates had basically agreed to a straight-up swap of Buechele for Jackson. Simmons and Leyland talked one last time before making the deal official. They both realized that given Jackson's losing record (4–9) and his injury-plagued past, and given that Buechele was somewhat popular in Pittsburgh since being acquired the previous year, the move might not be immediately well received. But there was still little hesitation by either Simmons or Leyland.

Said Simmons, "It comes down to this: Are we better with Buechele at third and Cole or Robinson in the starting rotation, or are we better with Wehner or Young or maybe King at third and Jackson in the rotation? To me, we have to have the pitcher. Buechele's all right, but we don't lose a lot defensively with whoever we put out there. We'll just have to see about replacing his bat."

"We gotta make the move, Teddy," said Leyland. "We gotta have the pitching. We can replace Buechele. He's a good player and a good guy, but we can replace him. But we can't win without getting some pitching."

So the deal was announced on July 10 and there were immediately some raised eyebrows. However, Leyland never wavered. "Buechele's not easy to part with, but it should be obvious to everybody that we needed another veteran-type pitcher," Leyland said on his radio show that night. "Pitching is the name of the game, pitching and defense. And Danny Jackson is a quality pitcher."

Upon Jackson's arrival, he was met by Miller and the two went off into the Pirates' weight room for a long talk. "I just wanted to get to know him and see what he's been working on," said Miller. "If the guy is healthy, then we got ourselves a darn good pitcher."

The Pirates meanwhile sent Victor Cole back to the minors and recalled Kevin Young, their promising Triple-A third-base prospect. However, Leyland was pretty much convinced who his third baseman would be within a matter of days.

"King's finally started hitting the ball," he told Donnelly. "The Buffalo people say he's started to really swing the bat again. You watch, he's gonna be back here in a few days and he's gonna have a helluva second half."

The Pirates reached the All-Star break looking revived, winning three out of four at Cincinnati. But they were still just a .500 team since their 15–5 April.

Still, it was good enough to keep them in first place. A Cincinnati reporter asked Leyland in the presence of his coaches if he felt his team was lucky to still be in first. Donnelly immediately looked at Virdon and Virdon left the room, suppressing a laugh.

The coaches knew what was coming as Leyland predictably sputtered.

"Why are we so lucky? We've more games than anybody else, haven't we?" said Leyland. "That's why we're in first place.

"Yeah, we have some holes, just like any other club. But we've battled our tails off and we've been in first place almost the entire season so far. Hell, it's not my fault that no one else has made a run against us. We're where we deserve to be. The rest of the teams are where they deserve to be. If another team had played better than us in our division, they'd be in first place, not us.

"I'm sick and tired of people trying to make it seem like we're so lucky. That really rubs me the wrong damn way. It's an insult to the guys on this club when people continue to question whether we're a first-place club. The goddamn answer is right there in the damn standings. We're in first, it's right there in black and white.

"And I'll tell you one more thing. We might have played .500 over the last period or whatever, but this ain't no .500 team. We're not a great team. But we're a damn good team."

With that, Leyland snatched on his hat and bounced out of his office. Baseball was set for a three-day holiday. But Leyland couldn't wait for the stretch run to begin.

Chapter 9

"He Sure Got Here at the Right Time"

◆ Zane Smith's first start after the All-Star break was scheduled for Sunday night against the Cubs. He had rested his tender left arm during the three-day break, but since it was normal procedure for Pirates pitchers to throw two days before their next start, Smith threw Friday in the bull pen hours before the game.

It was not a fruitful session. Smith's sore shoulder continued to plague him, and after about 15 minutes Miller told him to stop. "Let's pack it in, see how you feel tomorrow and go from there," said Miller. "This isn't helping anybody."

When Smith arrived at Three Rivers Stadium Saturday afternoon, his shoulder was still sore. Miller started making plans for who would take Smith's place Sunday in the Pittsburgh starting rotation. It seemed a simple matter. Danny Jackson, who was scheduled to make his Pirates debut Monday in Houston, could have his start moved up a day, and Pittsburgh would fill in on the Monday with a makeshift starter like Jeff Robinson, buying time to further assess Smith's condition and weigh their options.

But that would mean Jackson would be making his first Pirates start at home. And it would come against the Cubs, his former team. That was a combination of circumstances that Miller had hoped to avoid. The trade for Jackson had not been well received locally; Steve Buechele got a big ovation when he batted for the Cubs on Thursday in Pittsburgh. Miller was hesitant about putting Jackson in a situation where not only would he be facing the Cubs and Buechele, but if he didn't pitch well, he faced getting booed by his new hometown fans.

So early Saturday afternoon, Miller and Leyland weighed their options. "It's not that he can't handle it, it's just putting a lot of extra stuff on him when we have the option of avoiding it," said Miller.

Leyland agreed up to a point. However, he preferred using the makeshift starter in Houston for a number of reasons. For one thing, the spacious Astrodome can be friendly to pitchers. The Astros were a Western Division club, and he would rather gamble with an emergency starter against a team from the other division than against the third-place Cubs in his own division. That indeed was the bottom line. The Sunday night game was an ESPN national telecast, but much more importantly, it was against a division rival.

Miller didn't argue any of the points. But he asked Leyland to delay making the announcement of the pitching change until after Saturday night's game. "At least then Jackson won't have to sit here all day today, talking to the Chicago writers and radio about what it will be like pitching against his old team," said Miller. "I mean, we're not being dishonest. We're just waiting to announce something a little later. I just want to keep the heat off Jackson as much as I can. I want to give the guy a chance to get off to as good a start as possible. He can be really important to us over the next few months."

To the uninitiated, all this might seem like inordinate concern for one player's feelings. Danny Jackson was a ten-year major-league veteran, playing for his fourth different team. It should be old hat for him to face the pressure of pitching for a new team in a new city. Why all the worry?

However, Leyland and Miller were firm believers that you

should always try to put players into situations where they have the optimum chances for success. And Miller in particular did not discount such nebulous factors as atmosphere and his own gut feelings.

All Pirates coaches were given the freedom to work their particular areas, but Miller was undoubtedly the most visible. Some detractors, who go back to his days as pitching coach with the Baltimore Orioles, claim that Miller is all too willing to talk to the press, that he is something of a self-promoter who never fails to remind the listener of all the 20-game winners and Cy Young Award winners he's coached through the years.

But those detractors can't deny Miller's track record with pitching staffs. Miller had loads of talent in Baltimore, but he also was able to extract career seasons from a number of pitchers like Steve Stone, a journeyman who had a 25-win Cy Young season for Miller in 1980, reliever Don Stanhouse, left-hander Scott McGregor, and others. Miller's work has helped land the Pirates annually among the league pitching leaders despite constantly changing staffs and the lack of a dominant bull-pen closer.

Those detractors fail to mention that in every one of Miller's conversations about the Pirates' pitching, he will invariably mention that the keys to success are "our defense and Jim Leyland, who is the best manager at handling pitching that I've ever seen."

There is a whole dynamic between a manager and his coaches that does not immediately meet the public eye. All that is usually seen is a manager flashing signs to his third-base coach or sending a pitching coach to the mound to calm a struggling pitcher.

But much more goes on behind the scenes. On some clubs, there can develop back-channel intrigue, with coaches circling a struggling manager like sharks, seeking the big job when the boss is obviously in trouble.

Take the story of the 1983 Phillies, then managed by Pat Corrales. By late May, at the end of a West Coast trip, word circulated that Corrales could be in trouble. One of the Philadelphia coaches at the time was Dave Bristol, who usually had little time for the media. But on the last day of the road trip,

Bristol effusively greeted some of the traveling writers in the morning and said, "How about some coffee, guys? Let's talk about what's wrong with this team." Corrales eventually did get fired, but he was replaced by Paul Owens, then the Phillies' GM, not by Bristol.

Baseball is rife with such stories of coaches who develop cliques within a club to supply them with ammunition for getting the manager's job should a change be made. A manager like Leyland is secure in his position and thus has little to worry about palace coups, but many managers aren't so lucky.

"I've had a lot of young managers ask me how to put together a coaching staff," said Sparky Anderson. "Some things are obvious. A young manager needs help with his pitching because pitching decisions are the toughest decisions for a manager to make. He needs someone who's been around and knows the league and knows the umpires. And he needs hard workers. Heck, every manager needs all that.

"But what I tell them is first of all, he needs one coach who he knows he can trust without any questions. Sure, you want all your coaches to be loyal and you hope you can trust them all. But every manager needs at least one guy who he knows without a doubt is in his corner, someone he can talk to without worrying about it going anywhere else, someone who you can tell your frustrations or your worries or whatever.

"I tell ya, a manager has got to have that guy. This is a tough job. You have to be a lot of things to a lot of different people. And a manager needs to have someone around him who he can be himself with once in a while."

Anderson has such a confidant in Tigers coach Billy Consolo. The two were high-school teammates in Los Angeles, and Consolo was the first coach Anderson hired when he took the Tigers job in 1979.

However, in many cases, new managers are nowadays not given the freedom to hire all their own coaches. They are instead given holdover coaches from the organization or asked to hire certain people by their GM. As a result, such managers must take on their new job while playing "whom do you trust" with their own coaching staff.

Then there are new managers who are given the freedom to hire their own coaches but try to avoid hiring anyone who could be perceived as a threat. They instead load up on inexperienced hands from the minors, recently retired players with whom they might be familiar, or veteran coaches who don't have managing in their future.

And the irony is that those managers who are the most secure in their profession thus often end up with the best coaching staffs. For example, Atlanta's Bobby Cox didn't worry about putting together a staff that includes two former managers in Jimy Williams and Pat Corrales; he wanted two good baseball men whom he knew well as his line coaches. The possibility that either could be able replacements for him didn't worry Cox.

LaRussa's staff in Oakland includes two former managers in Rene Lachemann and Doug Rader, plus pitching coach Dave Duncan, who is highly regarded as a future managerial prospect. But none are threats to LaRussa's job, because of his stature and also because they are very loyal to LaRussa personally.

Leyland, although having a solid rapport with all his coaches, was until last year always closest to Gene Lamont, who left to become manager of the Chicago White Sox. Leyland would use Lamont as his sounding board for ideas. He could vent his anger or frustration at Lamont.

Although few managers in baseball are more secure in their jobs than Leyland, when Lamont left, Leyland still felt the need to replace him with somebody he could lean on at times. Leyland hired Bill Virdon to fill much of the void left by Lamont. Leyland has huge respect for Virdon, a veteran manager himself with Montreal and Houston whom Leyland brought to spring training every year to assist himself and his coaches. When Leyland would be particularly wired after a tough loss in 1992, it was Virdon with whom he knew he could unwind.

Donnelly was also very close to Leyland, having been with

Leyland for all seven of his years as Pirates manager. In fact, when Leyland was given a cruise for two couples by a travel agent, he invited Donnelly and his wife to join the Leylands for the postseason trip. Donnelly is well known around baseball for being one of the funniest interviews in the game, someone always ready with a one-liner or offbeat observation. Donnelly adapted quickly in 1992 to his new duties as third-base coach. He was aggressive in sending runners, mirroring Leyland's style when he was LaRussa's third-base coach for the White Sox. Leyland's philosophy as a coach was, "You can't score if you're held at third," which meant when in doubt, send the runner. Donnelly knew that he would have his manager's backing to err on the aggressive side, a major help for someone new in what can be the very sensitive third-base coaching job.

Donnelly also had to carry a heavy burden all season. His oldest daughter needed surgery for a tumor, and her condition required monitoring for several months.

Milt May, the batting coach, was also close to Leyland, with whom he's been a coach for six years. Leyland greatly respected May's instincts about people and game situations. May had had his own personal crisis: His son, an excellent high-school athlete and potential professional prospect, had suffered a serious auto accident last year. The boy was in a coma and hospitalized for several months but gradually made remarkable progress, which May would proudly acknowledge in his quiet way when asked about the boy.

Tommy Sandt was also in his sixth year with Leyland, a former manager in the Pittsburgh minor-league organization. He tended to be closer to Miller than to the manager, although there was never a hint of cliques among the Pirates' staff. Sandt is always smiling, but behind his sometimes slapstick facade is a solid baseball man and a tough competitor.

Terry Collins was the newest Pirates coach, having previously managed the team's Triple-A Buffalo team. He was quickly accepted as a worker but he needed time to earn his way subtly

into the inner circle. It was evident he had accomplished that
when Leyland let Collins manage the Pirates the day after the
club clinched the division title.

Miller was not one to socialize much with Leyland, and their
styles were different in many ways. But the two greatly respected
each other's opinions. "Mundo is as good as there is; when we
get a pitcher we just assume that he's going to make whoever it
is better than when we got the guy," said Leyland. And as Miller
often said, "When you have the best manager in baseball as your
boss and he lets you do your job like Jimmy does, it's the best of
all worlds."

It was significant that though Leyland and Miller weren't
bosom buddies, Miller was given a two-year contract extension
as Pirates pitching coach midway through the season. "Heck, I've
been in the game about 30 years now and I've finally got more
than a one-year contract," said Miller. "I didn't get that when I
was hired to manage the Twins."

But Miller's skill in handling a pitching staff was quickly being
tested as the season's second half began unfolding. The decision
to start Jackson on the Sunday night against the Cubs having
been made, Miller spent Saturday deflecting questions about
Smith and who might replace him.

Aiding him in that effort was the fact that the Pirates' clubhouse
was a zoo because of the presence of several former players scheduled to play in an old-timers game that evening. When rain held
up the proceedings, the ex-players camped out in the clubhouse.
One of them, Dock Ellis, held court in the middle of the room
with Barry Bonds, who spent at least a half hour loudly kidding
around with Ellis while swinging a new set of golf clubs delivered
that day.

And over in Leyland's office was former Pirates president Carl
Barger, now the president of the Florida Marlins. Barger and
Leyland were very close and it was not unusual for Barger, who
still maintained a home in Pittsburgh, to visit. This time, however, his visit had been preceded by speculation that Barger was

interested in hiring Virdon as his manager in Florida. Said Leyland, jokingly, as Barger entered his office, "You better not talk to any of our people or we're through. I'll get Teddy Simmons down here and we'll nail your ass for tampering."

The mood was therefore light. But Leyland and the Pirates were on the verge of a terrible stretch in which they would fall out of first place for one of the rare times in the last three years. They managed to win two out of four that weekend against the Cubs, losing Jackson's solid debut on Sunday when Ryne Sandberg hit a two-run homer in the ninth inning off reliever Stan Belinda. They then lost two out of three in Houston, giving up 22 runs in the three games with Robinson getting bombed in his emergency start. And they went on to Atlanta where they lost two out of three, and then to Chicago where they were swept in a three-game series in which their reeling pitching staff was ripped for 20 runs.

Pittsburgh had meanwhile made pitching moves to at least change the mix. Robinson and left-hander Jerry Don Gleaton, who was being used infrequently, were released. The Pirates dipped into their farm system for youngsters Steve Cooke and Blas Minor. Leyland didn't kid anybody about the moves' significance. "I don't think these moves are anything real relevant as far as the success or failure of our club goes right now," he said.

In effect, the Pirates were simply replacing their bottom two pitchers with kids whom Simmons in particular wanted to see in the majors with an eye toward whom to protect in the fall expansion draft. At the same time, Simmons kept bringing in more veterans to the minors in Triple-A hoping to get lucky with someone who could be useful in the stretch drive. The lastest two added to a list that already included names like Dan Petry and Oil Can Boyd were John Cerutti and Fred Toliver.

However, by then it was evident that Zane Smith's problems were more serious than originally believed. In a meeting with Simmons and Leyland, trainer Kent Biggerstaff and other medical personnel broke the news that Smith would be missing indefinitely and it was immediately decided to place him on the disabled list.

So a starting pitcher was needed. Simmons had been trying to talk trade for weeks, but the Pirates had basically shot their bolt when they obtained Jackson. So the move needed to be made internally. And during the series in Chicago, Simmons had made his decision. "Jim, it's gotta be the kid Wakefield," said Simmons. "He's been pitching the lights out in Buffalo."

Tim Wakefield was not just another pitcher. He threw a knuckleball, a capricious pitch thrown by only two active major leaguers, Charlie Hough and Tom Candiotti. It is a pitch that's difficult to learn and just as difficult to catch. Thus, despite its effectiveness when thrown well, knuckleballs are not taught in the minors. Indeed, Wakefield was signed by Pittsburgh as an infielder. He fooled around with throwing knuckleballs in warm-ups and one day his manager at the time asked him to try and throw it for strikes. When he was hitting only .189 in the minors and was close to being released, Wakefield asked for a chance to pitch and began his trip through the Pittsburgh minor-league system.

Leyland had never seen Wakefield pitch and had never managed a knuckleball pitcher. Leyland's only real knowledge of Wakefield came from Don Slaught, who had caught Wakefield in Buffalo when Slaught was there on a rehabilitation assignment. Reported Slaught to Leyland, "He has a good one, Skip. I completely missed the first dozen or so he threw. If he throws it for strikes, he's not going to get hit."

Still, Leyland had to rely largely on Simmons's judgment, for this was the rare Pirates personnel move on which Leyland did not have any real input. Although such situations became tense issues back in spring training, Simmons and Leyland had long since developed a solid working relationship.

Simmons was not a prototypical GM. He had his own unique lingo that delighted Leyland. Before leaving for their road trip, Simmons had been regaling Leyland and some visitors with one of his theories of hitting and pitching. "When a guy comes to bat in a tough situation, he has that monkey on his back," said Simmons. "And the pitcher in that same situation has a monkey on his back. The guy who wins is the guy who can make the other guy keep his own monkey and put his own monkey on the other guy, too. The guy with two monkeys can't win."

After a distinguished playing career, Simmons had been a baseball executive for only three years as player development director of the St. Louis Cardinals before coming to the Pirates as GM. After the rocky spring training start, he had eased into his job. And he had no problem staying out of Leyland's way and working with his manager.

"We talk when we have to talk, but I'm not one of those GMs that has to talk to his manager every day like some guys," said Simmons. "What am I going to tell Jim Leyland about managing his club? I'm not going to call him to cheer him up after a loss or pump him up after a win. That's bull. He's a professional and I know damned well that he's the best in the business.

"But when we have to do something, we talk and we're usually on the same wavelength. We have no trouble listening to each other. He respects my position and I respect his. As far as I see it, we've been working great together."

A manager–GM relationship is one of the more difficult in baseball because ultimately it is the GM who is going to end up firing the manager. Even in cases when the two are friends, the relationship inevitably is tempered by the realization that if things go bad, one of them has to go, and in more cases than not it's the manager. Probably nobody second-guesses a manager more than the GM, because this generation of ownership has put the GMs under the gun, just like managers. As managers must often walk on eggs in their relationship with their GMs, a GM must similiarly get along with his club president or owner. If a club owner or president has a different opinion of a manager than the GM, the tension grows on both sides.

In 1992, such a situation unfolded in San Diego. Manager Greg Riddoch was inherited by Joe McIlvaine when McIlvaine left the New York Mets to become the Padres' GM. Riddoch at the time was solid with the Padres' ownership, and largely at his instigation, a veritable purge of the organization unfolded upon McIlvaine's arrival after the 1990 season.

It became evident during the '91 season that McIlvaine and Riddoch were not always on the same page. However, Riddoch had ingratiated himself to segments of the Padres' ownership group. As the 1992 season went on, there developed factions within the organization, some pro-Riddoch, some anti-Riddoch. Eventually Riddoch was fired when the Padres failed to make a run at first place despite the best batting order in the league. But the various back-room machinations had effectively paralyzed the organization for months.

However, just because a team wins doesn't mean that the GM and manager are getting along. Actually, when you talk of the GM, it really means the whole organization—the minor-league staff, scouts, and front-office assistants of whom the GM is the titular head. And many managers, even successful ones, have been known to pay little heed to the front-office staff.

Earl Weaver was famous for his heated arguments with the Orioles' superscout Jim Russo. The two loved to argue and were friends, but there was also an edge to their discourse. Weaver had little patience for being told about players he saw himself. He had his own opinions and could rarely be argued out of them.

Weaver had a frosty relationship, especially in his later years, with then-Orioles GM Hank Peters. The two had one of the more public scenes ever witnessed between a manager and GM. At the baseball winter meetings one year, Peters had negotiated a trade with Montreal that would bring Gary Roenicke and Don Stanhouse to the Orioles. However, he could not find Weaver to run the details past his manager. Weaver was at a managers' reception in another section of the resort hotel where the meetings were being held.

The Expos were meanwhile pushing Peters to finalize the deal and announce it. Rather than lose a trade he felt was helpful, Peters accompanied Expos officials to the press room to make the announcement. Just as the announcement was being made, Weaver appeared at the back of the room and confronted Peters. "How the hell can you make a trade without talking to me first?" yelled Weaver.

Peters tried to pacify his manager. "Earl, we couldn't find you anywhere and we had to give the other club an answer or the thing would fall through," said Peters. "It's a deal you'll like."

"You don't make trades without me knowing them," said Weaver. "If that's the way it's going to be, then I quit right here, right now." With that Weaver stormed away and started making plans to return home. To his credit, Peters didn't accept Weaver's hasty resignation and eventually the dispute was smoothed over. Roenicke and Stanhouse eventually became key elements in several successful Orioles teams.

But Weaver and Peters maintained a shaky relationship. Weaver felt Peters was too timid about making moves. Peters didn't always appreciate Weaver's crusty persona. They endured because the Orioles kept winning between 90 and 100 games year after year.

Davey Johnson was similarly winning every year with the Mets. But he and Frank Cashen were often at odds over player moves and Johnson's managerial style. Johnson eventually alienated many in the Mets' baseball operation, so when the Mets were dethroned in 1989 as NL East champs and then got off to a 20–22 start the next year, Johnson was fired and he had no organizational allies to stand up in his defense.

But many of baseball's most successful franchises have a GM and manager who closely work together. So it is in Oakland, where LaRussa and Sandy Alderson are well matched. So it was in Cincinnati where Piniella and Bob Quinn worked together to make over the Reds into 1990 World Champions and then again worked closely together to instigate Cincinnati's many off-season moves prior to the 1992 season. (Of course, by the end of 1992, both would be gone.)

There was not yet the personal rapport between Leyland and Simmons and Mark Sauer, the club president, that Leyland had with Barger. "I've never had dinner with these guys yet, but that doesn't mean anything, really," said Leyland near the All-Star break. "What matters is that we work together as professionals. And I think Teddy is going to be a helluva general manager. Mark Sauer is outstanding. They're going to be around a long time and I enjoy working with them."

Now at a very crucial point in the 1992 season, Leyland had to trust Simmons's judgment and bring in the unknown named Tim Wakefield to join a Pirates rotation that needed help.

Wakefield would make his first start on Saturday, July 31. Leyland had him join the club in Chicago to give the rookie a chance to get acclimated to the major-league atmosphere that he had never been a part of, even in spring training.

The 26-year-old proved to be a revelation, and his arrival coincided with a Pirates hot streak that reestablished their control of the NL East race. Wakefield was brilliant in his debut, pitching a complete-game 3–2 victory over St. Louis in which he struck out ten batters. Leyland, who is a constant picture of nervousness in the dugout anyway, chewing his fingernails and smoking cigarettes even during a typical game, was a nervous wreck throughout Wakefield's first start. He had started Slaught at catcher, even though the Cardinals were pitching right-hander Jose DeLeon, because of Slaught's experience in catching Wakefield. Then Leyland gnawed his fingers and smoked butts as he watched Wakefield throw knuckleballs to get out of early-inning jams with runners on third, just a wild pitch away from scoring.

When the one-run game reached the eighth inning, Leyland toyed with removing Wakefield so as to not risk the rookie losing a tight game that might damage his confidence. Leyland queried his coaches as the late innings unfolded, and May had the answer that made up Leyland's mind. "All I know, Jim, is that if I were in that other dugout trying to hit this guy, I'd be very happy if you took him out," said May. So Leyland stuck with Wakefield and got a complete-game victory out of the rookie.

Leyland was exhausted after the game. He sat with Donnelly and Miller and wondered aloud about the vagaries of managing a knuckleballer. Such pitchers are unlike other pitchers. For one thing, a knuckleball pitcher will likely throw many more pitches in a game. Indeed, Wakefield would throw 141 pitches in his second start, an eight-inning outing that earned him another victory. That would usually be far too many for a conventional pitcher, but since the knuckleball is thrown with an effortless motion, pitch count is not as important a factor.

Also of no importance is the speed of his pitches. Many managers and pitching coaches will compare early-inning radar gun readings with the speeds clocked in later innings. If there is a significant drop-off, then it is a pretty good gauge that the pitcher is tiring.

But the knuckleballs float to the plate at 55 miles per hour. And Wakefield was a knuckleballer who threw the pitch nearly 90 percent of the time. Candiotti, for example, mixes in far more fastballs and curves than Wakefield uses.

So Leyland wrestled with how he would handle the youngster. "This is tough. I might need another five-year contract extension if I'm expected to use a knuckleballer," said Leyland kiddingly. "By the time I have this figured out, I might look like Telly Savalas.

"I mean, I'm just not sure what to do. From now on, I think the only way I can go is to try and handle him like I would handle any other pitcher. If I think he's in trouble, I'll make a change. I don't know how else I can do it."

Said Donnelly, "Well, if he keeps pitching like this, it's going to be worth a lot of aggravation."

Wakefield's successful arrival proved to be a tonic for the Pirates. They proceeded to run off their longest winning streak of the season in the days following his debut.

Wakefield's first start was part of a four-game sweep of St. Louis. New York next arrived in Pittsburgh and the Pirates took both games of a two-game series with the reeling Mets, Wakefield pitching one of the victories.

The Pirates then traveled to St. Louis and swept four more games from the Cardinals to end any chance of the Cardinals mounting a pennant run. That series sweep gave Pittsburgh a ten-game winning streak and a three-and-a-half game lead over Montreal.

From St. Louis, the Pirates went on to New York, where they won two out of three. Then it was back home to Pittsburgh and a weekend series with Atlanta. On Friday night, the powerful Braves bombed the Pirates 15–0, a rout in which several Braves showboated and high-fived as if to rub the Pirates' noses in the defeat. It was more of the same next night when the Braves scored five runs in the first inning, eventually hanging on for a 7–5 victory.

It was time for Wakefield on Sunday, August 16, in a game that meant something to the Pirates. Leyland had nothing to say about the Braves' on-field antics, but several of his players were seething. Said Jay Bell, "Some of their guys took things a little too far. We're not exactly some little team that rolls over for them."

Wakefield again came through. He quieted the Braves and got the Pirates back on track with a complete-game 4–2 victory. It was his third victory and it convinced Leyland and Miller more than any other that Wakefield was indeed a unique rookie.

Long after the game, Leyland and Miller talked about the young knuckleballer. "I'm not sure how he throws that pitch," said Miller. "But he has unbelievable control with the thing. And the thing I like best is that he has as much poise as any kid I've ever seen."

Said Leyland, "He's something. I look at him in the ninth inning and I don't see any difference from what he looks like in the first inning. All I know is that he sure as hell got here at the right time."

Chapter 10

"The Game Part Is about the Only Fun Left"

♦ No team was hotter in August than the Pirates. But Montreal stayed right with Pittsburgh and as the end of the month approached, the Pirates, like every other club in baseball, were searching for a way to make some moves.

Because of baseball's trading rules, the last days of August are always a fascinating time for baseball. And that was never more true than in 1992.

Trading regulations require that players included in any deal after August 1 must have waivers from the other clubs. Teams that are smart enough to look far enough ahead often get waivers on their players in advance of having any trade talks. And just as often, prospective trades are blocked when a team claims on waivers a player they suspect might be headed to a rival. When that happens, the team owning the player will withdraw the player from the waiver list.

There is another wrinkle to the intrigues of August. Only players acquired prior to August 31 are eligible for the postseason, so a contender is under pressure to make their moves prior to that date or face making a deal for a player who might help them win a division but then not be available to help them reach the World Series. And few clubs are interested in acquiring a player for just the final four weeks of the regular season.

What makes all this so interesting is that virtually every team gets involved in some kind of August trade talks. Contenders are the most obvious; they all want to pick up added strength for the season's final push. But there is another side to these deals.

Teams with free agents who aren't likely to be re-signed will furiously shop such players. The hope is that a contender will be willing to give the club something in exchange for the prospective free agent. Whatever that "something" might be is likely better than the amateur draft choice, which is all the club will receive for losing the player to free agency. Clubs that are out of the race will make available most anyone on their roster in hopes that a contender, in the heat of a pennant race, might overpay to obtain that one missing ingredient.

Such deals can end up being important building blocks for those losing teams. For example, Atlanta came up big on their 1987 late-season trade of veteran pitcher Doyle Alexander to Detroit in exchange for a then-unknown pitcher named John Smoltz. Baltimore made what appeared to be a minor deal late one year when they dealt Fred Lynn to Detroit for young catcher Chris Hoiles.

The Pirates had acquired Zane Smith from Montreal for the stretch run in 1990 in exchange for three prospects who directly and indirectly helped rebuild the Expos. One was talented outfielder Moises Alou; the other two were pitcher Scott Ruskin and infielder Willie Greene, who were part of a later deal that brought John Wetteland, now the Expos' ace reliever, to Montreal.

In 1991, Larry Doughty made another late-season deal when he acquired Steve Buechele from Texas for two hard-throwing pitching prospects, Hector Fajardo and Kurt Miller, a Pirates number 1 draft pick in 1990. The wisdom of that move had since become murky. Pittsburgh quite likely would have won in 1991 without Buechele, whom they then dealt for Denny Jackson, on whom the jury was still out.

All this manuevering can be tough on managers. The manager of a losing club is often in a shaky position himself and feels the need to win as many games as possible. So when the losing manager's GM proposes trading off an established player for young players who are perhaps years away from being major leaguers, the manager is placed in a no-win position. On the one hand, he can't like the deal because it will hurt his chances of winning more games that season. On the other hand, if he objects too strongly, he will be criticized within his own organization for putting marginal short-term gains ahead of potentially significant long-term benefits.

Meanwhile, the manager of a contending club is usually pushing to obtain immediate help by any means necessary, even if it means trading prospects coveted within the organization by the GM, scouts, and farm director. In his early years with the Mets, Dave Johnson would privately fume when he'd be sitting in his office after another loss and have to listen to the Mets' brass come in and crow about how good the farm teams did that night. "Here we are getting our brains beat in and we're supposed to be happy about Tidewater or Jackson winning that night," Johnson would say to his coaches.

And for years, Dodgers scouts would claim that "we need a 60-man roster for all the guys Tommy [Lasorda] is pushing us to sign or pick up in trades."

The argument between a club's so-called development people and the major-league personnel is an ongoing one in most organizations. It sometimes goes beyond just the manager and includes the GM, who nowadays is under as much pressure to win right away as managers.

A few years ago, then-Cubs GM Jim Frey convened a meeting of his minor-league staff, coaches, and top scouts. For much of the day, they went around the room talking about the club's minor-league talent. In most cases, the final assessments were that such and such a player was "two years off" or another player was "three years away."

Finally, Frey had enough. He raised his arm for silence and

stood up at the end of the conference table. "All I've been hearing all day is that this guy is two years off, that this guy is three years off, that this guy might be ready in three or four years.

"Well, I'll tell you what three or four years away is." Frey started hobbling around the room. "This is what three or four years away is. It's Jimmy Frey in his walker, that's what it is. It's people saying, 'Hey, Jimmy, what are you doing nowadays?' It's 'Hey, Jimmy, remember the good old days with the Cubs?' That's what three or four years away is."

The conflict between winning now versus having the patience to build for the future is present in every organization. Toronto manager Cito Gaston was being sniped at throughout the 1992 season, not only by Toronto columnists but also by baseball people in his own organization, for his persistence in playing the same lineup every day, in particular playing veterans like Candy Maldonado and Pat Borders while blue-chip prospects like Derek Bell and Ed Sprague sat on the bench.

In meetings, top Blue Jays brass on the one hand complained that their top minor-league talents were being wasted. On the other hand, they suggested to Gaston that anything short of a World Series appearance would make the 1992 season a failure.

The fact became clear in late August with the year's first big pennant-race deal. Without any public warning, the Mets suddenly dealt away David Cone, their best pitcher and a free agent-to-be, for two young Toronto prospects, infielder Jeff Kent and outfielder Ryan Thompson.

From the perspective of the two managers involved, the surprising trade was a mixed bag. For the Mets' Torborg, it was the final recognition that the 1992 season was a washout. Torborg was not even consulted during the whirlwind negotiations but instead was told just prior to its public announcement. Torborg had had a testy relationship with the headstrong Cone, but he also knew how much Cone meant to the Mets' pitching staff and had hoped that the Mets would be able to re-sign Cone.

For the Blue Jays' Gaston, the deal gave him a huge additional pitching weapon for the pennant race and more importantly for the play-offs. Indeed, this was a deal made with an eye more on the postseason than the rest of the regular season. Since Gaston was well aware this was a must-win season for Toronto, he was pleased to be given one more arm with which to win it all.

When Cone was dealt, two very interested parties were Oakland's Tony LaRussa and Sandy Alderson. They both were convinced that the patchwork A's had built enough of a lead in the AL West to hold on in the division, especially after a dramatic three-game sweep of the Twins in Minnesota had sent the A's into August with an eight-game lead.

However, LaRussa was looking ahead to the play-offs and was getting uneasy. He had been juggling his pitching staff all summer with almost miraculous results. At times, the A's were carrying as many as 12 pitchers, an extraordinarily large number, especially in the AL where the designated hitter reduces the need for a lot of extra pitchers if a club has strong starting pitching; with no pinch-hit moves necessary, a strong AL pitching staff could get by with nine pitchers.

However, every AL club carried at least ten pitchers, with many NL clubs like Pittsburgh carrying 11 pitchers at any one time on their roster. LaRussa's thinking in carrying 12 was related to his shaky starting pitching. He found himself using three or four relievers every night, and without extra arms, such a regimen would wear out a staff quickly.

But LaRussa and Alderson felt they couldn't go with such a patchwork staff in the play-offs. So Alderson had been talking to other clubs for weeks in hopes of landing some pitching.

When the Cone deal was announced, Alderson complained, "I'd have liked a chance to make an offer. Maybe I couldn't have given the Mets as much as Toronto, but I sure would have liked to have tried."

How much the A's were willing to give up in a trade became evident a few days later. LaRussa's patience with Jose Canseco had been exhausted over the season, indeed over the last few seasons. What was evident was that several A's veterans were tiring of Canseco as well. Some still seethed at remarks made by

Canseco late in 1991 after Oakland had been eliminated from the AL West race. Canseco told some teammates that he was glad the A's for once didn't have to keep playing into October.

Canseco's frequent absences in '92 also upset many A's. And when he left the ballpark one night before a game had been completed, both LaRussa and many A's players felt betrayed by Canseco's apparent lack of interest in the team's ongoing effort to hang in the race.

Moreover, Canseco's absences put an enormous strain on everyone else in the lineup, not to mention on LaRussa himself. Before one midseason game he sat in the dugout pondering his options out loud.

"Here we are an hour before a game and I don't know who can play," he said. "Canseco's out. Hindu [Dave Henderson] is still out. Rickey [Henderson] won't know if he can play until he runs in batting practice. But he ran yesterday, so chances are he won't feel like running today. So he's probably out.

"I'd love to give McGwire a rest, but if I do, this is already a day when I have to sit out Steinbach. And who's going to drive in any runs? But McGwire is dragging. This is one of those things that can be a win–lose thing. If I sit him out, then I know I win because I'm giving him rest he needs. So if I lose the game, I at least win something because I gave McGwire a rest. If I play him and we still lose, then it's a lose–lose day. But I better play him today and look for the rest in a few days."

Unable to give McGwire the rest he needed and still field a respectable lineup, LaRussa had watched McGwire aggravate his own injuries and wear down further. In his view, Canseco's lack of effort was hurting the team, both figuratively and literally.

So when Alderson approached LaRussa with the possibility of trading Canseco, LaRussa didn't blink in telling his GM that if the right deal could be made, he would be in favor of trading the superstar right fielder. There was of course more to this than just personality differences. The Oakland franchise, like so many others in baseball, was faced with a money crunch. Their success of the last five years had swelled attendance, but it had also sent their payroll hurtling past the $40 million mark. Alderson maintained to the press that the club could lose between $5 and $10 million in 1992.

So the payroll would have to be cut. And flexibility had to be created in the A's salary structure for the winter ahead, when as many as 15 different A's could be free agents.

Alderson began making it clear in conversations with other GMs that Canseco could be had. But as great a talent as Canseco is, his marketability was greatly limited. For one thing, only a handful of teams could afford the roughly $12 million owed Canseco over the life of his remaining contract. For another, his frequent back problems made him something of a physical risk.

But coincidentally enough, the Texas Rangers were shopping Ruben Sierra, their own superstar right fielder. Sierra was struggling through what was for him an off-season. He was eligible for free agency after the season and was getting booed at home. The Rangers were convinced they could not re-sign him, so with Texas out of the race, Grieve was shopping Sierra.

The year's biggest deal had been set into motion. Alderson was talking frequently with Grieve because of the availability of two interesting pitchers. One was starter Bobby Witt, a hard thrower with whom the Rangers had become frustrated because of his persistent control problems. The other was reliever Jeff Russell, Texas's closer who was headed for free agency and whom the Rangers were unsure about re-signing.

Grieve and Alderson bounced back and forth different names in hopes of finding a mutually acceptable package. But when Grieve kept mentioning Sierra, Alderson had an idea. He asked Grieve if he would be interested in Canseco, and Grieve was immediately intrigued.

Grieve knew he was losing Sierra, so Canseco filled the right-field hole with a player who had more power and more stolen-base credentials. And Canseco had a star quality that was virtually unequaled in baseball. Like him or hate him, Canseco was one of those athletes who transcended his sport. He was of rock star celebrity. Heck, he even dated Madonna once.

The Rangers will open a new stadium in 1994 and they needed to start marketing season tickets and luxury boxes. With another losing season almost completed, those might be tough sells. A star of Canseco's magnitude had to help.

So Grieve was interested. He and Alderson exchanged several lists of players, but the deal finally came down to Sierra, Witt, and Russell for Canseco.

From Grieve's perspective, he was giving up fairly little. He was going to lose Sierra for a draft choice in the free-agent market. He was also likely to lose Russell in the same way. Although Witt was a young enough talent to still have a successful career, the Rangers had pretty much exhausted their patience with the right-hander.

The deal was much more anguishing from LaRussa's and Alderson's point of view, beginning with how it became official. Alderson completed the deal at roughly 8 P.M. West Coast time on August 31. He immediately called down to the dugout to inform LaRussa. Ironically enough, Canseco was in the on-deck circle. So in an uncomfortable scenario for everyone, LaRussa immediately whistled Canseco back to the dugout, where he was told he was now a member of the Texas Rangers.

The Athletics appeared to be taking a huge gamble. There were no guarantees that Oakland would have Sierra or Russell beyond the 1992 season. If they did leave, then the A's would have traded their marquee player for in effect six weeks of service from Sierra and Russell, Bobby Witt, and some extra amateur draft picks.

But Alderson would cogently point out that the A's needed to cut their payroll and that the deal's impact couldn't be completely gauged until the following season at the earliest. Baseball economics were on the verge of a massive readjustment and an organization like Oakland needed to get ahead of the curve and create some flexibility in its budget. Dropping Canseco created $12 million worth of flexibility.

Lost in all this was the feeling among the A's baseball people that Witt could blossom into a big winner under LaRussa and pitching coach Dave Duncan, who had worked wonders over the years with pitchers unwanted by other organizations, pitchers like Dave Stewart, Dennis Eckersley, Storm Davis, Scott Sanderson, and Ron Darling.

However, not surprisingly, the deal was instantly controversial in the Bay Area, especially when the A's lost their first five games following the announcement of the trade. LaRussa kept stressing that from his perspective, the primary reason for the trade was to help Oakland get to the World Series in 1992.

"Everybody keeps wondering about the free agents involved, but ever since Sandy and I started talking about all this, the main worry I've had has been this season, about getting this division won and then on into the play-offs," said LaRussa. "We'll deal with next year when we have to, but right now I'm concerned about what we do in the next few weeks.

"Before we made this trade, I could not look my team in the eye and truthfully tell them that we could go all the way through the World Series. Anyone who's seen our pitching in the last few weeks should know why we made this deal. We needed another starting pitcher. And we needed help in the bull pen.

"Heck, for a lot of this season, we've been an eight-game losing streak waiting to happen. We've been walking a fine line all year because of our pitching. We've done a heck of a job to this point. But neither I nor my coaches nor Sandy could realistically say we could win it all without getting some added pitching.

"Sierra? Well, we got a pretty darned good player to play right field. Sierra doesn't hit as many home runs, but overall, I think we're as good if not better with him in right."

However, it was a difficult selling job in the days immediately after the trade, as the A's were booed in their own stadium and ripped by a lot of the area's columnists. Canseco, who was being booed by his home fans prior to the trade, was now a hero in absentia. Sierra hadn't even joined the club yet because of a mild case of chicken pox. Witt was scheduled to start his first game for Oakland in a Sunday night game with Boston. Sierra was due into town the same day with the outside chance he might be able to play.

But as LaRussa sat in his office that Sunday afternoon, he could barely contain his emotions. A visitor stopped by and LaRussa, tossing a newspaper at him, said, "Have you seen this?"

It was a front-page exclusive interview with Canseco in the *San Jose Mercury-News*. Canseco ripped the Oakland organization and LaRussa specifically. "He's supposedly a players' manager but Tony goes out of his way to embarrass players when they make mistakes," said Canseco. "No one is allowed to have fun there. It's always this super serious, must-win atmosphere and it's all because of him."

Canseco went on to say he had never been respected or supported by LaRussa or the A's organization, hinted that his treatment might be the result of racism, and said the A's obviously intended not to be competitive in the coming years.

For LaRussa, the printed words were like a physical blow. He had always prided himself on being a players' manager, on always being available when a player wanted to talk or serving as a counselor if the player had some personal problems that he needed to discuss. LaRussa was also proud of being able to push the right buttons to motivate individuals.

He rarely, if ever, publicly criticized his players, preferring to keep that in his office or in the dugout but always away from the media. When meeting with players individually, LaRussa will often be brutally direct. But when he talks about his players to the press, LaRussa will not comment at all rather than criticize someone.

LaRussa had expected and had usually received loyalty from his players in return. However, it was something that was becoming increasingly rare in modern baseball. With players changing teams more than ever and earning million-dollar salaries after only a handful of seasons in the majors, players' loyalty to teams had deteriorated. And handling those players who were stars had become an increasingly complicated job for managers.

It was something LaRussa often discussed with Leyland. The two talked to each other three or four times a week. They'd talk about their own teams or maybe a particular strategy; they'd read each other's box scores and when they noticed something out of the ordinary, they'd call. And when Leyland had his problem earlier in the year with Bonilla, LaRussa had called to commiserate.

Now LaRussa felt wounded by Canseco. As he sat at his desk, LaRussa wrestled with his emotions.

"You know, there's a lot about this job that can be really tough to handle," said LaRussa as he fiddled with his lineup card. "I talk about this all the time with Jimmy. You might have some guys in the media who go out of the way to give you a hard time no matter what and that's something you have to try and deal with as best you can. Some managers might have owners or general managers who are tough, who might not trust you or listen to you, who might give you coaches you don't want or make player moves without consulting you. And that can be difficult to handle, though thank God it's not a problem here because we have such great people running this franchise.

"The strain on a manager's family can be brutal even if he's winning. You need to be blessed with a great wife and kids who understand the pressure and understand that someone changes during the competition of the season and is able to put up with that. All that is very, very difficult.

"But you know what I think is the worst thing to handle? It's when a player betrays you like this. Here's Jose mouthing off about not getting supported and that really gets to me. I think of all the times I've gone out to the press and if not lied to protect him, then at least not told the whole truth. And I'm not talking about once. I'm talking about a lot of times over the years.

"I never asked for thanks. But at least, I thought I deserved some respect or some loyalty. I'm putting my own integrity on the line, something that means an awful lot to me. My credibility is on the line to protect the player's reputation. And then he goes and turns it around like this when he gets the chance. Do you know how it makes me feel? It makes me feel physically sick.

"My first reaction is that I'm going to go out there when the press arrives and just lay it all out about Jose. I'll tell all the stories, I'll blow him away. I'll tell about all the times I've protected his reputation by not telling the whole truth. Let the public decide who has supported who over the years. I want to go after him with everything I have."

By then, some of LaRussa's coaches had filtered in. And as LaRussa went on, it was suggested that by going after Canseco, he would in effect give the whole story a new life.

"I know, that's what so damned tough about all this," said LaRussa. "If I fire back like I want to so much, it will keep this crap alive at a time when we should all be focused on winning this thing. And if I keep this alive, no one wins. They'll say I'm trying to justify the trade by bringing stuff up. And in some people's eyes, it will make him a victim or something.

"So what do I do? I wait until we clinch and then maybe have my say. But in the meantime, I have to hold all this and I'll feel it eating away at me like an ulcer and I won't be able to do a damned thing about it. And that really stinks."

LaRussa looked down at his lineup card and wearily shook his head. "What gets you is that the game part of this job is about the only fun left," he said. "I bet if you asked all 26 managers in the major leagues, they'd tell you that those three hours or so when the game is being played are the best hours of this job. All the other stuff, the press, the front office, the personalities, all are shut out then. When the game's being played, all you have to worry about is competing and winning. And that is still the greatest thing about all this, the chance to compete at this level every night for six months.

"But there's so much going on around the game now that it's tough to keep that in focus. And dealing with the big players is something that just keeps getting tougher all the time."

Throughout baseball history, one of a manager's toughest jobs has been his relationship with his stars. Going back to Babe Ruth's skirmishes with Miller Huggins, managers have had to grapple with the star syndrome.

There was no more visible star–manager feud in recent history than Reggie Jackson and Billy Martin in New York. The pictures of Martin and Jackson having to be separated in the Yankees' dugout one day in Boston will live forever.

However, their feud was atypical of the normal star–manager relationship. The immediate cause of that skirmish was Jackson loafing after a fly ball, but the animosity was rooted in each's need to dominate the spotlight. Neither would relinquish attention without a fight. But the tension was not wholly negative. Jackson fed off the atmosphere to be a dominant player, while Martin's own self-destructive tendencies would have sought out someone else if Jackson had not been in pinstripes.

While Martin and Jackson were feuding, over in Baltimore Earl Weaver and Jim Palmer had a running battle that lasted for over a decade. In many ways, they were like oil and water—the short, raspy, and often profane Weaver versus the tall, elegant, and erudite Palmer, who had very definite ideas of how to run a baseball team and specifically a pitching staff and was never afraid to express them.

The two would run afoul of each other on any kind of strategy. Weaver would often chide Palmer in the press, suggesting he was too often concerned with his own physical condition and not the welfare of the team. Palmer in turn would question Weaver's strategy and go out of his way to get under Weaver's skin with personal digs such as "Do you ever notice how when Earl comes to the pitcher's mound, he finds the highest place to stand so he won't look so short?" Invariably when Weaver came to the mound to remove Palmer from a game, the two would stand and debate for a few minutes before Palmer would relinquish the ball and leave the game.

The two were highly intelligent and highly stubborn. Weaver would never acknowledge that Palmer might have a point about anything. Palmer would never acknowledge that maybe Weaver might know what was best for the team as a whole. The two would debate on the mound, in the dugout, in the clubhouse, on the team bus, and while waiting for their room keys in a hotel lobby. Fortunately for all concerned, the Orioles of that era were loaded with savvy veteran players who watched the Earl–Jim show with bemusement. It had little effect on the team itself.

As the years went on, the two seemed to disagree with each other just to disagree. But it had largely become an act expected of them for public consumption. The years of sparring over every minute bit of strategy evolved into a grudging mutual respect. Even at the end of Palmer's career, Weaver always viewed him as his number 1 pitcher. For example, when the Orioles brought the 1982 AL East race down to the final day by sweeping the first three games of what was for them a single-elimination series with Milwaukee, it was Palmer whom Weaver had saved for the final game, which the Brewers won.

Weaver would never second-guess himself for that decision. To him, Palmer would always be the quintessential ace even if he would never say as much to Palmer himself.

Although Weaver never bended in his long debate with Palmer, other managers have coped with their superstars with more of a laissez-faire approach. When Chuck Tanner managed the Pirates, he had a star-studded crew that included Willie Stargell, Bill Madlock, Dave Parker, Phil Garner, Tim Foli, Manny Sanguillen, and others. It was a free-spirited team that was resistant to rules and regulations. Instead of trying to bend their collective will, Tanner coexisted with his stars by basically turning over the keys of the asylum to the inmates. The Pirates' clubhouse of that era vibrated with loud music right until minutes before game time. Tanner let go without comment all kinds of free expression in dress (earrings in the late 1970s were very radical, for example). His approach translated into excellent relationships with his players and a 1979 World Series Championship.

Sparky Anderson during the Big Red Machine days had an even more illustrious cast that included superstars like Joe Morgan, Pete Rose, Johnny Bench, and Tony Perez. However, this was more of a serious bunch, players who were highly intelligent and absorbed with baseball.

Anderson, although well established even then as one of the

game's best managers, did not try to impose his will on this collection of headstrong talents. Instead, he would in effect make things a committee effort. He would make sure that he talked to Rose or Morgan before many decisions. He'd invite postmortem debate over strategy. As Morgan said, "When we thought Sparky had screwed up, we didn't hesitate to tell him. And because he invited that kind of give and take, it helped the players get on each other about doing things the right way."

The atmosphere between the Reds' stars and Anderson was unencumbered by any debate over the sensitive area of off-field rules. The conservative Reds management insisted on trimmed hair, no beards, and traditional black baseball shoes. Since the players knew such edicts were out of Anderson's hands, they did not become issues between the stars and the manager.

However, both stars and the nature of the game have changed over the last dozen or so years. And the ability of managers to develop meaningful rapport with their stars has greatly diminished.

For one thing, players, even superstars, move around much more frequently. And managers are fired more quickly, so there is not always an opportunity for relationships to develop as they did in the past. And nowadays, the stars have multiyear contracts worth millions whereas many managers work on a one-year deal for a fraction of the money. Managers in such situations are loathe to confront their stars, who in many cases have more clout within the organization than the manager does.

Early in the 1992 season, Seattle manager Bill Plummer rightly went ballistic when his pitching ace Randy Johnson threw two listless innings and then took himself out of a game. After the game, Plummer called Johnson "a quitter who let down his whole team." But the end result was that two days later, Plummer was forced by his front office to apologize to Johnson, and whatever credibility Plummer had in his clubhouse was largely shattered.

A few years ago, Boston's Roger Clemens and Dwight Evans raised a stink over the details of a Red Sox road trip. In a snit over the travel plans, they got off the team plane and made their own arrangements. Although the press demanded penalties, then-manager Joe Morgan sought to maintain a fragile peace with his stars and did not make a major issue of the whole affair. There are still superstars like Ryne Sandberg, Robin Yount, Kirby Puckett, Cal Ripken, Jr., Roberto Alomar, Ozzie Smith, and others who play the same no matter who manages and who don't expect special treatment. But they have fast become an exception in an age when the relationship between stars and managers has never been more tenuous, even for someone as established and successful as LaRussa.

Still seething over the Canseco interview, LaRussa's mood eased when he realized how much respect for Canseco had deteriorated among his former Oakland teammates.

That had become clear the previous day when LaRussa ventured into the clubhouse before heading to the field. A group of players and coaches were watching Canseco's Rangers playing in New York. Ironically, Canseco was hitting and he grounded out.

Mark McGwire was among the group and he said, "How'd you like what Josey told Toby Harrah [Texas's manager] when he got there? He told him not to expect much from him because he was still hurting and that he might only be at 50 or 60 percent. I bet that made Harrah real happy. Here they trade three guys for someone and the guy comes in and tells him not to expect much."

LaRussa listened and then turned to walk toward the field without commenting. He thought of how McGwire had played all season through a variety of injuries and was having his greatest season until suffering a painful pulled rib cage muscle. McGwire had been sidelined for two weeks but had begun hitting. LaRussa kept telling McGwire not to rush things, but McGwire kept pushing to do more. McGwire's obvious disdain for Canseco made LaRussa smile in spite of himself.

LaRussa was finally diverted from Canseco when Sierra arrived for an examination by team physicians. When told Sierra had been medically cleared, LaRussa wrote him into the lineup as DH. And when a clubhouse attendant told LaRussa that Sierra had come to the clubhouse, he immediately left his office to greet the new outfielder.

LaRussa had different greetings for the three new players.

In Witt's case, he and Duncan were careful not to push their ideas immediately upon the pitcher. As Duncan said, "It's too late in the season for us to do anything really significant with him. I need to see him pitch for me a few times and we can't really load him up with any stuff now. It will have to wait until spring training."

In Russell's case, LaRussa's main job was making sure Russell knew that his job in Oakland would be different from what he did in Texas. In Texas, Russell had been the closer, but in Oakland, he would set up Eckersley, baseball's best closer. This change in role did not bother Russell; all he wanted, he assured LaRussa, was a chance to pitch in the play-offs for the first time in his career.

Sierra arrived with an aide-de-camp who was carrying a jewelry box filled with Sierra's baubles, watches, earrings, and gold necklaces that had to be worth thousands. The man Friday told an A's clubhouse attendant that the box needed to go into a stadium safe. A club official had to be found for approval.

As ludicrous as that scene was, Sierra was quiet and almost shy as LaRussa put his arm around his shoulder and whispered a few words. "If you feel okay, you'll DH tonight," said LaRussa. "Don't worry about anything. Just be yourself. That's plenty good enough. We're glad to have you here."

The night turned out to be productive for the A's. Witt pitched a solid seven innings in his Oakland debut. Sierra would win the game with a daring baserunning play as he scored from first on an outfield single that was then botched up by the Boston defense. LaRussa, Lachemann, and several A's players all hugged Sierra as he left the field. The A's had finally won a game without Canseco.

. . .

There was meanwhile no such late-August trade drama surrounding the Pirates. Coincidentally, the only rumor connected
with Pittsburgh involved Sierra. When it was originally reported
that Texas was shopping Sierra, there was speculation that the
Pirates had offered infield prospect Carlos Garcia in a package
for Sierra.

On the surface the rumor made some sense. The Pirates sorely
needed a hitter like Sierra. Leyland had exhausted virtually every
possible option in finding someone to hit fifth behind Bonds,
who was on his way to being intentionally walked nearly three
dozen times.

Leyland tries to stay on top of who is available and who isn't
around baseball. Leyland, like a lot of other managers, wouldn't
hesitate to suggest specific players for his GM to pursue. More
than any professional sport, baseball was always awash with daily
gossip. Most managers love to hear rumors about other teams,
about what players are available, about who is on the trading
block. And just like scouts, GMs, and sportswriters, many managers have their own sources of information.

Leyland was always looking for information that could lead to
a beneficial deal. For example, it was he who initiated the Pirates'
acquisition of Zane Smith in August of 1990 during a late-season
brainstorming session in his Three Rivers Stadium office.

It was obvious then that the Pirates needed a starting pitcher
if they were to hold off New York down the stretch. Drabek was
on his way to the Cy Young Award, but the rest of that 1990
rotation was shaky, with John Smiley not fully recovered from a
broken thumb and Walk suffering recurring groin pulls. Neal
Heaton had been a first-half All Star but couldn't win at all after
June.

So Leyland was becoming desperate for a veteran pitcher and
he knew the Pirates' best chance was to pursue someone who
would be a free agent after the season, someone whom Pittsburgh
could in effect rent for the stretch drive and worry about re-
signing later. And as August '90 wore on, Leyland was becoming

increasingly restless about the Pirates' inability to zero in on a pitcher.

"Larry [Doughty] goes slow sometimes but jeez, Geno, there ain't a whole lot of pitching out there anyway," said Leyland to Lamont. "I talked to Jimmy Frey when the Cubs were in. And he tells me that they need pitching themselves, yet clubs are coming to them about their pitchers. It's crazy."

"Who's Larry talking about?" asked Lamont.

"Well, he wants us to look at Triple-A, but you know and I know there just ain't anything there to help us the way we need help," said Leyland. "I'll tell you the name of a guy we might ask about. It's Mike Scott. I hear from some of the writers that Houston wants to move him. Couldn't he win us a few games? I just wonder how much money he's making."

"Well, ask Larry, because if we go to Triple-A, that's going to mean Rick Reed again," said Donnelly, who had joined the conversation.

"The heck with that. I'll call Scott's agent," said Leyland. "Alan Hendricks is a good guy, I know him. I just gotta get his number."

With that, Leyland walked to the doorway and shouted into the clubhouse, "Spanky, get in here."

In walked LaValliere, who declared, "What's up, you want me to play against Dennis Rasmussen [that night's starter for San Diego]? Well, you can shove it. I'm not messing up my stroke trying to hit that big SOB. My knee's sore anyway, so keep Sluggo in the lineup."

"Will you shut up?" said Leyland. "I need your agent's phone number. No, I'm not trading you, I just want to ask him a question."

LaValliere thought for a moment. "God, what is his number? I can't remember it," he said.

Sitting on the couch nearby, Donnelly let out a huge sigh. "Don't you love these players?" he said. "Here they trust some guy in Texas with hundreds of thousands of dollars of their own money and they can't even remember the guy's phone number.

If it was my money, I'd have that guy in Texas's phone number tatooed on my forehead."

"Hump, Alan's number is 713-555-6200," said LaValliere. "And tell Donnelly I'm not talking to him again until he apologizes."

Leyland was dialing the phone and got Hendricks on the line. The conversation was brief. "What's the story with Mike Scott?" asked Leyland. "Is he healthy? How much is he making?"

Leyland hung up a few minutes later. "Scratch Mike Scott; he's making a ton and his shoulder has been a little tender.

"I have another idea that makes more sense anyway. Montreal has got to be shopping Zane Smith. That guy could really help. For one thing, we get him and now we can fire another left-hander at the Mets. I talked to Dave Dombrowski [Expos' GM] when they were last in here. He was saying they were looking to drop some contracts and some free-agent guys and they were just looking for prospects."

So Leyland got together with Doughty and the two agreed that the club would check out Smith, and the deal was eventually completed, helping the Pirates win the 1990 division.

But in August of 1992, things were different for the Pirates. Leyland had seen the long list of possible free agents and had heard the reports about Sierra being available. But Leyland knew there was little chance the Pirates could make such an expensive move.

There was no question how well Sierra would fit into the Pittsburgh lineup. But Leyland also knew that Bonds and Drabek were already headed for free agency and the Pirates were unlikely to re-sign either. So, the club wasn't going to give up a prospect like Garcia for a player like Sierra, who would have to be paid close to $1 million for the final six weeks of 1992 and would also likely leave after the season.

Simmons quickly squashed the rumor, anyway. "The only time I've talked to Tom Grieve was to try to find out if he had any idea where all this insanity was coming from," said Simmons. "There's nothing to it, nothing at all. The only major-league person who's going to manage Carlos Garcia is Jim Leyland."

So Sierra wasn't headed to Pittsburgh. And neither was anyone else. Their pennant-race move, for better or worse, would be the recall of Wakefield. Montreal meanwhile made a move shortly before the August 31 deadline when they acquired veteran left-hander Bill Krueger from Minnesota.

However, that didn't tip the delicate balance between the two NL East contenders as they headed for the stretch. For Leyland, his biggest chore continued to be juggling his shaky bull pen. One example was his use of Danny Cox, one of the veterans signed during the season to Triple-A contracts. Cox saved two games at a time when Leyland had lost confidence in his other relievers.

It was another element in how Pittsburgh continued to be resourceful in grinding out wins when they needed them the most. The Pirates seemed to be barely hanging on. They came out of the Atlanta series in late August having gone 7–5 over their last 12 games. They followed that with a five–game winning streak but then hit a stretch when their bull pen completely collapsed, getting ripped for a collective 6.75 ERA in one ugly first week of September.

What kept the Pirates in first place were big performances at the right time. One of the biggest came on September 8 from Drabek. Pirates relievers had pitched eight innings the previous day in a 6–5 loss to Chicago, and over the last six games, Pittsburgh's bull pen had been used for 20 innings. So several relievers were unavailable when Drabek took the mound that night.

Miller was very blunt with Drabek as the right-hander began warming up 20 minutes before the game. "Doug, you know the situation we're in tonight," said Miller. "You're about all we have tonight. If you're in trouble, you're going to have to stay in there."

Like clockwork, Drabek and the Pirates responded to this mini-crisis. Bonds hit a two-run homer in the first inning and Drabek pitched a complete-game three-hitter.

Leyland puffed on a cigar later and admitted that it could prove to be a pivotal night for the Pirates. "That was one of those which wasn't huge in the sense that we have to win it," he said. "But it was a huge game in the sense that we needed Doug to be really strong.

"The bull pen was short. And Doug gave us exactly what we needed. If he had struggled early, I don't know what I would have done. All I know is that we would have been in big trouble. I wouldn't have had any choice but to leave him out there for a while. But the guy has been a heck of a big-game pitcher for us. And he rose to the occasion and really came through when we needed it."

The Pirates were also showing an uncanny knack for coming back to win games. They would end the season with 21 victories earned in their last at bat, a big reason being Leyland's willingness to use any of his players in tough situations and the Pirates' ability to keep themselves focused on just the game at hand.

The holes were evident in the Pittsburgh lineup. As well as Jeff King was playing since coming back from Buffalo, he hardly filled the void in the lineup left by Bobby Bonilla. At times, especially in June and July, the Pirates fielded incredibly weak lineups with four or five players batting .200 or lower, and such lesser lights as Gary Varsho batting cleanup. The Pirates had survived nearly three weeks without Bonds. Their pitching staff continued to withstand the loss of a 20-game winner in Smiley and a 20-save reliever in Landrum.

Through it all, the one constant was Leyland. As Donnelly would say, "He's unbelievable. He just refuses to let down. He keeps everything so simple but when you look at it from a distance, you realize that he is the same as any of the great managers through history. He does things the right way. He doesn't embarrass anybody. He doesn't let himself get discouraged ever. He doesn't take credit away from anybody who deserves it. He handles everything the way you were taught to handle it.

"And he never stops believing in his own club. He will put guys into situations where other people would be afraid to use them. He uses starters as relievers. He will spot a guy in a game who no one would even think of using there. To watch it every day makes every player start thinking that he's always going to think of something that will work. And that gives the individual player a little more confidence when he's the guy Jimmy calls on.

"Heck, I'm the most biased person in the world because Jimmy's my boss and I think he's the best manager I've ever seen. But all I know is, to watch him work every day is to watch someone doing an unbelievable job.

"It's to the point now with the players where Jimmy can get a point across with them just with a look or a glance. He doesn't need meetings. There's no rah-rah stuff. But it's incredible how he always seems to know when to talk to them," he said. Donnelly was onto one of his favorite topics. "And it's remarkable how he has the knack of always saying the right thing.

"I'll never forget back in 1990. Jimmy never said a thing all year about winning it all. He would just keep on them about grinding it out day after day. It was the thing about how if we play our best, then we can't complain about where we end up.

"Well, on this one day, we had just lost a game in Chicago. It was something like our seventh loss in a row, but the Mets had only picked up a game in the whole stretch. And after that seventh loss, he came into the clubhouse, Jimmy got them together and just said, 'All I know right now, more than at any other time this season, is that you guys are going to be the National League East champions.' That was it. And then we won something like six of our next eight to break the thing open."

Like any manager late in the season, a big concern for Leyland was making sure his everyday players were not overly tired as the club hit the stretch. He was always willing with some players to sit them for one game in exchange for knowing they might be fresh for the next three weeks.

Leyland had a unique way of handling such decisions, which often can create tension between managers and players.

One such incident occurred in the second week of September as the Pirates headed closer to a big series with Montreal. It involved shortstop Jay Bell, who was playing his best baseball of the season but had also not been rested for even an inning in weeks. Leyland was toying with giving Bell a night off.

Some managers will simply sit down the player and let him find out the news when he arrives at the clubhouse and sees the lineup card. But that's not Leyland's way. Instead, he will always try to twist around the decision so the player leaves thinking the final decision was his.

On this particular September day, Leyland wrote out his lineup card but stuck it in the top drawer of his desk until he could first bring Bell into his office.

"Jay, you've been in there every day for weeks and I think you're tired," said Leyland. "So you won't play tonight. I want you to take the night off."

"Skip, everybody is tired, but I don't need any night off," argued Bell. "I'm going too good to sit down. It's no rest sitting, anyway, because I get nervous watching the darned game from the bench. What good is it to sit me out for one game?"

That was, as it turned out, exactly what Leyland wanted to hear. The two argued back and forth for ten more minutes. Finally, Leyland feigned exasperation and said, "All right, enough's enough. Get out of here. I'm tired of listening to all this. You win, you're in there."

Bell left, and then, smiling, Leyland opened his drawer and pulled out the lineup card he had written before seeing Bell. There was Bell, playing short and in the number two spot of the lineup, just like always. Leyland wanted the decision to be made by the player. He had suspected Bell was all right, but he wanted him to argue the point. If Bell had been less adamant, then Leyland would have scratched him.

Days later, there was another example of Leyland's methods. When the club began a road trip in Philadelphia, several players were scheduled to hit early. Major-league rosters can be expanded after September 1 and with several extra players, extra sessions of batting practice are often needed to accommodate the overflow.

On this night, several players were a few minutes late getting on the field for extra hitting. Nothing was said at the time, although the tardiness did irritate the coaches, who themselves had to be at the park early to throw batting practice and shag balls.

The next afternoon, Leyland came pacing through the clubhouse at a time when virtually every player was in the room. He was talking loudly to himself and was obviously irritated. "Goddamn it, I ask them to bring some reports sent to the hotel and they're late," said Leyland, loudly enough for most of the room to hear him as he grabbed a cup of coffee.

"How the hell can someone with this club mess up like that? What the hell. How hard is it to get out here at the right time? It ain't no big deal to be on time, is it? This club runs so well. Everybody does their job and then someone screws up like this by being late with something I need. Hell, you learn how to be on time when you're in high school."

Leyland retreated back into his office, slamming the door for effect. Meanwhile, back in the clubhouse, several players, particularly the younger ones recently recalled, looked at each other, obviously wondering at which of them Leyland's minitirade was aimed. Thus was the question of being on time put to rest.

As Donnelly put it, "Jimmy has that knack of talking to 25 guys, but also speaking to one specific guy at the same time."

Chapter 11

"That's One I'm Going to Be Thinking about for a While"

◆ Every pennant race eventually boils down to a final, *mano a mano* collision of the two top contenders. And so it was September 16 when the NL East race arrived at its crossroads. The second-place Montreal Expos had arrived in Pittsburgh for a two-game series, trailing the Pirates by four. The two clubs would meet a week later in Montreal for two more games, but if the Expos were going to make a run, it had to start now.

The national media, at least those not already consumed by football, were in town. And three hours before the game, dozens of baseball's repertorial bigfeet were crowded in Leyland's office hanging on his every word. Never mind that Leyland had been giving the same down-to-earth answers for months. They did not become Big News until they were reported by *The New York Times*, the *Los Angeles Times*, the *Philadelphia Inquirer*, *Sports Illustrated*, *The Sporting News*, or any number of other publications.

On most nights, Leyland's coaches drift in and out of the manager's office, but on this late afternoon, with the reporters draped in all the chairs and on the couch and standing along the walls and near the doorway, the coaches largely stayed away unless a visit was absolutely necessary.

Miller popped in briefly to hand Leyland a sheet of paper that had that day's bull-pen pitchers listed along with when they last pitched and also when they last warmed up. Miller quietly told Leyland that Randy Tomlin's sprained ankle would not allow him to throw on the side on what was his scheduled day to throw between starts.

Leyland didn't even look up at Miller. Leyland was a picture of pennant-race frenzy, sitting behind his desk wearing a T-shirt. With one hand, he was scratching his upper arm where he wore the nicotine patch that had briefly done its job but was now a long forgotten effort to cut down on Leyland's smoking. TV viewers were frequently treated to shots of Leyland in the dugout, stealing puffs from a cigarette cupped in his hand. On this night, a lit cigarette was burning in his ashtray while a lit cigar was stuck in the corner of his mouth. So until the season was over and Leyland again made his annual attempt to stop smoking, for the duration he would continue to look like a poster boy for the National Tobacco Institute.

The reporters were peppering Leyland with questions, since most had early stories to write that would plug their pages for the later game story. He was asked in at least six different ways if he was surprised that Montreal had surfaced as the Pirates' main contender. Leyland, playing the pennant-race game to perfection, was lavish in his praise for the Expos.

"They just don't go away, they just damned well won't go away," he said. "I've been saying that nearly all year and it's still true.

"I thought before the season that the Mets might run away with our division because of their pitching. But if they didn't, then I thought every other team had a legitimate chance. I thought Montreal had the potential to be outstanding this year and I was right, damn it."

Leyland went on to laud Expos manager Felipe Alou and the Expos' excellent young talent. He downplayed the importance of that night's game, saying, "We could win tonight and tomorrow night and it won't mean a thing if we then lose three over the weekend to Philadelphia. You can't look ahead or look behind. You have to play the game you have that night. And that's something that my club has learned how to do."

Leyland dismissed the suggestion that the Pirates' pennant-race experience gave them an edge down the stretch. "Hell, look at it the other way—maybe the Expos are too young to know how tough it's supposed to be," he said with a hint of Stengelese logic.

Such praise of the enemy is typical of pennant races, when most managers would sooner have their tongues imprinted with a branding iron than say something that could inflame the enemy, although there have been exceptions to this rule. In 1990, Lou Piniella and Roger Craig sniped at each other as the Reds tried to hold off Craig's Giants.

Earl Weaver was always known to tweak his rivals, especially if they were the Yankees or Red Sox. In 1979, when the Orioles were drawing away from the AL East pack, Weaver would frequently say, especially in Boston, "It's hard for me to understand how a team like the Red Sox isn't closer in this thing. They have the best lineup in baseball. How can we be in front of them?"

In 1980, when his Orioles would end up winning 100 games and still finish second, Weaver kept the heat on the Yankees to the bitter end when New York was forced into the final weekend before clinching. Weaver would say, "You know, that Steinbrenner made all his money building ships. Well, I got this feeling that this ship he has in New York is called the *Titanic* and it's going to start sinking any day now."

But Leyland wasn't one to try and get under his rivals' skin, so he continued to spout platitudes about the Expos, whom he genuinely respected and whom he targeted as the division's sleeper way back in spring training. He also continued to be wired with anticipation.

Lanny Frattare, the Pirates' chief play-by-play broadcaster, worked his way through the clog of reporters. Frattare taped Leyland's daily pregame radio show. "If you don't mind, will you guys clear out so I can do this?" said Leyland. "I'd let you stay in, but Lanny would get nervous and we can't have that."

Leyland was kidding, as he often did with Frattare. It in fact was one of his frequent pregame rituals to start the taping and then drop an obscenity into an answer just to make Frattare restart the tape. Or he would keep dropping a ball on Frattare's foot as the broadcaster tried to tape the introduction of the show without laughing. On this night, though, Leyland was much more businesslike, doing the show in one take.

Leyland was very skittish coming into the series. The Pirates had doggedly been treading water in the race for the last ten days. The lead over Montreal had basically stayed the same for weeks, and Leyland was getting anxious about breaking the race open once and for all. But he also knew that his club, as it had all year, was balancing on a fine line between holding on in the division and falling back to the pack.

He ironically had heard the exact same thing days ago from his friend LaRussa. "Tony was saying the other day how this has been a year when he's never felt like he could relax with any lead," said Leyland. "And he said that all season long, he always felt like his club could at any time hit a seven- or eight-game losing streak. I've felt the same way sometimes.

"We've got a damned good club. But we're not the kind of great club with which you can sort of sit back and feel relaxed if you can get up four or five games in the division."

The Pirates entered the Montreal series with less than their best starting pitching. Leyland was a firm believer in not juggling around starters for a particular series. As both he and Miller often discussed, "You set things up to get one guy to face a certain club, and you can end up fouling up the routine of the other three or four guys," said Miller.

So the Pirates' starters remained in order, and that meant that they would have Walk and Jackson starting against Montreal in the two games, not Leyland's two most reliable starters—Drabek and Wakefield.

Leyland meanwhile didn't have to consult statistical charts or play any hunches in writing out his starting lineup. Indeed, there were no real lineup decisions to make. With Expos left-hander Chris Nabholz starting, Leyland would use the lineup he usually used against left-handed pitching. So shortly after Leyland arrived at Three Rivers Stadium at around 2:30, he had the lineup posted on the wall just inside the entrance to the Pirates' clubhouse.

It read this way:

- Gary Redus would lead off and play first, where he platooned with left-handed hitting Orlando Merced.
- Jay Bell would bat second and play short, as he did every day.
- Andy Van Slyke would bat third and play center and Barry Bonds would bat fourth and play left, just as they always did.
- Batting fifth was third baseman Jeff King, who besides Bonds was the Pirates' hottest hitter and who had become the regular fifth hitter after Leyland had tried a half-dozen others in that key spot.
- Batting sixth was Lloyd McClendon, who platooned in right field with left-handed hitter Alex Cole.
- Batting seventh was catcher Don Slaught, who platooned with Mike LaValliere.
- Batting eighth was second baseman Jose Lind, with Walk batting ninth.

For years, baseball people had generally believed that the Pirates were weaker against left-handed pitching than against righties. That impression was largely caused by Bonds and Van Slyke, both left-handed hitters who devastate right-handed pitching. With the switch-hitting Bonilla gone, the impression was even more pronounced that the Pirates were vulnerable to lefties. And now that Cole, the club's one true leadoff hitter, would sit on the bench against left-handers, that was added evidence in many minds that Pittsburgh was weaker versus the left-handed starters.

But in the last several weeks, the truth was actually the opposite. Bonds had always hit left-handed pitching well, and this season was no exception. But Van Slyke was making the biggest difference. Prior to 1992, Van Slyke was a notoriously poor hitter against left-handers. He batted only .195 versus lefties in 1991, the lowest such average in the majors among everyday players. His career average versus left-handers before '92 was .218.

Since his spring training back problems, Van Slyke was under doctors' orders to be careful. And, working with May, the batting coach, Van Slyke had concentrated on a more compact swing to lessen the pressure on his back. The result was that Van Slyke was hitting far more balls to left and left-center fields. And the shorter stroke allowed Van Slyke to have more success against left-handers, because instead of trying to pull pitches, he was simply trying to put the ball in play and hitting it where it was pitched. Van Slyke was hitting left-handers consistently at a .300 clip all season, and in the process he made the Pirates much less vulnerable to southpaws.

There were other factors as well. Cole, after a solid start in Pittsburgh, had hit a serious slump, which at one point resulted in a 1-for-31 streak. McClendon meanwhile was more of an extra-base threat, and so the Pirates in recent days were more dangerous with McClendon in the lineup than with Cole. And after struggling for much of the season, Redus had gotten hot, so there was little lost with him in the lineup instead of Merced. Slaught meanwhile was having a solid season, and the defensive gap between him and LaValliere was largely negligible.

So the bottom line was that Leyland had no qualms about having to face the left-hander Nabholz in the series opener. And since his roster had several extra men (the result of the rule that allows clubs to expand rosters from 25 men to as many as 40 after September 1), Leyland had a myriad of options for in-game moves when the Expos made a pitching change.

By the time the Pirates were ready to start batting practice at 4:45, Leyland headed to the field, his dealings with the media basically concluded except for three different television interviews still to come. Before leaving his office, he double-checked with traveling secretary Greg Johnson to make sure he had left the names of the people for whom he was leaving tickets.

As he always did, Leyland bounced all over the field during batting practice. He spotted young Expos outfielder Moises Alou and gave him a big hello. Alou, the son of the Expos' manager, was a former Pirates farmhand included in the 1990 trade for Zane Smith.

Leyland then headed for the outfield for a long talk with Van Slyke. The center fielder was bothered by a chest cold, and Leyland spent several minutes finding out if the cold had weakened Van Slyke in any way. Leyland then headed back to the infield, where he picked up a fungo bat and hit some grounders to rookie infielder Carlos Garcia.

Later, Leyland sat with trainer Kent Biggerstaff, who updated him mainly on Tomlin's sprained ankle.

By the time Montreal started hitting around 6:10, Leyland was headed to the clubhouse. A few straggling reporters remained, but the clubhouse was cleared of outsiders shortly before 6:45.

Miller had earlier met with the catchers and pitchers to go over the several Expos who were new to the club since the Pirates had last faced Montreal in late June. Donnelly had similarly gone over defensive positioning with the infielders and outfielders. The coaches and Leyland maintained such information, which was supplemented by Pirates special assignment scouts Lenny Yoachim and Ken Parker, who had done advance scouting on the Expos.

Now, in the minutes before Walk would go to the bull pen to warm up, Leyland, along with Slaught, LaValliere, and Miller, reviewed the Expos' batting order.

The lineup was as follows:

- Leading off was center fielder Marquis Grissom, the league's leading base stealer and one of the most talented players in baseball.

- Bret Barberie, who was replacing injured second baseman De-lino DeShields, was batting second.
- Left fielder Ivan Calderon, recently back from the disabled list, batted third.
- Batting fourth was Larry Walker, Montreal's best all-around player and one of the best players in the league.
- Rookie first baseman Gregg Colbrunn was batting fifth.
- Batting sixth was veteran third baseman Tim Wallach.
- Batting seventh was left-hand-hitting catcher Darrin Fletcher.
- Shortstop Spike Owen, having the best season of his career, was batting eighth, with Nabholz batting ninth.

Keeping Grissom contained was obviously one of the keys. But Grissom had also blossomed into a power threat, and there were warnings to Walk about not leaving any fastballs up and over the plate or Grissom was capable of driving them with power.

The book on Owen had always been to get him out with off-speed stuff. He had been hitting those pitches better in recent weeks, a main reason for his hot streak. But there was agreement that he primarily remained a fastball hitter.

Calderon, according to the reports, was not 100 percent and his injured wrist appeared to limit his ability to drive the ball for power. But left unsaid was how Calderon was a solid clutch hitter in RBI situations, with the discipline to work deep counts.

Less was said about the younger hitters like Colbrunn and Fletcher, and the review session was actually quite brief. The main reason was Walk, an unflappable veteran who had long ago learned that while there were certain things to remember about individual hitters, he ultimately had to pitch to whatever was his own strength on a given night.

Walk had always been one of Leyland's favorite players, one of the few remaining Pirates who went back with Leyland to the early days when Pittsburgh was the worst team in the NL. Since Walk returned from the disabled list, he had been used both as a starter and reliever. Leyland felt confident about using Walk as a utility pitcher, not only because of Walk's experience but because he knew the pitcher would never complain and would give complete effort to whatever job he was asked to do.

"He's one of the special guys," Leyland acknowledged earlier. "He's a guy who truly cares about only one thing, helping the team win. You say to Bobby Walk, 'You're going to be the long man.' He says, 'Okay.' You say, 'Hey you're my closer.' 'Okay.' You say, 'I'm going to start you again.' 'Okay.' Where do you find guys like that anymore?

"His own numbers naturally can suffer because of how I use him, but I've never heard him complain. Most guys'd be in my office. 'Why aren't I starting?' Not Bob Walk. If he comes into my office, it's to bum a cigarette. People always try to get rid of him for us, but he always comes back to help us win.

"And no matter how he's going, I always feel good about Walky starting a big game for me."

So although Walk was not Pittsburgh's best pitcher, he was someone whom neither Leyland nor Miller had to worry about being rattled by the importance of the game. "He might not win, but you know that he's not going to go out there and beat himself by getting nervous," said Miller. "Heck, he started the first game of a World Series in what was the sixth or seventh appearance of his career (in 1980 with Philadelphia). Walky doesn't scare."

With the first pitch of the game scheduled for 7:35, Walk headed to the bull pen with Miller at 7:15. Several other Pirates were already in the dugout watching the upper deck to gauge what kind of crowd would attend the game. The Pittsburgh attendance was a frequent topic of conversation for Pirates veterans; on this night, LaValliere and Van Slyke looked out to the outfield bleachers and were pleased to see the seats filling, indicating a big crowd that would be announced later that evening as being 37,436.

Having won games the previous two days after he had taken the lineup himself to the umpires at home plate, Leyland bowed to the demands of superstition and walked out this evening as well to exchange lineups. Whenever the Pirates lost, someone different would carry out the lineup card before the next game.

Most managers were similarly superstitious, even LaRussa, who was widely perceived as being the ultimate in modern cerebral baseball. When the A's lost a couple of games, LaRussa would make sure he found someone other than himself to tape that night's lineup to the wall. One night in Cleveland last year, after the A's had lost to the Indians the previous two evenings, LaRussa held the lineup in his hand for nearly a half hour until he could find Oakland's veteran equipment manager Frank Ciensczyk, to whom the lineup card was handed for posting. The A's won that night, which meant Ciensczyk would put up the lineup until Oakland lost again.

A month later in Kansas City, Oakland lost two in a row to the Royals. A visitor half kiddingly reminded LaRussa that maybe Ciensczyk could break the losing streak. LaRussa brightened up and responded, "Hey, that's a heck of a memory you have, I'd forgotten that. If we win tonight, that reminder is worth a dinner." LaRussa wasn't completely kidding.

Earl Weaver had countless similiar superstitions. He would use the same pen to write up his lineup card until the Orioles lost a game, whereupon the pen would be thrown away. He would play a game called home run derby with one of the traveling writers in which he and the writer would each pick three Orioles they thought might hit a home run that night. The writer and Weaver would get a dollar for each correct guess, and if the Orioles won the game that particular night, the writer would have to play home run derby the next night and so on until the Orioles lost.

While money never changed hands and the exercise was strictly for amusement purposes, Weaver's home run derby was serious business. One night in Anaheim, against all logic, he picked his light-hitting outfielder Larry Harlow to hit a home run. The selection was derisively received by the writer, who picked the usual suspects like Eddie Murray, Doug DeCinces, and Ken Singleton.

The press box in Anaheim is situated in such a way that you can see directly into the visiting dugout. So when Harlow proceeded to homer in the fifth inning, Weaver leaped to the top step of the dugout, starting waving his arms until he was noticed by his home run derby foe, and when eye contact was made, Weaver thumbed his nose at the writer.

Ray Miller, who was Weaver's pitching coach for many years, learned his superstitions well. Whenever he returns to the dugout after after a visit to the mound, he always pauses right before the baseline, bangs his fists together, steps over the line, and then trots the rest of the way to the dugout. And Miller will have the next day's pitcher (on this evening it was Jackson) who charts the game's pitches use the same pen until the Pirates lose a game.

Nobody really believes such rituals actually influence games, just as nobody believes that a player who makes sure his T-shirt is not washed during a batting streak actually gets extra hits because of such a phobia. But on the other hand, on those occasions when Weaver would misplace a pen that was on a winning streak, clubhouse boys and coaches would tear apart lockers in an attempt to find the hot pen.

The lineups were exchanged and the national anthem was played. ESPN cued the umpires, and Walk got ready to throw the first pitch.

Leyland as usual sat at the far right end of the Pirates dugout if you were looking in from the field. To his right, as usual, was Bill Virdon. To his left, sitting on a stool a few feet closer to the field from the bench, was Miller.

Leyland and Miller often go through a series of signals from the bench. Sometimes they're calling pitches for whoever is catching. Sometimes, with a runner on base, they signal for pitchouts, throws to first, or for the pitcher to step off the rubber. At other times, they're signaling nothing but rather are simply decoying the opposition.

But right away in the top of the first, Leyland and Miller were signaling in earnest after Grissom led off the game with a bloop single to center.

Walk, with each move called from the bench via Slaught, tried to keep Grissom close to first. In the course of pitching to Barberie, Walk threw to first five times. He also stepped off the rubber three times. But on a 2–2 pitch, Grissom stole second for his 71st stolen base of the year.

The pitch meanwhile was called a ball, a close call by home-plate umpire Steve Rippley that had Miller and others on the Pirates' bench yelping. The noise from the Pirates' dugout was pretty minor, and faded after Barberie flew out to Van Slyke on the next pitch for the first out. However, Walk allowed Grissom to get too much of a lead off second, and with Calderon batting, Grissom stole third.

Walk pitched to Calderon carefully, finally walking him to bring up the dangerous Walker. Too early into the game for a cigarette, Leyland chewed his fingernails as Donnelly got up to move McClendon slightly more toward the right-field line. There was little for Leyland to do. Walk wasn't being hit hard. No bull-pen action was warranted. Neither was a visit to the mound. However, Leyland signaled Slaught to stay alert to Calderon at first. It wasn't likely that Calderon would run; by staying at first and being held by Redus, he would keep a hole on the right side of the infield for Walker to pull a ball through for a hit. And should Calderon steal second, there was the possibility that Leyland could intentionally walk Walker with first base open, thus taking the bat out of the hands of the Expos' best hitter.

Nevertheless, Slaught went to the mound and the Pirates infielders joined him, making sure they knew whether Slaught would throw through to second or hold the ball to prevent Grissom from trying to steal home. Bell and Lind made sure they knew who would cover second.

But the big task was Walker, and Walk pitched him well, getting the Expos' outfielder off balance with a change-up and inducing Walker to hit a pop to shallow center. With the big crowd loudly yelling, Van Slyke came in on the ball while Bell retreated into the outfield. It should have been Van Slyke's ball to catch; his momentum was coming toward the plate and he had an excellent arm, a combination of factors that would have either kept Grissom at third or allowed Van Slyke a good chance to throw him out at home if Grissom tagged up and tried to score. However, Bell wouldn't peel out of Van Slyke's way. And when the Pirates' shortstop made the catch, Grissom didn't hesitate; he tagged up and scored just ahead of the throw from Bell, who had to regain his balance after making the catch.

It was the kind of fundamental mistake that the Pirates rarely make. But Leyland was more irritated by what happened moments later, when Walk hung a curve to Colbrunn who pulled it into the left-field corner for a double that scored Calderon and gave Montreal a 2–0 lead.

Miller, sensing Leyland's irritation, had a brief word with Walk as the pitcher reached the dugout after retiring Wallach for the third out. As for Bell, Leyland said nothing. He assumed the shortstop knew he had made a mistake. And with Bell batting in the inning, Leyland was careful not to disrupt his concentration for the at bat ahead.

As was their style all year, the Pirates came right back against Nabholz, never giving the young left-hander a chance to settle into the game despite the quick 2–0 lead. Redus led off by doubling to left. Leyland went through a series of signs to Donnelly, but the only possible play was a Bell sacrifice, and being two runs down, Leyland didn't even consider such a move. So all the signs were decoys.

Bell came through with a single and Donnelly held Redus at third. Redus had not gotten a good jump on Bell's hit. And because there were no outs, because the ball reached Walker quickly, and because Walker has one of the best arms in baseball, Donnelly quickly determined that Redus had no chance of scoring.

Van Slyke was next. Using his new compact swing against the left-hander like he had all season, Van Slyke slapped a single to left that scored Redus, with Bell stopping at second when the throw from Calderon came quickly to third.

In such an inning, everything is on autopilot in the dugout. There were no outs, two men on, and Bonds at the plate. It was time for the Pirates to wait and watch their cleanup hitter, who had a chance to at least tie the game and put young Nabholz on the ropes.

Bonds delivered as he did throughout the stretch run, drilling a single to center. But for the second time in the inning, Bell committed a rare mental error. Grissom had charged the ball quickly and with no outs, Donnelly determined that sending Bell home was hardly worth the gamble. He'd have the bases loaded, no outs, and the hot-hitting King coming up. The Expos' bull pen hadn't started warming anyone up, so Nabholz would have to pitch to King and at least McClendon as well.

So Donnelly came a third of a way down the third baseline and held up both hands as a stop sign for Bell. However, Bell disregarded it and charged around third and on to home. Grissom's throw beat him by ten feet and Bell could only run into Fletcher in hopes of dislodging the ball. However, the Expos' catcher held on to the ball and Montreal had a very big first out.

Leyland did not say a word to Bell as he passed him in the dugout. It was rarely Leyland's style to berate players for mistakes during a game; if something needed to be said, it was usually a coach who did it during the game. Leyland would save his rebuke for when he could talk to the player in private. And Bell, who was in the midst of a 20-game hitting streak, was one of those players who knew when he made mistakes, who was never a problem for anyone, who was a reliable presence day in and day out. As Leyland said later, "He knew he screwed up. He was trying to make something happen when it wasn't the right play. I can't undo it by yelling at him. He felt worse than anyone else when it happened, anyway."

However, Bell's second mistake of the inning ended up killing the Pittsburgh rally. Nabholz retired King on a fly to semideep right that would have easily scored Bell from third had he stopped there. And McClendon grounded out to Owen at short to end the inning.

Donnelly came back to the dugout, eyed Leyland, and shrugged. Leyland muttered, "Damn it" under his breath and then reached for the first of what would be many cigarettes.

The mood wasn't helped in the top of the second. Walk threw a 3–2 fastball over the inner half of the plate, and Fletcher yanked it over the right-field fence for only his second home run of the season. Leyland hardly changed expression, but Miller briefly lowered his head and said, "Darrin bleeping Fletcher."

Walk was meanwhile disgustedly throwing dirt on the mound. Miller eyed him, but neither he nor Leyland felt a trip to calm Walk down was necessary. And Walk settled down to retire the next three Montreal hitters to end the second with the Expos holding a 3–1 lead.

Walk would go on to retire the Expos in order in both the third and fourth innings. However, Nabholz, given a reprieve by Bell's base-running gaffe, settled down himself.

He set down the Pirates in order in both the second and third. In the fourth, Bonds led off by reaching first on a third-strike wild pitch. Leyland signaled that Bonds, as usual, was free to steal when and if he saw the chance. But Bonds never had time to measure Nabholz because King grounded the first pitch to shortstop Owen, who started a 6–4–3 double play.

But Leyland didn't second-guess himself for not giving a take sign to King, allowing Bonds a pitch to steal. King had been swinging a hot bat and especially with a left-hander pitching, Leyland wasn't going to curtail King's aggressiveness, since the third baseman could tie the game with one swing of the bat.

Nabholz finished out the inning easily and then Montreal padded its lead in the fifth. With two outs, Grissom ripped a gapper to right center and only Van Slyke's quick retrieval and throw back to the infield prevented an inside-the-park home run as the fleet Grissom eased into third with a triple. When Walk then walked Barberie on four straight pitches, Leyland quickly said to Miller, "Get Mason and Patterson going." Miller grabbed the phone, which had a direct line to the bull pen. Collins answered and Miller merely said, "Mason and Patterson."

The two relievers started loosening up immediately as Walk continued to labor. Calderon lined a single to left, scoring Grissom, and the big Pittsburgh crowd started to rumble for Walk's removal. But Lind prevented further damage by ranging far to his left to grab Walker's grounder and throw out the Expos' outfielder for the final out of the inning.

Leyland was then faced with a decision. His bottom third of the lineup was due up, Walk batting third in the bottom of the fifth. Leyland did not want to go to his bull pen this early, but the Pirates were now three runs down. If either Slaught or Lind got on base, Walk would have to be lifted for a pinch hitter. So Leyland told Miller to have Mason and Patterson stay loose just in case.

However, Nabholz easily retired both Slaught and Lind. So with the bases empty, Leyland stayed with Walk and had him hit for himself. He grounded out to give Nabholz 14 straight hitless batters since Bell was thrown out at home in the first inning.

Walk settled down to pitch an easy sixth, and the Pirates finally twitched back to life in the bottom half of the inning. Redus led off with a single. Leyland immediately wanted to go into action, perhaps waiting a pitch and then putting on a hit and run. But Bell singled to left on the second pitch and the Pirates now had runners on first and second.

Van Slyke then reached when Colbrunn booted a grounder and the bases were loaded for Bonds. However, he ripped a one hopper to Barberie, who was able to step on second and throw to first for a double play that scored Redus.

So the inning was short-circuited. But the Pirates got a break when Nabholz hit King with a pitch to put runners on first and third. Expos manager Felipe Alou gave Nabholz a quick hook, bringing on right-handed set-up man Mel Rojas, who was part of a double move, entering the game to bat in the seventh spot replacing catcher Fletcher, and new catcher Tim Laker entering the game and batting ninth.

The so-called double switch was part of managing in the NL and was one of the biggest differences between the two leagues. "You have to be alert to so many more different possible moves in the National League than you do managing in the American League," said the Reds' Piniella, who had previously managed the Yankees. "The double-switch stuff isn't tough, but it is something you always have to look for, because in the NL, you simply have to be ready to make so many moves with your pitchers. It takes getting used to because until you feel comfortable with it, it can be easy to miss something."

The night's first pitching change meanwhile triggered what would become a flood of player moves. When the right-hander Rojas entered the game, Leyland sent up Cole to pinch-hit for McClendon, who was already heading for the dugout when Rojas reached the mound, so sure he was that Leyland would make the obvious move.

Cole, who would remain in the game in right field, failed in the pinch-hit appearance, flying out to center to strand two runners and end the inning with Pirates managing only a run to trail, 4–2.

But Walk wouldn't survive a seventh inning. He had appeared to be easily through when he retired Owen and Laker for two quick outs. Walk hung a slider, and the ubiquitous Grissom blasted a home run over the left-field fence to make it 5–2. Barberie followed with a single, and the crowd started booing for Walk's removal.

Leyland had Mason and left-hander Denny Neagle now warming up. But he was hoping to get Walk through the inning. Walk was scheduled to bat third in the bottom of the seventh, and Leyland did not want to waste a pitcher for what could be only one batter. Nor was there anywhere he could logically double switch the pitcher into the game.

However, when Walk walked Calderon to put two runners on and Walker at the plate with a chance to blow the game wide open, Leyland had to make the move. He walked briskly to the mound and said to Walk, "That's it for tonight." Walk handed him the ball and walked off the mound, getting a pat from Leyland as he left. Neagle came on and was basically told that Walker was the guy he was in to get. Neagle did his job, retiring Walker to strand the two runners.

Only a handful of managers come to the mound to remove

pitchers. Most send their pitching coaches for a first visit. Occasional managers will make visits that don't result in removing the pitcher; such visits are either for the purpose of tongue-lashing a pitcher or perhaps calming down a younger one.

But managers' visits don't always go smoothly. Back in 1982, Giants pitcher Jim Barr tossed the ball to Frank Robinson before Robinson reached the mound. As Barr started walking off the mound, Robinson grabbed him by the front of the shirt, spun him around, and started screaming, pointing a finger into Barr's face as television cameras recorded the whole scene.

In some cases, such visits, either from the manager or the pitching coach, result in humorous exchanges. When George Bamberger was Baltimore's pitching coach in the mid-1970s, there was a night when left-hander Ross Grimsley was getting hammered. Grimsley was known around the Orioles for occasionally using a spitter. On this night in Milwaukee, Bamberger strode to the mound and said to Grimsley, "Ross, I know that sometimes you have thought of trying to cheat out here. Well in case you're wondering, if you're ever going to cheat, now would be a good time because you ain't throwing shit out here tonight."

Some managers visit the mound undecided on a pitching move and ask pitchers how they feel. And there are some visits when the manager or coach might try to loosen up the pitcher with idle chatter or perhaps try to pump him up with some inspiration. And many visits are made simply to impart advice on how to pitch to a specific batter.

But the majority of trips are matter-of-fact visits like Leyland's in the seventh inning. It was as obvious to the veteran Walk as it was to Leyland and the stadium crowd that Walk was done for the night.

The crowd came back into the game in the bottom of the seventh when Slaught opened the inning against Rojas with a shot into the left-field corner. Moises Alou, who had pinch-run for Calderon in the top of the inning and then remained in the game to play left, allowed the carom to skip past him and roll several feet toward left center. That allowed Slaught to reach third with a leadoff triple, just ahead of a brilliant throw by Alou.

Leyland now started making moves with his bench. He called Lind back from the on-deck circle. "Chico, I'm going to hit for you," Leyland told him. Leyland then called, "Come on, Varsh, let's go," sending up left-handed hitter Gary Varsho to pinch-hit.

Varsho was another of Leyland's favorites, a fringe player who had gotten some big hits over the last three years, who never complained about playing time, and who was the butt of constant good-natured kidding from Leyland. Leyland would pass Varsho in the clubhouse or perhaps on the bench and say, "Varsh, you better hide because Teddy [Simmons] is headed down here. If he sees you, you're gone. He doesn't know you're here so lay low." It was something of a running joke.

But there was no banter in the bottom of the seventh. Varsho was up in a key situation and his main mission was to put the ball in play. Montreal was playing the infield back: with a three-run lead, Alou was willing to concede Pittsburgh the run in exchange for an out to avoid a big inning. But after yanking a deep shot just foul down the right-field line, Varsho struck out.

Leyland then had Neagle come back from the on-deck circle and called on Cecil Espy to pinch-hit. But the hard-throwing Rojas blew Espy away on strikes and Slaught remained at third.

Leyland then made his third straight pinch-hit move, calling back Redus and sending up Merced to pinch-hit. Rojas walked Merced. Bell followed with another walk to load the bases for Van Slyke.

However, Alou didn't stand pat. He went quickly to the mound to remove Rojas and replace him with left-hander Jeff Fassero, whose mission was to retire the left-handed hitter Van Slyke. Fassero won the confrontation, inducing Van Slyke to ground to first where Tom Foley had replaced the rookie Colbrunn for defensive purposes.

So the Pirates had left the bases loaded and had stranded five runners in the last two innings, something they had not been doing with much regularity. "It's one of those nights, one of those nights," Leyland muttered to Virdon before taking his lineup card to home plate and outlining all the various changes to Rippley after the inning's moves. Merced stayed in the game to play first, still batting in the leadoff spot where he had batted for Redus. Roger Mason, who had warmed up three times now, would pitch the eighth while being inserted in the eighth spot in the batting order vacated when Lind was removed for pinch-hitter Varsho. John Wehner entered the game as third baseman and was batting in the ninth spot. Jeff King was moved from third base to second, replacing Lind.

Every major-league dugout has a large lineup card taped to the wall. The bench coach keeps track of who's been used by both teams, scratching off pinch hitters who have appeared and inserting new names in the lineup on the field. But the manager also has a lineup card. Leyland is constantly looking at it to check whom the opponents might have available for a pinch-hit move in the coming innings or what the opposing lineup looks like an inning away so that he can plot his bull-pen moves.

Such strategy becomes a little easier in September because of the extra complement of personnel. Where Leyland placed Mason and Wehner was illustrative, since he intended to lift both for pinch-hitters whenever their turn in the order arrived. If this had been prior to September 1, Leyland would have likely juggled things differently. With the normal level of player strength, Leyland would not have had the luxury of hitting for both immediately in the next inning. But with the bench loaded with September call-ups, Leyland didn't have to worry about where to put Mason and Wehner in the lineup.

Mason got through the eighth without damage, the only blemish being a gapper by Fassero, who stumbled rounding second, sprained an ankle, and got tagged out. The freak injury forced Alou to bring on his closer John Wetteland to open the eighth, an inning earlier than he would have preferred. Alou had hoped that Fassero could get through the eighth, then Wetteland would come on in the ninth. However, in a game of this magnitude, Alou was not going to risk bringing in anyone else, so when

Fassero couldn't continue, Wetteland was brought on to get the last six outs.

Bonds greeted him with a double off the right center-field fence that missed being a home run by a foot. King struck out but Cole singled, Bonds stopping at third on the hit to left. Slaught followed with a double that scored Bonds and sent Cole to third. So the Pirates were two runs down with runners at second and third.

Leyland whistled for Slaught to come back to the dugout and sent rookie call-up William Pennyfeather to pinch-run for him. He represented the tying run, and with the Expos' three outfielders Alou, Grissom, and Walker all possessing excellent throwing arms, Leyland wanted the extra speed on the bases that Pennyfeather could provide.

He also needed another pinch hitter since it was Mason's turn at bat. Leyland had been looking at his lineup card in between hitters for several moments and decided on Dave Clark. The simple reason was that Clark was a power threat and also possessed some experience. Clark had hit a big three-run homer in a rare start several weeks ago during an earlier call-up, so Leyland was hoping here for a big fly.

Instead Clark got ahead in the count 3–0 and looked to Donnelly for a sign. Leyland flashed a take sign. With someone with more experience, Leyland might have given the go-ahead for the batter to swing on the 3–0 pitch, but with a less established player like Clark up, Leyland wanted the pitch taken. Less experienced players when given the okay to swing on 3–0 often take that message as meaning they *have* to swing at the pitch. That often results in swinging at a pitch they have little chance of putting into play.

So Leyland put the take on for one pitch and it was ball four, sending Clark to first and loading the bases with Wehner scheduled to hit next.

There was no question in Leyland's mind that he would hit for Wehner with a left-handed hitter. His remaining choices were either LaValliere or rookie Al Martin. LaValliere was obviously the most experienced and also the more likely to at least get a fly ball to bring in a run. However, LaValliere was also the slowest Pirates runner and thus a threat to ground into an inning-ending double play. Merced was on deck and even if the hitter in Wehner's spot failed, Leyland wanted to at least preserve Merced's chance to hit against Wetteland with men on base.

All this was thought through in the 30 seconds or so that Leyland had to make his decision. He went with the rookie Martin, who the Pirates thought had excellent potential but who had struck out in his only two appearances to that point. Alas, Martin kept his record intact by fanning against Wetteland.

Leyland sat back, pulling his cap briefly over his eyes. Puffing cigarette after cigarette, he was already second-guessing himself as Merced came to the plate and grounded out to end the inning and leave the bases loaded for the second straight time.

The Pirates in the sixth, seventh, and eighth innings had sent a whopping 18 batters to the plate but managed only two runs. And when Merced grounded out, there was the palpable feel of a game that had been settled.

Montreal added a run in the ninth off Stan Belinda, the Pirates went out 1–2–3 in the bottom of the inning, and the Expos had apparently made it a real pennant race with a 6–3 victory that brought them to within three games of first place.

Leyland quickly walked into his office after the game. Little was said by anybody. It was as sloppy a Pirates performance as they had produced in weeks. When the writers descended into Leyland's office, he didn't pull any punches. "That wasn't Pirates baseball we played out there tonight," he said in a monotone. "We didn't get any key hits, we made mistakes in the field and on the bases, we made bad pitches at the wrong times. That's not how we usually play the game."

However, when some writers kept asking him about how resilient and tough the young Expos were, Leyland began to bristle.

"Hey, they've been outstanding, don't get me wrong," said Leyland. "But I'm getting tired of hearing about how outstanding everybody else is. We've been in first place for more than 155 days this season. And we're still in first place after tonight. We didn't accomplish that by being a bunch of damned donkeys."

It took nearly an hour for the last writer to leave. Donnelly had been sitting nearby, as had Virdon for several minutes. When they were finally alone, Leyland quietly began second-guessing himself. He had made dozens of decisions over the course of the game, but there was one he kept chewing over. He said, "Damn, maybe I should have used Spanky in the eighth. He never ends up in the game and he might have got a run in that situation. And if we get within a run, who knows what happens."

Said Donnelly, "Well, you got Merced his chance, and if Spanky hits into the double play, you don't get Merced the chance to hit."

"Yeah, I guess I thought maybe the kid would at least get it into play," said Leyland. "But that was a tough one. It's tough to look back and realize that we didn't get Spanky in there for one shot. That's one I'm going to be thinking about for a while."

With the victory, the Expos had closed to within three games and had their ace Dennis Martinez pitching the next night. The Pirates were hanging by a thread. But they remained confident. Simmons visited Leyland over an hour after the game and was upbeat.

"You know, a lot of the Expos really don't know they're in a race," said Simmons. "And until they catch us, they're not going to find out what kind of club they are.

"I remember when I was with the Brewers during the 1982 season. We led that thing most of the way and Baltimore kept coming and kept coming. Then we finished the season there and they won the first three games to catch us for the first time. And they came out Sunday a completely different team. For all those weeks they had nothing to lose but now they suddenly did and we just smoked them."

However, Montreal wouldn't fade away just yet. On the next night in Pittsburgh, the Expos and Pirates played a 13-inning, 4-hour 45-minute epic that eventually pivoted on a series of key plays and key managerial decisions.

Jackson stranded nine Montreal base runners in the first six innings. Along the way was a decision by Leyland to have Jackson intentionally walk Calderon and pitch to the dangerous Walker with the bases loaded and one out. Jackson fanned Walker and escaped the inning to keep the Pirates in the game. However, the Expos took a 2–0 lead against Jackson on Gary Carter's two-run single in the sixth inning. But the remarkable Bonds got a run back in the bottom of the inning by doubling home a run, one of his four hits. And the Pirates then tied the game in the eighth inning on an error by Owen.

The tie was preserved with some great defensive plays by Bonds, Wehner, Jay Bell, and Alex Cole. And the Pirates' bull pen shut Montreal out from the sixth inning on as Mason, Neagle, Belinda, Patterson, and Danny Cox combined for six shutout innings of two-hit pitching.

The Pirates won it in the 13th, largely because of Felipe Alou's fear of Bonds. Cecil Espy, who entered the game as part of a double switch in the ninth inning and was batting in the ninth position, led off the inning with a triple off right-hander Kent Bottenfield.

The routine managerial move is then to walk the bases loaded to set up a force play at the plate and thus choke off the game-winning run. However, Bonds would be the fifth hitter in the inning, and if Alou walked the bases loaded, then Bonds would be certain to hit. So Alou elected to intentionally walk just Alex Cole, a left-handed hitter, and have Bottenfield face the right-handed hitter Jay Bell.

"I walked Cole to save some room for Mr. Bonds," said Alou.

Bell made all the strategy moot by singling to end the game. "I wasn't surprised because if they walked me, then either the next hitter [it would have been pinch-hitter Lloyd McClendon] would have won it or they would have been facing Barry with the bases loaded and one out," said Bell.

Leyland said, "I think most managers would use a strategy that avoids pitching to a cleanup hitter with the bases loaded and less than two outs." Left unsaid, however, was that Leyland brought about that exact situation earlier when Jackson walked Calderon to face Walker with the bases loaded and one out.

Leyland would call the second Montreal game "one of the best I've ever been involved with. We did the next best thing by getting a split. A sweep would have been better, but at least we're the same as we were when we came into the series and we've run two games off the schedule."

The Pirates went on to reel off four wins in a row after that second game with the Expos to pad their lead to seven games when they arrived in Montreal for two games the following week. Leyland would still not concede that Pittsburgh could breathe easy, especially after the opener, when Moises Alou's 14th-inning grand slam beat the Pirates.

Montreal then came out and scored three runs in the first inning of the next game. However, Drabek shut them out the rest of the way on three hits, the Pirates went on to win 9–3, and as they boarded a plane for New York, Leyland could finally relax.

He settled into his seat in the front of the cabin, sipped on a beer, and said to Donnelly, "Richie boy, that was the big one. If we had left there only five up, who knows what could happen? We lose a couple and we're down to the last week. Yeah, that was the big one."

Chapter 12

"That's All I Can Ever Ask of Them"

◆ The Pittsburgh newspaper strike was in its fourth month with no end in sight. So when the Pirates returned home for their last three home games, there were no headlines about clinching a third straight division title.

There were no stories about how the big victory in Montreal had put this team on the threshold of the play-offs. There were no columns (except for the fax editions, which received scant circulation) extolling the virtues of a Pirates club of whom even its own executives were skeptical at the beginning of the season. Indeed, Simmons was privately admitting that "after the Smiley trade, I didn't think we'd have a chance of winning."

But the Pirates' drive to another NL East title wasn't the only story available only via TV and radio newscasts. The presidential campaign and Pennsylvania's big U.S. Senate contest went by without local newspapers to cover them. There were also no stories about the surprisingly unbeaten Steelers or the opening of another season of high-school football. Indeed, in normal times those stories would have likely been given top billing over the Pirates.

As always, the Pirates had to battle for local fan support. With the Pirates' magic number at three, they opened a weekend series September 25 against the Mets. But only 22,000 showed up at Three Rivers Stadium for a game that was going head-to-head with all the Friday night high-school football games in the area, games that are nearly a religious experience for their fanatical local followings. Even Donnelly was distracted by prep football miles away. Aside from the Pirates, the teams he follows the closest are the teams of his hometown Steubenville (Ohio) High School. "We're not loaded this year, so we might only go something like 8–2," said Donnelly.

The split in Montreal had drained the last remaining uncertainty from the pennant race. The only real challenge left for the Pirates was to clinch the division at home on what was their final weekend at Three Rivers Stadium, a week before the end of the regular season.

Leyland remained publicly superstitious prior to Friday night's game, even though he had a seven-game lead with nine games left to play. He deflected various questions about how the Pirates would match up against Atlanta. There was speculation about his right-hand-hitting platoon lineup having to play most of the League Championship Series because Atlanta had only one right-handed starting pitcher, John Smoltz. Van Slyke's improvement had helped make the Pirates less vulnerable to left-handed pitching, but in two of their three platoon positions (right field and first base) the Pirates' left-handed hitters, Alex Cole and Orlando Merced, were over the season statistically stronger than the right-handed platoon players, Lloyd McClendon and Gary Redus. Only the right-hand hitting catcher Don Slaught had better numbers during the season than his left-hand hitting alternate, Mike LaValliere.

However, Leyland wasn't anxious to discuss all that just yet. "We'll be all right. We have a lot of key guys, not just the guys who platoon," said Leyland. "Let's not worry about all that until it's time."

Leyland then scoffed at questions concerning the experience

factor in the play-offs. "All that's overrated," he said. "We have some experience, but we also have some younger guys in key spots too. Hell, Atlanta went to the World Series last year and most of their guys hadn't been there before. That experience stuff doesn't mean much.

"And I don't really want to talk about it much anyway. We're not there yet and neither is Atlanta. We could lose five in a row and all of a sudden this is a real race."

However, behind the scenes, the Pirates were getting ready for the play-offs. Their main concern was deciding upon a play-off roster.

Because the decisions can be complex, involving factors ranging from the strategic advantage of carrying an extra position player instead of a pitcher to the psychological decisions about keeping a struggling veteran instead of a promising but inexperienced youngster, setting the rosters is usually the subject of several meetings between GMs and the on-field managerial and coaching staff.

But in the Pirates' case in 1992, the decision would entirely be Leyland's, which became apparent when he stopped by Simmons's office earlier Friday afternoon. Leyland told Simmons he was going to bring in his coaches and talk about the play-off roster, and he asked Simmons what time would be good for him so he could join them.

Simmons stopped Leyland right there. "Whatever the roster is going to be for the play-offs is up to you and the coaches," said Simmons. "I have no input to give on that at all. What am I going to tell you about your own players that you don't know already?

"If I learned anything this year it's that I'll never question any managerial decision you make. So you guys figure out which way you want to go and get to me when it's all decided."

When Leyland brought in his coaches for the meeting, he briefly related the conversation with Simmons and said, "That really makes me feel good that he feels that way. We've come a long way together this year and I feel good about him.

"Now, let's get down to this. Mundo, I guess most of this depends on Zane."

Indeed, the one uncertainty concerning the Pirates' postseason roster revolved around the pitching staff and whether to carry 10 or 11 pitchers. If they carried 11, a position player (either John Wehner or Carlos Garcia, who had been recalled prior to September 1 to make him play-off eligible) would have to be dropped. If ten pitchers were carried, then one of them had to be dropped, with the candidates being Danny Cox, Bob Walk, or Zane Smith.

Walk appeared certain to stick. He had to leave his last start the previous Monday after two innings when he felt a twinge in his right groin, and his long history of groin problems made this a matter of concern. But he was apparently all right; he had thrown before Thursday's game in Montreal and had no discomfort. So Leyland scheduled him to start Saturday night against the Mets. If he had no problem then, Walk would be deemed ready for the postseason.

However, a bigger question mark in all this was Smith. He was healthy enough to pitch, but there was still some uneasiness about his strength. As Miller pointed out, if he were to be on the postseason roster, he would likely be used only in relief. And Miller didn't think Smith was strong enough to help in the postseason. "I don't think he's throwing well enough for us to use him," said Miller. "And I'd worry about warming him up a couple of times in the bull pen. You'd probably be in the position of having to use him any time you warmed him up or losing him for that game."

On the other hand, keeping Smith would give the Pirates a deep bull pen. The pitchers likely to start games were Drabek, Wakefield, and either Jackson or Walk. That would leave Smith, Randy Tomlin, Denny Neagle, and Bob Patterson as left-handers in relief, with Cox, Roger Mason, and Stan Belinda as right-handers. Leyland would have the luxury of left–righting to his heart's content.

However, their confidence in a lot of those relievers was waning, and if Smith were kept, Leyland would be reluctant to use

him as well. Plus, both Jackson and Walk would also be available
for relief duty since Leyland intended to have Drabek start three
games in the play-offs and Wakefield two. And in those games,
Leyland would almost certainly stay with his starting pitcher as
long as possible.

So even if Smith was 100 percent, 11 pitchers were an un-
necessary luxury. And with Smith iffy physically, the decision
became fairly easy. "We'll sit down Zane—it just doesn't make
sense to add him at someone else's expense," said Leyland.
"That's the way we'll go. I'll call Teddy."

The Pirates later that night cut the magic number to two with
a 3–2 victory over the Mets, Cox getting his third save in pre-
serving Tomlin's 14th victory.

The next afternoon, before a CBS national audience, the
Pirates humiliated New York with a brutal 19–2 rout in which
Bonds hit his 32nd homer and Walk passed his own test with six
easy innings. Montreal won for a second straight day, so the magic
number was down to one.

And so, for the third straight year, the Pirates arrived at a
ballpark on a Sunday morning needing a win to clinch a division
title.

In 1990, the Sunday had been in St. Louis when Drabek
pitched a complete-game shutout to nail down the clincher and
touch off an emotional postgame celebration in which the players
went bonkers. The proceedings were punctuated by a group of
Pirates led by Sid Bream hauling teammates one by one for a
dunk in the whirlpool bath, the first of them being a weeping
and red-eyed Leyland.

In 1991, the Sunday was in Pittsburgh when it was again
Drabek who went the distance to defeat Philadelphia for the
clincher. This celebration was somewhat less raucous than the
previous year, with the players splashing each other in an oblig-
atory clubhouse romp before many of them retired to the nearby
Clark's Bar, a restaurant partly owned by LaValliere, for a team
party.

On this Sunday in 1992, 31,000 fans arrived at Three Rivers.

That represented slightly more than half capacity, small by many clubs' standards. But for Pittsburgh, it was not altogether a bad crowd considering that the Steelers were playing. More encouraging, the front office sent down word that advance sales indicated that the three play-off games in Pittsburgh would likely be sellouts. Again, such news would not be remarkable in many cities. But Pittsburgh had been embarrassed last October when acres of empty seats were displayed to the nation during games six and seven of the riveting play-off series against Atlanta. And the Pirates were sensitive that their season attendance would represent a drop of nearly 200,000. They could rightly point to the effects of the recession and the newspaper strike as well as terrible weather during the season's first half, but it was still an irritant about which the players would often complain and about which Leyland had his midseason explosion.

Still, no one ever complained about the reaction of the fans who did come out to the ballpark. And with the Pirates holding a 4–1 lead on that final Sunday, the crowd was on its feet shrieking as the Mets came to bat in the top of the ninth.

Belinda, who had been so shaky for much of the season's second half, was on to save the game for Jackson, who had pitched seven solid innings. Despite allowing a run in the ninth, Belinda finished up. The final out settled into Van Slyke's glove, and the Pirates ran out of the dugout to celebrate another division title.

For a while, it was a typical scene. Leyland and his coaches embraced among themselves for several moments. "We all have the most in common, especially because Jimmy makes us part of every decision," said Miller. "And this was a season in which we all had to grind it out. So it was sort of natural that we looked for each other to congratulate first."

The players were meanwhile hugging together near the pitchers' mound, where they had converged following the final out. The coaches then worked their way out to shake hands and hug players as well. Several players were meanwhile saluting fans or looking for family members in the stands.

But as the celebration inched toward the dugout, something very unusual for professional sports unfolded. Bonds and Lloyd McClendon spotted Leyland and they grabbed the manager, raised him on their shoulders, and carried him off the field.

Now, you see such sights all the time in high school when coaches are the center of their teams' celebrations. And you see it in college after the big wins, especially in football. Occasionally in pro football, coaches are doused by buckets of water or even carried off the field themselves.

But such a moment is rarely if ever seen in baseball. Managers are almost never universally revered by their players. Indeed, this was the same Barry Bonds with whom Leyland had his ugly shouting match a long year and a half ago. Major-league players have become far too cool, far too cynical to do something so high-schoolish as to carry their manager off the field.

But here was Bonds, one of the coolest and most arrogantly confident players in the world, helping to carry Leyland off the field.

"I don't know, I guess I just felt that something should be done to put him in the spotlight," said Bonds later. "I mean, he never takes any credit for anything around here. He always gives all the credit to the players and sometimes we wish he would take some of that credit because he deserves it so much. Leyland is the best manager in baseball, man. But you never hear him talk about himself."

McClendon, a little-used player but always one of Leyland's favorites, was even more emotional when talking about why he helped hoist Leyland to his shoulders.

"It was done out of love and respect for the man," said McClendon, his eyes growing glassy. "Jim Leyland treats us the way we like to be treated and we reciprocate it. He's one of the few people I've ever come across in this game who realizes there are a lot more important things than winning and losing. And that's the friendships that this game can bring, the lifelong commitments to people you work with and get a chance to share some of your dreams."

Leyland, although a bit embarrassed as he rode on Bonds's and McClendon's shoulders, was grinning like a high-school senior as he was taken off the field.

The clubhouse itself was fairly subdued. "This is a heck of an accomplishment, we're all very proud, but I think we all feel like this is just a first step," said Van Slyke. "I mean, we've been here before and now we want to go to the World Series. It's like we've been a team on a mission all year and it's not over yet. That's why you're not seeing us jumping all over the place."

Leyland made his way to his office. With several TV cameras in place, he began talking about what this division title meant to him when his voice started cracking and he had to stop several times to compose himself.

"You know, back in spring training, a lot of people were laughing at us," he said, his eyes welling up with tears. "A lot of people were laughing at the Pirates' organization. And a lot of people were feeling sorry for the Pirates' organization.

"But here we are and I think this title, more than any of the others, means more to this entire organization. It's a credit to the front office and the scouts and the minor-league people and all my coaches. . . . These people work so damn hard . . . we were never given any chance . . . and here we are. It's just a credit to the Pittsburgh Pirates' organization and I mean that from the bottom of my heart.

"It's just been great, man, the whole thing. The whole grind of the whole season. You start in spring training on day one with the pitchers covering first and all the snowbirds watching us at Pirates City. Back in '86, I remember what it was like. We were lucky if our own grounds crew would watch us practice.

"We went through so much, but these guys kept going. They never gave less than all they had. I never once told them they had to win. That's not saying that you don't care what happens. But I never told them once they had to win this one. That puts pressure on the players they don't need. I tried to tell them in any way I could to have fun, to enjoy the game. Hell, that's what you're supposed to do, that's why the game was created, wasn't it?

"Sure, there's a lot at stake here. But I just want my players to relax and go out and play the game like professionals. And damn it, that's one thing I know for sure we did all season. My team went out and conducted itself like professionals. And as a manager, no matter where we might have finished, that's all I can ever ask of them."

Leyland was asked about his own role. As if to prove Bonds right, Leyland quickly downplayed his contribution.

He laughed at the question and said, "Hey, I didn't do anything to help the team win on the field—no manager does. But I can do things that sometimes help the team to lose. That's the way managing is. A manager can lose a game with what he does a lot easier than he can win one with what he does. Then why am I paid all that money? Hey, I don't get paid all that much, not what people say I get paid, that's for sure."

Weeks after the season, Leyland would be voted NL manager of the year in a landslide. Early in the season, the Pirates had certainly been helped by the mediocrity of the rest of their division. And yet Pittsburgh would win 96 games, and from July 31 until the clinching on September 27, they went 41–15 when it mattered most and when they were challenged most seriously by Montreal.

Elsewhere, the various division races all came to expected conclusions.

In Oakland, the Athletics clinched the day after Pittsburgh on what was an off day for them. LaRussa had gathered his coaches and several players at an Oakland restaurant to await the results of the Minnesota game, and when the Twins were defeated, the champagne flowed.

LaRussa had weathered a season every bit as demanding as his friend Leyland's. Both would acknowledge weeks later, after they had won their respective leagues' manager-of-the-year awards, that they had likely done their best job in the 1992 season.

As LaRussa said after clinching the AL West, "We never had our whole team together all year, and that meant that we had to turn to guys who we weren't always sure about. It was the toughest way to win we've ever had to go through here, but in a lot of ways it was the most satisfying."

Atlanta meanwhile rolled to its second straight NL West title under Bobby Cox, taking advantage of Cincinnati's constant injury problems and several key Reds losses at times when they looked like they'd make a run. Meanwhile, Cito Gaston won Toronto's expected division title in the AL East, holding off the surprising Milwaukee Brewers, who took the race down to the season's final weekend.

Like the Pirates, neither the Braves nor Blue Jays were going to be satisfied with just a division title. The Braves had played all season with the expectation of taking things one step further than their heartbreaking seven-game World Series defeat in 1991. And for the Blue Jays, nothing short of being in the World Series would be considered successful.

So there were very heavy expectations on the shoulders in Atlanta and particularly in Toronto where poor Gaston, a winner of two straight division titles, was hearing rumblings that he would be fired if the Blue Jays did anything less than win the World Series.

There were no such expectation games being played in Pittsburgh. Yet the Pirates players firmly believed that though this may well have been the least talented of their three straight division champions, this would be their year to go to the World Series.

They hadn't missed by much in the previous two seasons. In 1990, with the Reds leading the NL Championship Series three games to two, a sixth-game, ninth-inning blast by Carmelo Martinez was caught a foot below the top of the right-field fence, just short of what would have been a game-winning home run that would have sent the series to a seventh game.

In 1991, the Pirates arrived back in Pittsburgh with a three games to two lead only to be shut out in back-to-back games to lose to Atlanta.

Now they were back in the play-offs with a team that would likely be significantly broken up after the season. Bonds would surely leave as a free agent, and so probably would Drabek. With club officials maintaining that the franchise would lose anywhere between $5 and $10 million, speculation was already simmering over what other veteran salaries would be unloaded, with the candidates including Jose Lind, Mike LaValliere, much of the bench, and even the recently acquired Danny Jackson.

And that sense of this being a last hurrah and of the Pirates having their share of unfinished business combined to create the unusually low-key title celebration that Sunday in Pittsburgh. Plus, the Pirates had to get ready for a flight to Chicago where they would play three games, have an off day, and then finish the regular season with a weekend series in New York.

Before the flight took off, it was announced that the team ban on liquor was lifted in celebration of the division title. Few players partook, however, as most either slept, played cards, or exercised their Nintendo Game Boys.

Upon arriving at the hotel in Chicago, Leyland was greeted with several messages of congratulations from an assortment of people including Carl Barger, Gene Lamont, and some former Pirates players including pitcher Neal Heaton.

The final week played out uneventfully. Leyland gave the managerial reins that Monday afternoon to coach Terry Collins; it was his game to manage as he wanted, save for pitching moves since the Pirates were trying to limit innings for some of their pitchers and set the rotation for the play-offs. Collins managed the Bucs to a 10–3 victory and Leyland and the other coaches gave him hugs and handshakes after the game with mock enthusiasm.

The Pirates flew to New York immediately following the Wednesday afternoon game in Chicago. On Thursday, Leyland treated the coaches to a trip to Atlantic City.

On Friday night before the first game of the final weekend, Leyland got a surprise. He was sitting in the visiting manager's office when a ruddy-faced, burly man approached him. "This guy walked up to me and I didn't know who he was," said Leyland. "He said he was Nelson Doubleday. He wanted to congratulate me. Imagine that, the Mets' owner came all the way down to our clubhouse to congratulate me. That was a real thrill."

The Pirates then played out the final three games in dreary Shea Stadium. Throughout the weekend, Jeff Torborg stayed huddled in his dugout staring at the conclusion of what was a dreadful first season in New York. And as Donnelly said, "They've been the team that everybody has expected to win just about every year. And here we are, the team everybody counted out last spring. It sure is a funny game. That's pretty profound, isn't it?"

Chapter 13

"You Have to Turn the Page and Go On"

◆ By 12:45 A.M., the last member of the media had finally left the near-empty and somber Pirates' clubhouse. Pittsburgh had suffered a 6–4 defeat in the fourth game of the NL Championship Series, leaving the Atlanta Braves with a commanding 3–1 lead in the best-of-seven series.

Leyland had just finished a last interview, and before showering was sitting alone for the first time in hours. He was still dressed in various parts of his uniform, more hollow-eyed than usual and puffing on a cigarette when Barry Bonds appeared at his door.

"Skip, can you talk for a second?" said Bonds quietly.

"Sure, come on in and shut the door," said Leyland.

Bonds was very subdued, displaying a kind of vulnerability and depression he rarely shows to the public. Bonds can be, at times, engaging. He can also be arrogant. At times he will make insightful comments. At other times, he can make insensitive or rash statements that end up in controversy.

But Barry Bonds is rarely discouraged. He has supreme confidence in his own ability to perform, a trait that although at times can be overbearing is also the biggest reason why there has been no better all-around player in the game over the last five seasons.

However, Bonds was obviously distressed when he walked into Leyland's office on this Saturday night, and Leyland could see it right away. For the third straight year, he was having a woeful play-off series. Through the first four play-off games, Bonds had produced nothing. He had no RBI and was in the midst of a record postseason hitless streak with runners in scoring positions.

Many Pirates privately felt that his first at bat of the play-offs set a negative tone for the entire Pittsburgh club that lasted into the third game. During that first at bat days earlier against left-hander Tommy Glavine, Bonds had anxiously swung and missed at three straight pitches, two of which were far out of the strike zone. He then came back to the dugout muttering, "Those pitches broke from my head to my ankles. I got to swing at that shit because they won't pitch to me."

Pirates players, although in awe of Bonds's ability and appreciative of his performance, had long wearied of his complaints that he wasn't pitched to. When they read between the lines of such complaints, they took them as a slap at their own abilities, a suggestion that the rest of the Pirates lineup wasn't good enough for pitchers to take anyone seriously. So when that refrain was heard again in the first inning of the first game of the play-offs, it let down a lot of Pirates who felt this would be the year they would reach the World Series and were counting on Bonds to lead them.

Bonds didn't help the mood when he was later quoted as saying, "I told the guys that they'll have to get me to the World Series and once we get there, I'll carry them the rest of the way." Feelings were further frayed when it was learned and reported by the media that Bonds had gone on a house-hunting expedition in Atlanta, since the Braves were likely to be one of his most ardent off-season pursuers.

But Bonds was not the only reason why the Pirates had lost three of the first four games in the League Championship Series with Atlanta. Indeed, only another brilliant third-game pitching job by the rookie Wakefield prevented the Braves from sweeping the series in four straight.

Leyland had carefully weighed his decision on which game Wakefield would start. He originally had considered starting Wakefield in game two, but that game was in Atlanta and Leyland felt more comfortable having the rookie start his first postseason game at home. Also, the second game was a day game, and both Miller and Leyland felt that it was more difficult to catch the knuckler in the sunlight than at night. So Leyland decided to start Wakefield in the third game, and the rookie came through admirably.

However, Wakefield's performance was one of the only Pittsburgh bright spots through the first four games. Drabek, the Pirates' unquestioned ace, had not pitched well in either game one or four. Danny Jackson and the bull pen were embarrassed in a 13–5 Braves blowout in the second game. Van Slyke wasn't hitting and neither was Jay Bell or Jeff King. And the Pirates had been uncharacteristically sloppy in several fundamental areas.

But the most visible source of disappointment was Bonds. He was worn down by his play-off slump and the unceasing media attention it was receiving. With the Pirates one game away from seeing their season end, Bonds was also consumed by a wave of nostalgia. Game five on Sunday night would almost certainly be the last game Bonds would play in Pittsburgh as a member of the Pirates. And it could also be his final game as a Pirate, period.

Bonds had been close to Bobby Bonilla, but with Bonilla gone, Bonds did not have a lot of close friends in the Pirates' clubhouse. And on this Saturday night, with the end of the season and another awful play-off performance staring him in the face, Bonds had only one place to go—to Leyland's office.

Leyland himself was exhausted. Even the most cooperative managers find the play-offs to be a huge chore because of the enormous off-field demands that often arise. There are usually dozens of requests for tickets from long-lost cousins and casual acquaintances, not to mention the legitimate family, friends, and business associates who want to share the play-offs, so there is a constant barrage of phone calls both at home and at the ballpark and a constant search for tickets.

In addition, many managers as well as players often entertain family or friends at home during play-offs. And so Leyland, like many involved in the postseason, had several out-of-town relatives staying at his house. Sunday would be Patrick's first birthday, and Leyland's mother, many members of Katie's family, and friends like Carl Barger would be over for a party prior to Leyland's leaving for Three Rivers Stadium for game five.

Then there are the media responsibilities. There were well over 200 print and electronic journalists at the 1992 NL Championship Series. Clubhouses are closed prior to postseason games to limit the pregame distraction, but when a manager leaves the clubhouse, he is instantly descended upon by a swarm, all needing pregame stories. The swarm will keep coming in waves, with the interviewers who are inside the circle of humanity gradually leaving and then being replaced by the next group. So unless a manager is able to make his way to the outfield or throws batting practice like Minnesota's Tom Kelly, there is no escape from the constant barrage of repetitive questions.

In addition, CBS network telecasters Sean McDonough and Tim McCarver are granted a pregame session. And both local television stations and national outlets like ESPN and CNN request pregame interviews.

The media responsibilities are even more severe after games. When a postseason game is completed, managers run a gauntlet. If the network has time for a postgame show, the manager is usually required for an interview. The manager is then brought to a press conference at which he conducts a mass interview session with the answers being piped into the press box for those writers on severe deadlines. And after the press conference, there are usually requests for quick stand-up interviews with various television crews for which the manager is brought back to the field.

When the manager finally does get back to his clubhouse, it

is hardly time for a beer, conversation with his coaches, and a relaxing shower. Hundreds of media are waiting back in his office, many of them columnists wanting to obtain their own exclusive answer to their own exclusive (and, of course, penetrating) question. There are radio interviewers in search of a unique sound bite. There are writers from West Coast papers who have more deadline freedom and thus the luxury to sit in a manager's office for an hour to garner tidbits.

Given that most postseason games don't start until 8:30 P.M. eastern time, and given that postseason games rarely are completed in less than three hours, a manager usually doesn't get showered, dressed, and out to the parking lot until 1 A.M.—if he's lucky.

Also factored in are the demands that a manager's organization might create. Most teams have parties and other hospitality planned throughout the playoffs, some for media, some for baseball executives from other teams, and some for local corporate and civic bigfeet, many of them advertisers, season-ticket holders, or corporate box tenants. Most clubs expect their manager to at least show his face at a few of these functions at a point of the season when, as in Leyland's case, the only beings he wants to show his face to are his wife, his son, or a deer that he has in his sights on a hunting trip.

So on that disappointing Saturday night, with his team one game away from extinction, Leyland would have liked nothing more than to go home for a few hours sleep before Patrick got rolling on his first birthday.

However, Bonds was a very important priority. And their uninterrupted conversation ended up lasting nearly two hours. Later, Leyland would characterize it as a "father and son kind of thing. He just wanted to talk."

But there was much more to what was an emotional session. Bonds was also torn by the uncertainty of where he'd be playing in 1993 and all the good memories of having played in Pittsburgh for Leyland. At one point Bonds told Leyland, "Do you think we'll ever be together again after all this is over? Here I could be playing my last game for you tomorrow and I haven't done nothing. I've let you and the team down."

Leyland was moved by all this and he tried to calm down Bonds. As Leyland said later, "I told him that a lot of guys aren't producing, that he can't put everything on his shoulders. This is a guy who's been the best player in baseball for three years. He didn't let us down. And I told him that. I told him to quit thinking about that crap, just loosen up and play like he knows he can.

"Yeah, it all got pretty emotional. But it was all very nice."

Their conversation finally broke up after 2 A.M. Ironically enough, none other than Bobby Bonilla was waiting for Bonds, and the two went out with their wives for a very late snack and more conversation.

Leyland meanwhile got home at around 2:30. He was up with Patrick five hours later, and after the party he was back to the ballpark by 2:30 P.M. Leyland wandered through the clubhouse when he heard Bonds had arrived and saw quickly that Bonds was loose and in good spirits.

So was Leyland. He was bouncing around all afternoon. "Hey, it's Patrick's birthday. This is a big day," he'd say to all comers.

But after the club had returned to the clubhouse following batting practice, he also sent a message in his own way. Leyland walked through the clubhouse with traveling secretary Greg Johnson in tow. And in a loud voice that could be heard in all corners of the quiet clubhouse, Leyland said, "Now listen, Greggie, I want those planes ready when we get to the airport. We'll be on the buses 90 minutes after the last out, so you make sure those planes are ready to go. I don't want to sit on the ground for an hour."

The Pirates would be flying directly to Atlanta if they won Sunday night. And Leyland left no doubt in anyone's mind that that was where he expected to be heading after the game.

For this huge fifth game, Leyland had scheduled Bob Walk to pitch. He did not have many other attractive choices. Jackson was miserable in the second game, and the only other option was Randy Tomlin, who had been up and down all season.

Although Walk was ripped for a Ron Gant grand slam in a game two relief appearance, Leyland wasn't skittish about having Walk pitch such a critical game. There was a sort of symmetry to Walk, one of the last holdovers from the dismal mid-'80s Pirates, being the guy who was the last defense against a play-off elimination and the possible end of a Pirates era. "Hell, all I know about Walky is, he might not win, but he's not going to be scared by the situation and he'll give everything he has," said Leyland.

Walk would be brilliant on this cool Sunday night. But the tone for the game was set in the bottom of the first. Redus led off with a bloop double. Bell singled him home. Van Slyke moved Bell to second with a groundout and up stepped Bonds, who finally delivered with a double to right center for his first RBI of the series. Upon reaching second, with the sellout crowd screaming, he faced out toward center field and said to himself, "It's over, it's over." Leyland remained stoic on the bench. But when King followed with an RBI double that scored Bonds, Leyland was the first off the bench to reach out a fist for Bonds to slap as he returned.

It ended up being a four-run first inning for the Pirates off left-hander Steve Avery. Bonds would later add a single and stolen base while Walk pitched a complete-game three-hitter.

By the time the game ended, Bonds's late-night meeting with Leyland had become news. Leyland downplayed it in the postgame interviews, saying again, "It was a father–son kind of thing that was between us."

Bonds, hardly the sentimental type, wouldn't elaborate on what he discussed with Leyland in the wee hours of the morning. "All I know is that Leyland is the best in the business. You all should know that by now," said Bonds.

The whole Pirates club had seen a difference in Bonds when he first appeared at the ballpark before game five. He was ob-

viously much more relaxed and after he got his first-inning double, at least a half-dozen Pirates players were heard to shout
virtually at once, "Here we go." But there was no change in
Leyland's demeanor. He was upbeat before game five, sending
the constant message to his club that he had never lost confidence
in them. And before game six in Atlanta, he talked with the
media about being confident with Wakefield going that night and
Drabek ready for the seventh game. As he sat with Donnelly and
Virdon a half hour before game time, Leyland's tune didn't
change. "Boys, we're going to win this thing. I really believe
we're going to do it," said Leyland.

As game six unfolded, Bonds had a cathartic effect on the
entire Pirates lineup. He led off the second inning with his first
home run in 62 postseason at bats, and by the time the inning
had ended Pittsburgh had scored eight runs off Tom Glavine.
That was more than enough for Wakefield, as he pitched another
complete-game victory that sent the series to a seventh game.

Even before the seventh game began, the night, as Donnelly
later observed, summed up what the Pirates were all about.

First there was Leyland's lineup. The Pirates' right-hand hitting
platoon players—Lloyd McClendon, Don Slaught, and Gary
Redus—had been one of the main reasons Pittsburgh had come
back to take the series to a seventh game. But right-hander John
Smoltz would be Atlanta's starting pitcher in game seven, and
reporters were asking Leyland if he would deviate from routine
and start some of his hot right-handed hitters even though a right-
handed pitcher was starting.

For Leyland, there was no hesitation. "Hell, Merced, La-
Valliere, and Cole all were reasons why we got here," said Leyland. "You don't wait until the seventh game of the play-offs to
change what you've been doing all year."

Leyland did slightly alter his usual lineup. He moved Merced
into the fifth spot of the order behind Bonds, reasoning that
another left-handed bat there might be helpful. And he didn't

feel bad about LaValliere catching because he had always had an excellent rapport with Doug Drabek, the Pirates' starter.

True to their character, the Pirates stayed loose even during the game. Home-plate ump John McSherry became ill in the second inning and had to leave the game. During the ten-minute delay for Randy Marsh to put on equipment, Van Slyke, Lind, Merced, and Cole all sat on the grass in shallow center and played an imaginary game of cards.

And Drabek was true to his reputation as their ultimate big-game pitcher. He had earlier pitched two so-so play-off outings, but on this night, he came up big like he had so many other times for Pittsburgh. He constantly pitched out of trouble through eight shutout innings, seemingly killing off the Braves when he got out of a bases-loaded, none-out jam in the sixth inning. Meanwhile, Merced had a sacrifice fly to help the Pirates to a 2–0 lead. Merced also got thrown out at home in the seventh, but Drabek pitched on, entering the ninth with a two-run lead and the Pirates three outs away from the World Series.

Through it all, Leyland hardly budged from his spot at the home-plate end of the third-base dugout, saying very little during the game. This was Drabek's game to win or lose. He had thrown 120 pitches entering the bottom of the ninth, but the Pirates' bull pen was quiet.

But when Terry Pendleton led off with a drive down the right-field line that bounced a foot fair and went for a double, Leyland had Stan Belinda start warming up. David Justice followed with a ground ball to second baseman Jose Lind, who won the NL Gold Glove for fielding excellence at his position. He bobbled Justice's grounder for only his seventh error all year.

Drabek then walked Sid Bream on four pitches. The bases were loaded, the stadium that had been almost eerily quiet earlier was rocking, and Leyland knew that Drabek had run out of time. So he came slowly to the mound, waved in Belinda, and then retreated for the finish.

Ron Gant greeted Belinda with a shot to deep left that just

missed being a grand slam and was caught at the fence by Bonds, Pendleton scoring to make it 2–1. Belinda appeared to have Damon Berryhill struck out on a 2–2 pitch, but umpire Randy Marsh called the pitch ball three and Berryhill then walked.

But Belinda came back to retire pinch-hitter Brian Hunter on a pop-up, and the excitement built in the Pirates' dugout. "We all looked at each other and we all thought that when Hunter popped out, we were going to make it," said Donnelly.

But then, on a 2–1 pitch, pinch-hitter Francisco Cabrera, in his only series at bat, lined a single to left. Bonds made a great play to cut the ball off in left center and then deliver a perfect one-bounce throw to home. Justice had already scored, and on toward home came Bream, the popular ex-Pirate and one of the slowest runners in baseball. Bream beat Bonds's throw and LaValliere's tag by inches to give the Braves the pennant and a 3–2 victory.

For the first time in postseason history, a team that was leading lost the deciding game on the final pitch. The way the final inning unfolded, the way in which inches and fate played such a role, made it almost impossible to comprehend.

Pendleton's ball could have just as easily been foul. Lind is the most reliable of infielders, and Justice's grounder should have been an out. If it had, would Drabek have had better control with Bream? Gant's ball could have been a home run, which probably would have been easier to swallow in the long run. If McSherry hadn't been ill, would he have called the 2–2 pitch to Berryhill a strike instead of the ball called by Marsh? And would Cabrera have ever batted?

All in all, given the circumstances, it was as devastating a loss as any athletic team could possibly suffer.

Van Slyke and Bonds fell to the ground in the outfield and remained motionless for several moments as the Braves celebrated near home plate and the crowd went nuts. Many Pirates couldn't move from the dugout. Pitching coach Miller just stared transfixed at home plate. Said Donnelly in the silent clubhouse, "This is something I've never felt in my 46 years."

The despair in the clubhouse was so deep that virtually no one could speak for several minutes. Miller, after finally walking from the dugout, turned to Virdon and said, "Bill, this will either make a man out of you or kill you."

Bonds sat quietly, staring into his locker. Van Slyke, Bell, and Drabek were weeping. Most of the players were in the trainer's room or the players-only lounge. The silence was constant, except for sniffles. And when Leyland viewed the scene as the media entered, he asked the reporters to leave. "Media out, we need some more time in here," he said.

As if in a trance, Leyland performed his own duties. He went on live with CBS five minutes after the game ended and, keeping himself barely under control, he told interviewer Tim McCarver, "Atlanta won it, they deserve credit," in a low monotone. "It's the toughest loss I've ever had, but it just wasn't meant to be for us and you have to give credit to Atlanta."

Leyland was then hustled to the interview room for a mass question-and-answer session with over 300 reporters. Again he said, "It was the toughest loss I've ever had and it is difficult to handle." Leyland's voice cracked and tears started welling in his eyes. The media sat almost embarrassed at having to question Leyland now.

Then, as he was about to leave, Leyland said, "Well, if that's all, I want to thank you all for your coverage. I appreciate it and so does the Pirates' organization. I hope our guys all treated you professionally."

As he started walking out of the room, a strange thing happened: Sportswriters, who among them are some of the most cynical people on earth, started applauding.

Only a few players were able to emerge from their daze to talk about their feelings. One was LaValliere.

"I really don't know if any of us will ever recover from this," he said an hour after he just missed tagging out Bream. "But there are a lot of people in worse shape than we are. The sun's going to come up tomorrow. I might never get back here again but at least I made it this year. I was here tonight and it was exciting and it was something I'll never forget. The bad guys won, but I wouldn't trade this for anything.

"But you know what? All that probably sounds good. But this really stinks."

Leyland kept the clubhouse closed for 30 minutes. And it would be an hour before he could put any of his feelings into words and even then, the sentences came haltingly when he talked to Paul Meyer.

"It's hard to sum up how you feel. I guess it's disbelief or something," he said. "I know it won't be easy tomorrow."

Leyland was asked what was the first thing he thought of when Bream slid into home. He thought for a moment and then looked up with those sunken eyes and replied, "I thought he was safe."

And then he began talking about dealing with it all. "You have to think back to things that happen and realize that after a period of time, you have to turn the page and go on," said Leyland. "And as difficult as it seems right now, I know I'll be able to do that. As tough as this is, you have to remember that it's only temporary.

"You have to turn the page and go on. You can't look back. A lot of people are always telling you that they're there when you need them. Friends will always stand by you. But it comes down to you having to handle something like this yourself. And I'll have to face this myself.

"But this team will achieve things again. It will just be different. We'll make moves, we'll make trades or whatever, and when we get to Florida, this will all be behind us and we'll just be there giving things our best shot."

Indeed, the atmosphere around the Pirates was one of an era ending. The stunning defeat would have been more than enough to handle by itself. But there was also the likelihood that many players would not be Pirates in 1993.

Bonds was assumed to be headed elsewhere. And Drabek, who loved his home in suburban Pittsburgh, who wanted nothing more than to pitch for Leyland and Miller, had also played his last game for the Pirates. Red-eyed, he sought out Leyland, who put his hands on Drabek's shoulders and whispered a few words.

Other veterans, the fringe players like Varsho, McClendon, Roger Mason, and others, were likely all to be dropped or dealt after the season. So too would be the high-priced Lind, who, distraught over the error, sat next to Miller and told him he'd take any cut in pay just to remain with the Pirates.

Leyland meanwhile did not seek out players, but as they gravitated toward him, he tried to offer some comforting words. He would not break down in front of his team. Rather, he seemed to be in a trance, saying a few words here and there to those who sought him out.

Watching it all was Pirates president Mark Sauer, a stranger just months ago. "It was the saddest place I've ever been, other than with people who had just had a personal loss," he said. "And as much as he was hurting, as traumatic as it was for everyone in our organization, he was just magnificent. I truly believe that a lot of people would not have gotten through that night without Jim."

Finally, excruciatingly slowly, the Pirates gathered themselves and their wives and boarded the bus for the airport and a flight back to Pittsburgh that Van Slyke would later call "the flight to nowhere."

Leyland was one of the last onto the plane. His coaches as well as Katie eyed him closely for any reaction. Other than briefly breaking down at the mass press conference, Leyland had kept his emotions in check. Donnelly looked at him and said to himself, "He's not doing so good."

As the plane took off, Leyland took out his briefcase and started occupying himself with figuring out which 15 players the Pirates would protect in the upcoming expansion draft to stock the two new franchises in Florida and Colorado.

"That's Jimmy, he turns the page and goes on," said Donnelly. "But no one will ever know how much he was hurting."

The plane arrived in Pittsburgh and the 1992 Pirates began scattering. The days immediately following the play-off loss were difficult for many of them. "People don't understand that my feelings of sadness were greater than the Braves' feelings of excitement," said Van Slyke. "I felt worse than they felt good."

Donnelly related how friends swamped him with calls to commiserate. "It was strange, like there was a death in the family," said Donnelly. "I kept expecting someone to drive up and deliver flowers. My son Bubba cried so hard he got his eye infected and he had to go to the doctor. The doctor asked him what happened, and Bubba started crying again and then the doctor started crying.

"I wanted to go eat at my favorite restaurant but the owner had closed for the day. He said he couldn't take it, that people were taking it too hard. Heck, for the first time in my life, I didn't watch the first game of the World Series. I just couldn't bring myself to look at a baseball game."

Leyland, by his and Katie's estimation, received over 100 calls in the two days following the play-off loss. And there were likely twice as many that weren't made by friends or acquaintances who didn't want to intrude on Leyland's depression or didn't have the words to express their feelings.

One of those who called a number of times was Lamont. "I know a lot of people who wanted to call him but didn't," said Lamont. "But I have a little different relationship with him. If I knew I could have gotten through, I would have called him in the clubhouse that night of the seventh game.

"But we talk all the time. He'll call me just when he wants to talk to somebody. He's a little more open with me. And when I got to him the next day when he had gotten back to Pittsburgh, I really think he was in a state of shock. I knew he was really hurting. I ended up calling him later than same day to see if he was all right."

Barger also talked to Leyland several times in the days immediately following the loss. "He went through some very difficult days," said Barger. "This was the toughest thing Jim's ever faced other than losing his child. And I tried to put it in perspective for him."

Leyland stayed in his house with Katie for days after the play-off loss, in his words, "mourning." Said Leyland, "The minute I'd go out, everybody was saying how bad they felt and I felt bad for them too. It was tough."

But after a while, he started to get restless. "I had been discussing the thing with just Katie for two or three days and after a while, I started thinking, 'This is getting crazy.'

"You know, it was like when I walked on the plane that night in Atlanta. I could see the faces on the people, on even Katie, all wondering what I was going to do. And I thought, 'This is nuts.' I mean, it's tough but this is ridiculous. We have to snap out of all this.

"I ended up watching every inning of every World Series game. And damn right, I rooted for the Braves. They were the National League Champions and Bobby Cox is one of the best guys around. Hey, the world didn't end that night in Atlanta."

Leyland soon began emerging from the depression. And he was quick to become uncomfortable with the sympathy that friends and acquaintances kept offering.

"I don't want anyone to feel sorry for me. I mean, that's ridiculous," he said, days after the seventh game. "We've been in the play-offs three straight years. We played in two seventh games. We played in 20 of 21 possible play-off games.

"I'm being paid very well. I have a great contract. I have a beautiful family. We're all healthy. Hell, I don't need any sympathy. That's not what that game was all about.

"What happened was that we needed 27 outs and we got only 26. I can understand people's loyalty and concern and all that. I appreciate it very much. And I appreciate all the good friends who called me to tell me how bad they felt.

"But it's a little weird, like people are saying to me not to get down. They seem to imply that there was something unfair about it all, and that's what I don't understand. Things were fair. We played nine innings and they got one more run than we did. I have no problem with that at all. We played 162 plus seven but we didn't get done what we had to do. And that's the game."

. . .

And in the end, that's what it was all about, the rhythms of the game that sustained Leyland. Every game is played to a result and then it's time for the next one. It is the way of baseball and of life. And it's the way of managing.

"We were down three games to one and my guys played their heads off to get it to a seventh game," said Leyland. "That's part of life. Then those same kids of mine were crying in the locker room. Well, that's part of life too, and I enjoy life.

"Sure it was heartbreaking. There's no question about it being the toughest thing that ever happened to me on a baseball field. But if people are waiting for me to let it dampen my spirit or ruin my enthusiasm for the game, then they can forget it. Things in the game are great. No one, least of all me, should dwell on that one game. To me that wasn't a negative anyway. That was a team out there that won 96 games that was supposed to finish fourth or fifth and had people laughing at it in spring training. All of a sudden that team was ahead 2–0 with three outs left to go to the World Series. How the hell can that be a negative?

"I was asked the night of the game by the writers, I was asked by friends and people later, if it bothered me that we didn't win that game. Well, of course it bothered me. But it wasn't because I started thinking that people thought, 'Maybe he isn't that good a manager because he didn't get to the World Series.' It bothered me because I wanted to get to the World Series, because it's the ultimate for any manager to get there.

"It's what you shoot for right from those early days of spring training. And I wanted it. But I didn't want it any more than Cito Gaston or Bobby Cox or Tony LaRussa. They all wanted it just as much. And that's what this game is all about."

So Leyland had got past his depression, bringing with him a Pirates organization that would begin changing as predicted. But Donnelly couldn't let 1992 completely pass from memory.

"Now, I'm biased about all this because I work for Jimmy and I'm a part of this team and all the rest," said Donnelly. "But I was sitting in that clubhouse that last night in Atlanta and the thing that I thought of right away is how now no one will ever know what kind of job Jimmy did. Because we didn't get to the World Series, no one will know how he took a team that lost so much from the year before and just about took that team farther than the last two more talented teams had been able to go. That's what made me the saddest about it all.

"It's hard to put into words what he did last year. I mean, if you wanted to put together a motivational video for a company or something, you should show how Jim Leyland dealt with those 25 guys all season. You wouldn't need any speeches, just a look at how he did his job day after day. He had lineups that had six guys batting under .200, he had Gary Varsho batting cleanup, he had all different kinds of pitchers running in and out of there. And day after day, he kept believing with all his heart that this team would go all the way.

"You go back and look at all the great managers in history. There was a common thread of having a work ethic, of not seeking credit for themselves, of just doing things the right way. They don't embarrass anybody; they just worked hard and believed in their team. It's all so simple, yet it's something you just don't see very much of anymore. And to see Jimmy do it day after day was so neat. And that's why it bothered him and so many of us to lose like that at the end. Because, even when we had that lousy West Coast trip in May, when we were struggling to hold off Montreal, when we were down 3–1 to the Braves in the play-offs, all along he truly believed in this team. He believed 100 percent that somehow or another we would get where we wanted to be.

"And when it ended like that, I cried for him because if we had got there, then maybe everyone would have known that the way he does things is the right way, that the job he did was unbelievable. I could have told everybody, Milt May would have told everybody, and so would have a lot of the players. But now, we don't have the chance to tell people what Jimmy did last year and that's so damn disappointing."

However, Donnelly got over his own distress. Helping him

along was an early November cruise to the Caribbean with his wife and the Leylands. "Yeah, I thought for sure that with our luck, at the first island we stopped, Cabrera would get on board," said Donnelly. "And I would have just gone over the rail."

As Thanksgiving approached, Leyland was already looking ahead confidently to spring training.

"There's absolutely no way we can replace Barry [Bonds, certain to leave as a free agent]," he said. "And we don't know what will happen with other free agents and whatever deals Teddy might be able to make.

"But I feel really good about our club. Honest to God, I really believe we're gonna be a good club. Now, it's two different things to talk about being a good club and about winning. Hell, if we had Smiley and Bonilla and Landrum and Kipper and Heaton last spring, I wouldn't have told anyone we were going to win it all because you never know in this game.

"All I know is that I believe we're going to be a good club in 1993. It's going to be exciting for us to see these kids like Kevin Young and Carlos Garcia and Albert Martin and our young pitchers may be all on the verge. And we have some damned good players coming back. I liked what I saw of some of these kids, and there are too many good reports on them from our people and the people in other organizations not to think they'll be able to help us fill some holes.

"That Atlanta game is history. So is 1992. Me and Katie and Patrick are having a good winter and a great off-season. And then I'm going to go to Bradenton and work my tail off to make my contributions to the Pirates' organization. Hey, that's what managing is all about, ain't it?"

"The Worst Feeling Is to Know You Ain't Got No Shot"

◆ By the end of the 1992 season, Cito Gaston was finally getting the respect that had been denied him, having taken Toronto to the World Championship, besting the Braves in six games.

Meanwhile, Tony LaRussa lost a frustrating six-game series to the Blue Jays in the AL play-offs, one in which Oakland's trusty bull pen let them down. After the season, LaRussa faced the prospect of managing a whole new club when 15 Athletics filed for free agency.

Lou Piniella, tired of managing amid the circus atmosphere created by owner Marge Schott, asked not to be considered for a new contract and days later signed a lucrative new three-year deal to manage the Seattle Mariners. Schott meanwhile became embroiled in controversy after racist remarks were attributed to her by several sources.

And Tommy Lasorda was re-signed to manage the Dodgers for yet another season amid renewed speculation that 1993 would be his last year with Los Angeles.

As for Leyland, the crushing seventh-game loss to Atlanta proved to be only the beginning of a difficult winter.

With losses estimated between $8 and $12 million, the Pittsburgh organization went on a cost-cutting binge. Lind and his $2 million salary were traded to Kansas City for a pair of young pitchers. Patterson, Espy, Varsho, and Palacios were all released.

No effort was made to even discuss a new contract with Bonds, who ended up shocking the baseball world by signing a $43 million deal with the San Francisco Giants. When the final deal was announced at the baseball winter meetings in Louisville, Leyland stood quietly at the back of the room watching the press conference without any expression whatsoever. He knew for months that Bonds was long gone from Pittsburgh.

Leyland was more stung by the loss of Drabek. To the end, Leyland thought the Pirates had a reasonable chance to keep the right-hander. But they never offered more than a three-year contract, and Drabek took a four-year $19.5 million offer to play near his off-season home for the Houston Astros, quite likely the only team for which he would have forsaken Pittsburgh.

Meanwhile, Jackson and Cole, the 1992 season's key in-season trade acquisitions, were left unprotected in the expansion draft and both were lost. In all, 12 players from Pittsburgh's play-off roster were either traded, released, or not re-signed in the month following the end of the World Series.

However, Leyland kept his cool while conferring with Simmons on moves the Pirates could make to patch the holes while maintaining their austerity budget. "Sure, all this is frustrating," said Leyland, constantly puffing on one cigarette after another. "Heck, I have no idea who will be in my lineup, who will be my leadoff hitter, who will be in my bull pen. And it's frustrating nowadays that it seems players really have no pride in being part of one organization. There's no sense that 'I'm proud to be a Pirate and want to always be a Pirate.'

"I'm disappointed but I'm not mad. I understand what the organization is doing. Our organization is putting into action what a lot of organizations only put into words. I'm disappointed that the situation has to be this way, but I understand it. I'm a Pittsburgh Pirate and I won't bite the hand that feeds me.

"The thing is that I want to be able to compete. I want to be able to sit in my dugout and know I can compete with the team on the other side. And I hope I can still feel that way next year. And I know that I will work to the best of my ability to make that happen.

"But like I've told a lot of people in our organization, the worst feeling in the world is to sit in that dugout and know you ain't got no shot. Back in 1986, I'd be in my dugout and we'd be playing the Mets and I knew that we had no chance to win unless something freaky happened. And that just kills you inside. But I understand what we have to do and hopefully we'll be able to make it work because we still have some damned good players out there. And we ain't gonna completely strip down and give ourselves no chance. We still think we can be a competitive club."

Nevertheless, Leyland was wondering what would happen to the Pirates' already shaky fan support. "Yeah, I keep hearing a lot of people saying how they agree with what we've had to do," he said. "And what I wonder is if that same guy who says he agrees with us says in June that 'I'm not going to go see those assholes play because they can't win a game.' Those guys who agree with us in December, I wonder if they'll be there in June. Because what's the difference when you draw 2.5 million people, lose money, but win, or if you draw 800,000, lose money, and lose?"

But whatever anxiety Leyland felt over the disintegration of the Pirates' roster was largely overshadowed by two personal events, one joyous and one tragic. During Thanksgiving week, the Leylands learned that Katie was pregnant and Leyland was telling the good news to all when he arrived at the winter meetings.

Leyland left the Louisville headquarters hotel midmorning on Wednesday December 9. He was paged at the Pittsburgh Airport and told that his friend Carl Barger, the Florida Marlins' president, had collapsed during an owners meeting back in Louisville. Leyland learned with the rest of baseball that Barger had passed away on an emergency room operating table after suffering a heart attack.

Leyland sobbed when asked for comment, saying Barger "was one of the closest friends I had in this world."

Much was made later of how Barger was a chain smoker and how the stress of running a franchise was evident on him in recent weeks.